Keep Turning the Pages

Anita L Cobbins

Published by Purpose Publishing
1503 Main Street #168 ❧ Grandview, Missouri
www.purposepublishing.com

ISBN: 978-0-9828379-9-3
Copyright © 2014, Anita L. Cobbins

Cover design by: Sharon Bailey Designs
Cover Photo by: Christine Hines
Editing by: Anita L. Cobbins

Printed in the United States of America

This book, or parts thereof, may not be reproduced, stored in a retrieval system, or transmitted in any form or by means – electronic, mechanical, photocopy, recording, or any other without the prior permission of the publisher.

This book is available at quantity discounts for bulk purchases. Inquiries may be addressed to the publisher.

Stay Connected at:
www.AnitaCobbins.com

Foreword

When I was but eight or nine years of age, I recall times that my great-grandmother would take me by the hand during harvest time and lead me around through her garden. As she gathered the produce from the garden, she would talk to me. I did not understand, at the time, many of the things she was saying. However, one of her many sayings has stayed firmly in my mind and resonates with me even today. I remember, very vividly, "Baby you got to learn how to stand on your tippy toes 'cause when you stand on your tippy toes you can see a lil-bit furder..."

One of the brightest parts of my pastorate was meeting, becoming acquainted, and working with individuals like Anita L. Cobbins. As her pastor, counselor and friend of more than 25 years, it has been a joy to know Anita; and watch her transformation from a young girl into a mature, spiritually convicted woman. Teaching, preaching, and ministering the powerful redemptive message of Jesus the Christ, Anita lives in the creative potential that the Creator has given her.

Keep Turning the Pages affords the reader the opportunity of being introduced in a very personal way to the author, and become acquainted with some of the inner workings of God in her life. This is Anita's story: life experiences that challenged her to stand on tippy toes to look further, to look beyond present circumstances that would seemingly debilitate, subdue, and cancel one's resolve to live by faith.

With each turn of (life-changing) event, Anita's indomitable spirit, undergirded by her continued faith in God, has enabled her to stand on tippy toes...transcend present life adversities to see further.

In the pages of her book, the author gives us small glimpses into her life sufficient enough for us to know that everyone has a "valley of shadow." Her courage and faith will inspire you, for pain and conflict are parts of being human, and this is where God meets us.

With the substance and content of this book, we are now able to read and preserve in literary form the proclamation of an able, young mind eager and earnest to fulfill her calling. This book will take her important witness to more places and reach more people than any one person can go, even one with the gifts, the dynamism, and energy of the author of this book.

I believe, *Keep Turning the Pages*, can be of service for anyone at any time who has either contemplated or actually given up their pursuit of an authentic relationship with God. Read and benefit from what the author openly shares. There is joy in these pages. There is reality. There is hope. There is encouragement. There is direction. There is love.

Rev. Wallace S. Hartsfield, Sr., Pastor Emeritus
Metropolitan Missionary Baptist Church
Kansas City, Missouri

Thank You

To God be the glory for the things He has done through two spiritual leaders whose ministries, support and personal counsel served as the foundation and furtherance of my faith in God and love for Jesus Christ:

My beloved uncle, the late Rev. O.L. Cobbins, Sr.

&

My Pastor Emeritus, Rev. Wallace S. Hartsfield, Sr.

Also, if I had 10,000 tongues it still would not be enough to thank you for some of the best times of my life. Your friendship means more to me than you realize:

Alma
(love the 'play dates')

Curtis
(deep appreciation for making things easier for me)

Edwina
(for walking with this co-worker
through many dark days)

Gwen
(hang in there, our health challenges
are worth the fight)

Stan
(I call you 'my brother'...and I mean it)

Virginia
(my 'twin sister' friend)

Dedication

I dedicate my first book to the memory of my loving and
devoted father, Rev. Cle Otis Cobbins, Sr.,
whose spirit rests in the Lord's presence
and forever remains in my heart.

I esteem and honor my surviving family:
My Mother, Essie Prince,
along with my sisters, brothers, in-laws,
nieces and nephews.

In this commemorative, inaugural publication,
I give you my words, my spirit, my heart.

I will always love you, family.

— Anita

A Sincere Dedication

"Love recognizes no barriers. It jumps hurdles, leaps fences, penetrates walls to arrive at its destination full of hope."
— Maya Angelou

One day to my surprise, Elbert said to me, "Cheryl thinks of you as the sister she never had." That comment at that moment defined for me a relationship I have treasured. Since day one, we hit if off. And throughout the years, I constantly find myself beaming with admiration and appreciation for the joy of our friendship.

She is my compassionate, caring confidante and advisor, my bold and energetic sister in Christ, an enthusiastic co-worker in God's work, my professional mentor and down-to-earth running buddy, who will freely let her hair down to have fun with the likes of me. I love Cheryl for who she is and all that she has done to enrich my life.

Cheryl unconditionally gives herself to our relationship. Whenever I am struggling with a side of myself that falls short of God's desires for my well-being, Cheryl encourages me to fight for the good she sees inside. In some of the darkest hours of my life, I will have a little talk with Cheryl and end up seeing light at the end of the tunnel. I would be foolish to pass up opportunities to take in her sage advice. So oftentimes I jump at the chance to pick up the phone and track her down calling all of her phone numbers until we connect.

Also, I can always exhale because Cheryl gets me. She knows I am about purposeful, fulfilled and focused living as an overflowing expression of my love for God and faith in Jesus Christ. She knows my heart. She is in tune with my unwavering desire to always emerge having pleased God— no matter the struggle and how much I hurt when facing opposition.

In another sense, whether we are shopping, or at a concert, at the movies, the theater, enjoying a meal, serving together in ministry or as colleagues, exchanging comical emails or just talking on the phone, I enjoy every moment we share.

For me, it is perfectly natural to hold Cheryl in high esteem for virtuous characteristics such as loyalty, respect and selflessness. She unwittingly and naturally carries herself with dignity and grace, but will shun arrogance in a heartbeat.

She has never given me reason to question where I stand with her. Cheryl is an inspiring supporter who assures me in words and deeds that I am worth her time, attention and energy. Cheryl has invested in my life more than she realizes.

The tie that binds our hearts is genuinely rooted in Christian love. A quote from the book *Girlfriends: Invisible Bonds, Enduring Ties* by Carmen Renee Berry and Tamara

Traeder says, "Sometimes our girlfriends are the ones who become our spiritual families — people to whom, for whatever reason, we feel more comfortable going to with our confessions, problems and achievements."

Clearly and sincerely I am indebted to God for allowing our paths to cross, our lives to touch and our relationship to flourish.

In sincere dedication to Cheryl, my trusted friend.

A Special Acknowledgement

With immense gratitude, I am also sincerely indebted to Denise Jordon, managing editor of the *Kansas City Globe*. As a follow up to several intimate conversations, one day Denise strongly encouraged me to "go public" with my stories. She then "gave me my space" in the *Globe's* "Church" section. Denise named the monthly inspirational column, "Expect A Miracle" because she wanted the readers to witness God working in my life, not only to restore my health but mainly to show what He was really up to from within.

As the months went by in my physical recovery, there were no shortages of Scriptures to turn to and claim as God's promises. One of which is in Philippians 1:6, "Being confident of this very thing, that he which hath begun a good work in you will perform it until the day of Jesus Christ."

God knew that there is something in me that needed to be released, exposed for His purposes. He knew it because He put it there—"a good work."

Don't misunderstand. It did not take the accident and my life as a paraplegic before God could begin the work. No, God determined that the good work would continue in spite of the accident and its results.

That work often calls for the assistance, empowerment and open opportunities others can provide.

Thank God for Denise. Her generosity and willingness to make a personal investment in my life set the stage for me to go to a new level. The pages of my life turned from accident victim to author, and Denise allowed God to use her so that I could make the transition.

I had never written extensively, but I am honored to be given a chance to impact lives in this area of my profession as a communicator and minister, using testimonies of my trials and triumphs. I learned to hone the skill and perfect the craft, to meet the readers on their levels. As the saying goes in the industry, "Write to express, not impress."

Writing the *Globe* articles has also been therapeutic, especially in times of struggle and even in response to my accomplishments. When the inspiration hit, I found myself in the moment, putting my thoughts on paper then tucking those inspired words away for just the right time to submit a full article. Some of the articles follow chapters of my personal stories because the articles' topics, messages and/or illustrations complement and connect with valuable lessons I have learned.

What I most treasure and cherish is the reality that this opportunity opened the door for a relationship between Denise and me, indelibly bonding us as Christian sisters, colleagues, as a mentor to a protégé, sorority sisters and dearest friends. Denise is all of that to me and then some.

I would be shamefully remiss if I failed to reciprocate and honor her by presenting *Keep Turning the Pages* to her. The value Denise has placed on me as a woman of faith and a vessel of God's good work is yet another demonstration of divine favor.

So here's to you, Denise.

Humbly from Anita.

Introduction

Sunday, January 29, 2006. If you can remember that far back, for you that was probably just another day. For me, I remember that day as if it was yesterday. It marked two years since Daddy went home to be with the Lord. It was a sad and solemn day, and I just wanted to be alone. Who? Me? The one who is outgoing and cherishes being with and around others? Although out of character, yes, that was me.

I went to Sunday School, did the best I could to facilitate the lesson discussion, and then I decided to just go home. I didn't have plans, nothing to do in particular. So I decided that I would attempt to honor Daddy's memory by at least penning the words to the book that I intended to dedicate to him. So eight years ago, I wrote:

I present this book in the spirit of my father, because it was during the days leading up to his homegoing services, that I sensed something. It was indescribable at that time. I struggled to devote my time and attention to preparing for Daddy's homegoing while also grieving. However, I could not shake this strange distraction that controlled my spirit.

Finally on the day of Daddy's homegoing celebration what I sensed became clearer. The family prepared to procession out of the sanctuary to the limos waiting outside the church. Now it was time to journey to Dad's final resting place. As we were being escorted up the aisle, my

Aunt Minnie who was standing at the end of the pew, leaned over to me and whispered, "You ought to write a book."

I believe that revelation came to her after listening to the words I shared during the services, "A Living Testimony," a tribute to Daddy. I faintly answered in affirmation, because I was still emotional. That day marked our final goodbyes to a man who meant the world to me. It was hard to think of anything else; I was preoccupied with my life without my Daddy.

Less than a week had passed since Daddy was laid to rest. What was happening in my spirit had intensified and I became sensitized to the prompting. God was calling me into the preaching ministry. What could I say? I remember responding, "Lord, if this is what you want me to do, then I'll do it." No resistance. No questions. Just a simple, humble "yes" with one minor consideration. My "pulpit" would have to begin with my spiritual writings published in the 'Kansas City Globe.' My church had yet to fully unite on the issue of women preachers; but that was okay. I was ready to assume this new role and begin wherever the opportunity presented itself.

Furthermore, it occurred to me that I could create my own opportunity and expand the ministry by publishing a combination of 'Globe' articles and my personal testimonies of major turning points in my life in my first book.

In order to read my *Globe* articles, readers had to turn the pages to the "Church" section. With that, I was inspired to title the book, *Keep Turning the Pages.*

This intimate labor of love has been 17 years in the making, beginning with my oldest sister Kathy's first encouragement to me to journal my experiences as I progressed. From there, *Kansas City Globe* Managing Editor Denise Jordon suggested and offered space in the weekly newspaper for inspirational monthly columns written by me. She named the column, "Expect A Miracle." Then my one of my closest friends and former roommate, Delores, gave me a combo devotional/journal for my birthday. I have already mentioned my Aunt Minnie who encouraged me to write a book in 2004. But in the summer of 2006, following an outdoor revival at my church, then-pastor, Rev. Wallace S. Hartsfield, Sr., hurriedly approached me as if he wanted to make sure I would not get away. When I stopped to see why he called out to me with such urgency, I vividly recall him saying insistently, "Daughter! You need to write that book! I saw it in a vision. You need to write."

Thus, *Keep Turning the Pages* is my first memoir. It is filled with my experiences representing major turning points towards discovering how and why Jesus Christ makes the difference in my life.

Keep Turning the Pages is my journey, my testimonies that led me to discover and define what it means to live by faith. You see, I am determined to reject the façade of a faith that is only marked by attending and working in church. On the contrary, I am stubbornly determined to know firsthand what it's like to turn adversities into turning points for purposeful living.

It's rather ironic that out of such a painful and difficult experience as grief came God's calling to preach and the inspiration for this publication ministry. Thus, *Keep Turning the Pages* is more than my first book. I consider it a new level of ministry, because my prayer is that you read something that propels you past your apathy, your complacency or the mediocrity, which keeps you from being your best self.

I also pray that *Keep Turning the Pages* will encourage you as you read what the Lord has given me to share since becoming a featured *Kansas City Globe* columnist in 1999. The stories represent real, down-to-earth experiences. I know that faith in God is real. In terms of sharing the ups and downs I have encountered, I have tried to keep it real, relevant and relatable. So turn the pages and read on.

Plus, *Keep Turning the Pages* was written so that the reader can choose to read any chapter anywhere in the book. No need to read chronologically, from the first to the last page. Choose from the table of contents or just flip through the pages to a topic that catches your eyes, stirs your intrigue.

But above all, *Keep Turning the Pages* and see how Jesus Christ has literally, faithfully proven Himself to me as my Lord, my love and my life—time and time again. You can choose to have your Bible handy and read for yourself the Scriptures I reference. Or, you can pause, reflect and allow God's word to permeate your thoughts and inspire you to be a better person, just as God's word has done for me.

Now it's time to turn the pages.

Table of Contents

Chapter 1
From Headlights to Head-on Collision..23

Chapter 2
I (GOD) See You in ICU...27

Chapter 3
Lord, I Need You..55

Chapter 4
Walk. By Faith...89

Chapter 5
I Lost My Job...123

Chapter 6
I Lost My Joy...159

Chapter 7
Sisters by Heart, Roles to Model..197

Chapter 8
Family Matters...249

Chapter 9
A Mother's Day Gift from God..295

Chapter 10
Daddy's Devotion..317

Chapter 11
Walk On. By Faith...357

Chapter 1

From Headlights to Head-on Collision

May 9, 1997, between 11:30 that night and midnight, is where my story begins.

My Friday was ending as normal as any day. I had just gotten off work from my second job and was on my way home. It was about a three-minute drive to my apartment. I ended my 11 o'clock part-time gig. After I got in the car, I searched for my billfold but could not find it. I needed to fill up my gas tank that night for my 9 a.m. shift the next day. *Where is it? Must have left it at work at my day job,* I thought to myself. I decided to go back to the day job near downtown Kansas City, but first, *I should call somebody.* After all, it was rather late.

I called my sister, Tressa, told her my plans and instead she suggested I come by and get gas money from her. The trip would have been much shorter because the day job was located farther into the city. Since it was relatively late to drive the distance, it made sense to take my sister up on her offer.

As I was on my way, I was about four minutes into the trip traveling north when all of a sudden coming south from behind a van and crossing into my lane...all I saw were headlights out of the blue. It was too late to react; our cars collided head-on.

I heard glass shattering, hissing sounds, the sounds of other automobiles slowing down and car doors closing. I recall having difficulty breathing, something was wrong with my legs and I felt a burning sensation along my neck where the seatbelt rested and down my back. At times I leaned forward to rest my head against the steering wheel then back against the headrest. I heard sirens getting closer and closer. Then I heard voices.

I could tell radio communication was at my car door so I concluded the voice asking me questions was a police officer. He tapped on the window. "Ma'am, where are you hurt?" Gasping for breath, I answered, "My legs." He asked my name and I answered. He assured me with "Hang on. We're going to get you out."

I heard other voices saying they would probably have to cut me out of the car. The sounds outside and voices grew faint. I struggled to follow the officer's instructions to stay alert and not lose consciousness. I recall the officer's last question because his reaction to my response was coincidental. When the officer asked me if there was someone I wanted him to call, I answered, "Yes. My father." I gave him my father's name, "Cleotis Cobbins." Then I clearly heard the officer tell someone, "I know him. I know her father." He asked for his phone number. I managed to give him the number with all the strength I had. At the same time, I knew I could have given him my mother's name and phone number. Ironically, the accident scene was only two blocks from where she lived. But I did not want my mother to see me in this shape. I wanted to spare her the panic, pain and trauma of watching me struggle to stay alert and calm while fighting to hold back tears from the pain I was experiencing. I did not want her to have a ringside seat observing paramedics' hectic efforts to help all who were injured, the extent of damage to our vehicles, emergency vehicles and flashing lights—that whole scene.

I heard another set of sirens approaching from a distance. By now I am in and out of consciousness, trying to use the little bit of alertness that I had left to pray, "Lord, help me. Help me stay awake." However, I remembered being pulled from the car, placed on a stretcher and lifted onto the ambulance.

That was the last I recall until hours later.

Chapter 2
I (GOD) See You in ICU

"She gave this name to the Lord who spoke to her: 'You are the God who sees me,' for she said, 'I have now seen the One who sees me'." Genesis 16:13

I am putting my heart on paper. I realize I am taking a risk sharing some intimate details of my life. But it's worth the risk. As you read about my trials and triumphs, it is my hope you will understand why.

I chose to share certain experiences because they represent turning points and periods of profound change. So profound until keeping them locked up in memory was not an option. These experiences revealed and redefined more about me than I knew about myself. Most of all, at every turn I became more aware and excited about living daily a life with faith in God; although it's a life rejected, neglected and abandoned by many.

And yet anyone who dares to live to the contrary would agree that the faith life makes the difference, just as God intended.

Now let us turn our attention to the experience that inspired me to invite you to *"Keep Turning the Pages."*

ICU. On the one hand, this was the place where I eventually became aware that my life had taken a drastic turn. It was also where God, in essence, spoke to assure me "I (God) see you." Either way, I was now in a place that signaled life as I knew it was a thing of the past.

Oh how I needed to know that God had a watchful eye over me. Based on all I could see, that is, the little I was able to see, I needed answers. There were thoughts and questions running through my mind because I believed the God I loved and served could have prevented the accident.

As I gradually regained consciousness in St. Luke Hospital's ICU, I discovered I had lost track of the days. I knew I lost at least one day. I slowly opened my eyes; my vision was somewhat blurred. I was surrounded by the eerie sounds of equipment in a quiet background. Medical devices were monitoring my condition. The room seemed airy. I became more alert. My eyes curiously cased the room from one side to the other, as far as I could stretch my eyes within the limits of my peripheral vision.

And then it happened. I tried to move. First, my arms and fingers, but I struggled to lift them; they were extremely weak. Then I tried moving my legs but could not, no movement at all. I tried lifting my head to look around only to realize I was in a restraint and furthermore I could not sit up.

I began trying to recall the events that led to this moment. Suddenly in a flash, I remembered the automobile accident. As I searched my mind to make sense of where I was and what I was currently experiencing, tears started streaming. In that moment, that's all I had. There were parts of my body that did not work and the parts that worked were too weak.

My eyes and my tears were the only movements. The flow of my tears formed a steady stream down my face, around my cheekbones, down my hairline and the sides of my ears. At times, I choked as I struggled to breathe through the breathing tube.

Then something else happened. As believers, we were taught not to question God. Well, that was one teaching that went out the window. I did what some might consider the unthinkable. I unloaded emotionally and I cried out in anguish, "Lord, why?!"

No one on God's green earth could have convinced me to just lie in bed and "la-dee-dah" accept what happened. If questioning God was an absolute "no-no," then I was going to break the rules. Scary thoughts ran rampant through my mind. With a mixture of tears over what had happened and fears of facing an uncertain future, "Lord, why did this happen to me?" seemed to be a naturally justifiable reaction. I knew I couldn't change a thing but I needed to know why.

I recalled all of the plans I recently made. A year ago, I had just completed a dual Master of Arts degree in Media Communications and Marketing. It was an intense three-year degree program but I accomplished my goal while working full-time. I had added a part-time job to pay off my school debts and in preparation to relocate to Dallas, Tx., so that I could pursue a profession in media and marketing communications. Like many young adults with goals and ambitions, I had plans.

I've always tried to live to make my parents proud, be an example before my siblings, nieces and nephews and make something of myself. I thought about how I felt. I had really devoted my life to the Lord, serving in ministries with sincere motivation and genuine passion. I wasn't perfect, but I lived my life as a 39-year-old single woman dedicated and committed to God.

In that moment I didn't officially know that I was partially paralyzed, but I was aware that when you cannot move; when your brain is saying to your body "move" and nothing happens, then something is seriously wrong. This experience in ICU was frightening.

In that very moment of despair, it was a still and small but clearly heard voice that responded, "You're going to recover." Almost instantly, when I heard those words, it seemed as though the tears on my face just dried up. Remember, I can't lift my hands to dry my face and eyes, but the tears just dried up. The emotions calmed down and on the one hand I felt a sense of peace, yet I felt a sense of uncertainty about the days ahead. God allowed me to have my anxious meltdown. God allowed the questioning. Distraught and confused, I simply was not in a good place.

And yet, God saw me. Just like Hagar whose story is told in Genesis chapter 16. The Bible introduces Hagar as the handmaiden of Sarai and Abram who gave birth to Abram's first son. Although God had promised the elderly and childless couple a son, Sarai jumped the gun and gave Hagar to her husband. Hagar conceived and the immediate consequence of their attempt to usurp God's plans was rival tension, aggression and conflict between two jealous women. Hagar flaunted her superiority over barren Sarai. Abram permitted Sarai to punish Hagar as she saw fit.

Consequently, pregnant Hagar the handmaiden became a runaway. She eventually encounters the Lord's angel, who instructed her to return but not without first revealing a promise from God. "The angel added, 'I will increase your descendants so much that they will be too numerous to count...you will give birth to a son. You shall name him Ishmael, for the Lord has heard of your misery." In response, Hagar "gave this name to the Lord who spoke to her: 'You are the God who sees me, for she said, 'I have now seen the One who sees me'."

This confession became a source of strength for Hagar that motivated her to return and deal with her problem despite an uncertain future.

Regardless the circumstance, Hagar looked beyond it and realized her situation had not escaped God's eyes. This was enlightening for her and that realization was the same for me as I lay in ICU.

Although God did not answer and explain why the automobile accident, His response was most reassuring. Addressing why the accident, why the paralysis and injuries pales in comparison to the response God gave that day. God saw me at that moment. More importantly, God saw my outcome as a full recovery. The amazing peace that came over me is described in God's word as surpassing understanding (Philippians 4:7). Instantly, I was no longer distraught. The future appeared bright and hopeful yet still uncertain.

God gave me a promise. It has been the basis for a new course of life that has brought faith and God front and center.

Overcoming paralysis has been the greatest, long-term challenge of my life. I am determined to go the distance until God's promise of healing is fully manifested. Beyond my physical health, I would still be less than I could and should be if I excluded my spiritual, mental and emotional well-being from the equation.

Undoubtedly, my healing and wholeness are in God's hands. Still God needs my commitment.

Thus taking steps towards healing and wholeness is the central focus I have adopted. It appropriately defines the physical and spiritual realities I am confronted with daily. I have had to adapt to a lifestyle as a paraplegic, learning to walk and regain use of my lower body.

However, I have discovered that within me lies an extraordinary motivation to exercise faith in God and His promise of full recovery.

I am taking steps towards healing and wholeness despite the medical contradictions. What keeps me on the move? A promise God gave by His grace and I received by faith. It is a faith in God that began when I first prayed "Lord, I need you," 18 years prior to the accident.

For out of that prayer, I accepted the Savior, Jesus Christ into my life.

If Jesus were one to pout, I imagine Him seated on His throne, arms crossed, shoulders tight, eyes squinted and mouth poked out over our constant tendency to trust people, situations and things over Him.

If God were to throw a tantrum, He would have every right. When you consider the fact that at every split second, somebody somewhere willfully passes on opportunities to simply take Him at His word and believe who He is.

How many times has God's Spirit prompted us with, "Here's your chance. Just trust Me. Seize the moment. You'll be glad you did!" And yet, we shrug off His promptings placing greater credibility upon other people, our careers, our own reasoning, our position in life – you name it (other than God), we'll trust it.

Even if we are sincere in the struggle to trust God, it is usually because there are other options cleverly flaunting their appeal. Only when those options fail to pan out, *then* maybe God will get His turn.

At times, we will be challenged to trust God even when life hurts. Out of a broken heart, we will have to decide to trust Him wholeheartedly. So if we are truly committed to living by the mantra *In God We Trust*, then perhaps it is time to take to task why we often fall short.

Rest assured, God sees us in every circumstance and offers another chance to trust Him for the answers, directions and blessings we seek.

Keep turning the pages as I share select *Globe* articles on *Trusting God.*

Trusting God
Originally published May 2001
Reprinted with permission from
Kansas City Globe

After being bedridden for about four-and-one-half weeks, it was time for me to progress to a new level of mobility.

I was well acquainted with using a wheelchair. It was a black high-back, vinyl chair. Among its many features was its adjustable back that allowed me to recline at a comfortable angle. So it was my very own recliner on wheels. And for about four weeks, that is how I rode around - reclined and comfortable.

Then one morning, my therapist walked in my room and delivered the news. I would have to start using the wheelchair in a complete upright position, no longer reclining. I was being stripped from a comfort level I had enjoyed for weeks.

I actually threw a bit of a fit with my therapist. It didn't matter to her. She casually went to the back of my wheelchair, released the levers and in one sweeping motion, adjusted the back so that I was straight up.

Suddenly, I became light-headed and nauseated. I began to perspire. The therapist ran to get a cup and called for medical assistance. I felt feverish. I missed the cup, but not the floor. When the drama ended I just knew the therapist would realize she made a mistake and return me to my comfortable, reclined position. But she did not—not that day, nor the days that followed. I experienced the same physical reaction each day until my body got used to being in this new position. I had to trust my therapist's judgment.

That experience is one of many that represents a personal parable of my physical recovery. These parables reveal truths that have helped me grow spiritually and become more intimate with God. Basically, we describe parables as earthly stories with a heavenly meaning.

The story that I just described can be related this way from a spiritual perspective: Sometimes, in order to experience God's better way, you may be forced out of your comfort zone. The process will be painful and unpleasant. The pain may continue longer than you like. You may need the help of others. But when you get right down to it, you're going to have to trust God.

Proverbs 3:5 and 6, "Trust in the Lord with all thine heart; and lean not unto thine own understanding. In all thy ways acknowledge him, and he shall direct thy paths."

It's a familiar Scripture. However, trusting God is perhaps one of the most neglected spiritual disciplines of the Christian faith. We give more attention to leaning to our "own understanding," although we know God is trustworthy. We know that there is absolutely, without a doubt no failure in God. We hesitate or ignore our responsibility to trust Him because we're challenged to venture into the circumstantial unknowns.

We face circumstances everyday. We may or may not know how we got into certain situations. We have our own ideas about how we would like things to turn out. We rehearse them over and over in our minds. The bottom line is we really do not know how to deal with our circumstances. We don't know the outcome. Ofttimes, there are a lot of unknowns attached to our circumstances; which sets up a solid case for trusting someone who knows all, sees all and has all power. And yet, we just won't surrender complete trust to Him.

Most of the time, when we say or hear "trust God" or "trust in the Lord," it is because something has happened to cause hurt.

When we express our emotions, we are actually revealing and releasing the condition of the heart. An aching heart usually releases emotional pain. And emotional pain comes from all sorts of disappointing, unexpected and sometimes tragic circumstances.

They may never make front-page news. There will be no books published. No Oprah Winfrey interviews. They are; however, typical circumstances common to human living. I call them low-key adversities that stir up then quickly bury certain emotions. Eventually, the heart reaches emotional overload and finally releases its pain.

They are situations such as an unhappy marriage, a miscarried pregnancy, an angry and rebellious child, the family breadwinner who lost his/her job, living with a terminal illness, a dead-end job, ongoing financial strain, constant rejection by someone you love, a physical disability from an automobile accident.

These situations, while they may not be major compared to school shootings, plane crashes and federal building bombings, are still events of daily life that produce heartache.

So how can one trust God with an aching heart? I'll share my views with you next time.

Until then, keep the faith.

Struggling With Wholehearted or Hole-hearted Trust In God

Originally published June 2001
Reprinted with permission from the
Kansas City Globe

Although God says to trust Him with all your heart (Proverbs 3:5, 6), the challenge and the question are how do we trust God with an aching heart - a heart that is fragmented...broken? There is a difference between wholehearted trust and hole-hearted trust.

I believe most of us are struggling through painful circumstances with hole-hearted trust. This type of trust makes it hard to fully trust God the way we should.

The ability to trust by itself is difficult. The difficulty intensifies when we are faced with trusting our way through adversity.

Trust is a behavior we value. We are selective and guarded when it comes to trusting human beings. If you're too trusting, you can easily be taken advantage of. If persons have a record of untrustworthiness, we say, "we don't trust them as far as we can throw them."

However, one reason God wants us to trust Him is so that we can be less inclined to take life for granted. He wants us to acknowledge Him in all our ways.

As I progressed in my recovery, I had to trust my physical therapist. When she said it was time to use the high-back wheelchair in its most upright position, I had to trust her judgment. When it was time to switch to a wheelchair with less support so that I could use more of my own muscles, I had to trust her. When the day came for me to begin working my way out of the wheelchair and practice walking inside parallel bars, while holding onto the railings; I had to trust her. Then one day she walked in my hospital room with a walker and a belt to strap around my upper body to hold me up, I had better trust her.

Finally, the day came when she took away the walker and handed me two canes, by then I was ready to trust her judgment. I knew that all she was trying to do was help me advance from one stage in my recovery to the next. It was painful. It required more work on my body. I got sick, dizzy, lightheaded and nauseated; but in the long run, it was for my own good.

Hence, acknowledging God "in all thy ways" is the pathway to a gradual, growing trust in Him. Experience after experience, you will become more sensitive to your need to trust Him. But that's OK. God knows that it is for your own good. And with each experience, God proves Himself undeniably trustworthy.

God, like my therapist, knows what is He doing. He is omniscient which means He operates out of all the knowledge He possesses. He is omnipotent meaning that He operates out of all the power that He has. He is omnipresent that means that there is no situation in your life or mine that occurs out of His presence. He is always right there. In fact, He was in the situation before it even reached you or me.

In our struggles to trust God, perhaps the following can help. We should trust Him because:

1) He is the one and only true God, whose very words we can trust. II Samuel 7:28 says, "O Sovereign Lord, You are God. Your words are trustworthy…"

2) He is the essence of truth. Hebrews 6:18 says that it is impossible for God to lie.

3) In Deuteronomy 32:4 the word says that He is a faithful God who does no wrong.

4) God has absolutely all power and ability. Ephesians 3:20, "Now unto him who is able to do exceedingly, abundantly above all we ask or think according to the power that works in us."

5) Lastly, we can trust Him because He loves us unconditionally. In John 15:9, Jesus says, "As the Father has loved me, so I have loved you."

The fact that the Lord puts no conditions on His love towards us is an encouraging starting point. He will accept us just as we are, regardless if He sees us living with wholehearted or hole-hearted trust.

Be encouraged to trust Him and as always, keep the faith until next month.

In God, We Trust (Part I)

Originally published October 30 - November 5, 2008
Reprinted with permission from the
Kansas City Globe

It was a popular Motown groove and back-in-the-day hit by R&B singer Marvin Gaye. "What's goin' on," crooned Gaye? These days, here's a rundown.

Nov. 4, Americans (and people around the world, for that matter) are poised to witness the most historic U.S. presidential election ever.

The nation is entangled in a mortgage crisis rooted in the subprime lending meltdown, billion dollar mortgage loan losses, a drastic decline in new home construction and purchases, and millions of home foreclosures.

Recently, news reports confirmed that more than 30 states are in a recession; more states are expected to join the list.

Consumers are paying record high gasoline prices, and way more for services, utility bills and retail prices compared to last year.

Company layoffs, more job cuts, business acquisitions and companies closing signal unemployment is steadily on the rise.

Racial tension continues to raise its ugly head.

And the rise in crime and violence will make you shake and scratch your head.

While at war in Afghanistan and Iraq, the U.S. can't seem to get ahead.

Back on the home front, the federal government recently had to step up to the plate to bailout American banks. (By now, we know that plan came with a $700 billion taxpayer-paid price tag).

All eyes are on Wall Street. People are losing their hard-earned retirement savings. Nervous investors watch as the stock market plummets again and again, further threatening global economies.

Add to the credit crisis, financial experts predict a consumer credit card crisis on the horizon, while consumer confidence is at an all-time low, even as the value of the American dollar diminishes.

And check this out. The U.S. national debt is so huge until the Times Square debt clock has actually run out of digits to display the country's growing $10 trillion debt.

That is a rundown of "what's goin' on."

Plus in recent weeks, we have either read or listened to troubling news. In some cases, there have been reports of people tragically taking their futures into their own hands.

For example, earlier this month, a CNN *Times.com* headline read, "Murder-Suicide in California: A Tragedy of the Financial Crisis?"

A former financial analyst, husband and father of three shot his wife, mother-in-law and three children before turning the gun on himself. "I understand he was unemployed and his dealings in the stock market had taken a disastrous turn for the worse," said the Los Angeles deputy police chief.

Situations of this magnitude make their way to the Internet, the news channels or Oprah's couch. But there are other lesser-tragic circumstances that come with their own share of pain, dismay, frustrations, disappointments and anxieties. They may seem ordinary and mundane. Obviously, they pale in comparison to the LA tragedy.

Nevertheless, when you assess these situations they raise a question worth contemplating.

What role does trusting God have in our lives? Come on believers. Given the difficulties our country, communities, families and churches face today, perhaps it's time we take to task our tendency to trust God.

We easily recite Scriptures such as:

"Trust in the Lord with all thine heart, lean not to thine own understanding," (Proverbs 3:5, KJV);

"In God have I put my trust: I will not be afraid what man can do unto me," (Psalm 56:11, KJV);

"Thou will keep thee in perfect peace whose mind is stayed on thee because he trusteth in thee," (Isaiah 26:3, KJV).

It's uplifting to sing: *I will trust in the Lord...until I die; 'Tis so sweet to trust in Jesus. Just to take him at his word* and *I trust in God...my Heavenly Father watches over me.*

But today's partisan political climate, along with a struggling economy, pressing community issues and more resonate a call to trust God now, more than ever.

In his book, *Trusting God Even When Life Hurts,* author Jerry Bridges wrote that "the question 'Can you trust God?' presents two possible meanings when trying to answer it." One meaning is Can you TRUST God? The other meaning is Can YOU trust God? Notice the emphasis on TRUST and YOU.

Both meanings are worthy of consideration especially during difficult times.

The first meaning examines our response to trouble. In life, we tend to sink our roots too deep. Then when there's loss of employment, dwindling savings, delayed plans, broken relationships, business losses, home foreclosures, etc., we see just how secure life is not. So when adversity arouses our insecurities, what do we do? Just trust God? Hardly.

Often, trusting God gets pushed to the back burner in exchange for what comfortably comes natural. We don't have to work up worrying; we've got that down pat. We'll plan our exit strategy right out of our troubles, using our timetable. We'll even script the desired outcome. All the while, we say we trust God (that is, with crossed fingers behind our backs).

Or, we'll excitedly express our trust in God. We easily anticipate our immediate, victorious deliverance. There's one problem, though. We just can't seem to trust what God is doing in the process. So in protest, we feel God takes too long, uses the wrong people and compounds the problem.

Trials come. Believe it or not, God is with us from start to finish. He doesn't allow our trials to start, then make a mad dash to the finish line to await our arrival once we've gone through.

Psalm 46:1 affirms, "God is our refuge and strength, a very present help in trouble."

Those trying experiences teach us the greatest lessons about God as He conforms us to the image of Jesus Christ, and as the Holy Spirit leads us into truth.

As we experience trials, we begin to realize the truth that comes from an old hymn, *through it (trials) all...(we) learn to trust in Jesus...learn to depend on God...learn to depend upon His word.*

I'll continue in November with more on the two meanings.

Until then, keep the faith.

Trusting God, Even When Life Hurts

<u>An update on physical healing</u>
Originally published March 5 - 11, 2009
Reprinted with permission from the
Kansas City Globe

In God, We Trust. We rarely pay attention, but this is printed or engraved on every piece of money.

Yet, when you consider recent events surrounding America's economic crisis, you will wonder if God really is the object of our trust.

Businessman Bernie Madoff (ironically pronounced "made-off") almost made off with fortunes after bilking billions from unsuspecting investors. The lineup of some corporations seeking a bailout from the feds can be traced back to some bad business decisions, exorbitant bonuses and the lack of vision for today's consumers.

But this month's column is not devoted to this country's money matters that continue daily to make news headlines.

Instead, I'm picking up where I left off a couple months back in a column titled, *In God, We Trust.*

I asked the questions: "Can God be trusted?" "Can believers really make trust a way of life?"

Or simply put, can you TRUST God? And can YOU trust God? The answers are best determined after going through situations where trust is put to the test.

Initially, both questions were posed in a book I read years back and still occasionally pick up. The book is titled, *Trusting God, Even When Life Hurts*.

The title alone is provocative. Just reading "God" and "When Life Hurts" in the same sentence intrigued me to purchase the book.

Up until then, when I encountered hurtful situations I would pray to God. I'd sing my God songs. I would turn to close friends and family to listen and bask in the encouragement of their God-inspired council. But to trust God? Honestly, I did if I sensed a guarantee from God that He was going to fix my problems my way and according to my schedule. So much for trust, *right?*

The book's author, Jerry Bridges, prompts readers to ponder another question: "Is the whole idea of trusting God in adversity merely a Christian shibboleth (or catchword) that doesn't stand up in the face of the difficult events of life?"

Usually during adverse times, God makes it as far as our subconscious minds can comprehend. Yet, when we finally come face-to-face with trusting God, we resist. We're challenged to put all on the line — preconceived notions, jumping to erroneous conclusions, second-guessing God and even our *Underdog* "here-I-come-to-save-the-day" mentality.

I've learned that trust is a necessary discipline, if I am going to be serious about moving from wishful thinking to genuine life-changing experiences God orchestrates.

However, I clearly understand the profound effect of troubling circumstances. The breadwinner of the home unexpectedly gets a pink slip from an employer of 20+ years. A loved one is diagnosed with a terminal illness.

After a period of hard work, there is a major setback in long-awaited, highly anticipated plans. A crumbling career path, business venture gone bad, coming to terms with self-inflicted failures or a sudden change in health can make adjusting to life's adversities stressful, overwhelming, traumatic and emotionally challenging.

I was in that situation almost 12 years ago. The paralysis I live with today is the result of a head-on collision by someone driving under the influence. Living with a spinal cord injury and related health challenges meant that every area of my life was affected.

No one had given me a playbook on how to adjust. I didn't know a soul in a similar condition. So, I had to start at ground zero and ferret out my faith in His promises to heal my body. There are several promises that I live by. But the main promise is, "'I will restore health unto you. I will heal you of your wounds,' declares the Lord," (Jeremiah 30:17, NIV).

Along the way, I also realized that I had to take God off my schedule and surrender my strategy to however He chose to bless through His healing grace.

So to the question, "Can YOU trust God?" Well, I had to, "Trust in the Lord with all thine (my) heart and lean not to thine (my) own understanding," (Proverbs 3:5, KJV).

To clarify, God didn't force me into this. I am determined to overcome the mistakes and missteps that keep me from receiving God's best. Therefore, "I" have to "trust."

Furthermore, I could not let moments of doubt, episodes of intense neurological pain and muscle stiffness prove to be formidable foes to my best intentions to trust God.

As He continues to impress upon my spirit to keep at it, the experience is worth the challenge. I'm excited to share with you that God continues to manifest healing in my body.

Earlier this year, I noticed more return of feeling on my left side. I am able to walk with greater balance. My left upper leg shows signs of more voluntary movement and the lower left leg has a trace of movement.

I'm eager to begin soon a therapy program designed to maximize use of muscle activity and feeling that has already returned.

It's been 12 years and counting, anticipating more healing while conscientiously learning to make trust a vital way of life. Actually, this is only one of many testimonies on trusting God, yes even when life hurts. I hope this encourages you, because I've discovered that when life hurts; He is always ready to heal.

Until next month, keep the faith.

God Sees You

Originally published August 5 - 11, 2010
Reprinted with permission from the
Kansas City Globe

It has been since April when I last shared with you in the monthly columns. I was hospitalized twice and underwent two surgeries. However, as I recover I am now ready and anxious to resume reaching out to you through, "Expect A Miracle." It just dawned on me as I typed the title words to the column. The outcome of my recent health experiences affirms that I can always expect God to work in ways that defy odds and dispel any doubts about His care for me.

God's word in Exodus 15:26b says, "...for I am the Lord that heals thee." And my steadfast yet humbled testimony is that I know I am one who is living by God's healing grace. So, I'm excited about this month's column simply because God has given me another opportunity.

I recently read in a devotional magazine I receive monthly about a wife and mother of four young children who lives with Chronic Lyme—a disease that causes extreme pain, fatigue and other symptoms. Also, she indicated that she battles discouragement because of her inability to live a "productive Christian life." For you see in the church, culture being a faithful follower of Christ is usually measured by active church involvement and consistent church attendance. She wrote, "Just taking care of myself and my family took all my energy.

The idea of 'Christian service' felt completely overwhelming when I was just trying to survive."

Eventually her contemplations gave way to divine insight. She discovered that "God sees the disabled as able." She realized she could still bear fruit (John 15) and influence those whose paths she crossed.

While in the hospital, I often meditated on Genesis 16, the story of Abram, Sarai and Hagar. This story highlights Sarai's scheme to jump the gun on God, give Hagar the handmaiden over to Abram so that Hagar would give birth to Abram's firstborn son, whom they thought would be the "child of promise," Galatians 4:28.

You may be wondering why on earth was I spending time in God's word on this particular story. Well, it is because of Hagar's response to the angel of the Lord that I could speak to my situation as I laid in my hospital bed.

"She (Hagar) gave this name to the Lord who spoke to her, 'You are the God who sees me,' for she said, 'I have now seen the One who sees me'." I remember praying repeatedly, "God, you see me."

And God sees you just as He saw Hagar in her dilemma. Many of us can recall times when we were frustrated because we thought God did not see enough into our troubling situations to do anything to turn them around. Hagar's testimony would fly in the face of our anguish.

She said God is the "God who sees me." This was the name she gave God although she had not experienced the better side of her circumstance. When she encountered the angel of the Lord, Hagar was a pregnant runaway, on the run from an oppressive Sarai. Hagar had no clue where she was headed (verse 8). The angel instructed her to return to that same hostile environment that she was running from. Yet, she still cried in awe, "God is the One who sees."

When we're experiencing problems, at some point, we must also realize our need to surrender our doubts, fears and speculations to the truth that God really "made us and knows all about us." Our parents in the Lord made this claim when they prayed. They had been through enough to know that God had every iota of their experiences under His watchful eye; just as He saw the Israelites in bondage in Egypt. "The Lord said, 'I have indeed seen the misery of my people in Egypt...I have come down to rescue them...'" (Exodus 3:7-8).

In Luke chapter 15, God is depicted as the father who saw. After a wasteful stint in the far country, the broken down prodigal son was closer in his return home. Verse 20 says, "But while he was still a long way off, his father saw him and was filled with compassion for him."

God foresaw and affirmed Peter's potential to recover from his faith failure and subsequently be effectively used in ministry to others. Jesus told him, "Simon, Satan has asked to sift you as wheat. But I have prayed for you that your faith may fail not and when you have turned, strengthen your brothers," (Luke 22:31-32, NIV).

The God who sees will also always be the God who knows how to address every issue we face and every need we have. Are you like Hagar needing God to work in the midst of a messy situation presented as a threat to God's plan for you? Do you need assurance that God sees you as once gone astray and now reaching out and running back to Him?

Like the Israelites, are you feeling the love of misery keeping you company while also feeling trapped, with no hope of freedom in sight?

Are you aware that like Peter, God sees the best in you when everyone else around only sees the worst in you? If so, be encouraged. God sees you. And if you let God show you, you'll eventually see what I mean.

Until next month, keep the faith.

Chapter 3
Lord, I Need You

"You deserve honesty from the heart..." Psalm 51:6

How many times have you prayed, cried out or silently admitted to yourself, "Lord, I need you" to do something or show me something? That something? You fill in the blank.

For me, the blank I filled in dates back to 1979. I was in the middle of my third year in college at Kansas State University in Manhattan, Ks.

In the spring of that year, I received a phone call one evening. It was Kathy, my oldest sister. The news was not good; the call sent chills through me. The short version of a long story — my youngest sister, Sharion, had to be hospitalized. At seven years old, she suffered a stroke that paralyzed her left side. She was unable to talk and diagnosed with a condition where her toes had decayed so badly until they separated from her foot while she was bathing. The same affected her fingers and eventually they were amputated.

All of this resulted over a period of time from a fall down the stairs. Eventually she was diagnosed with a condition known as Raynaud's Syndrome.

Kathy told me that I needed to contact our father, who at the time, was working construction out-of-town not far from Manhattan. She finally got around to telling me I needed to return home because it was questionable if Sharion (as she put it) "would make it."

Needless to say the news was upsetting. I called but did not know how to tell Daddy. I struggled to remain calm because I had to share the details of Sharion's condition with him as best I could. Voice trembling, I greeted him. Immediately he seemed to brace himself as I shared my conversation with Kathy. While I was describing Sharion's condition, I heard Daddy get emotional, his voice fading and he tried to carry on the conversation with me. Tearfully we ended the conversation and I spent the rest of the evening overcome with emotions, questions and trying to think through arrangements and plans to go home to Kansas City.

The news spread to some of my Delta Sigma Theta sorority sisters. I was a basket case and could not clearly think of what to do next. My roommate, Yolonda, who was also a member of our rival sorority Alpha Kappa Alpha, was sympathetically supportive and encouraging. These ladies were there for me, working together to help me get through the evening.

My sorors worked out a plan to drive me to Kansas City the next day. Obviously, I was in no shape for a three-hour drive home. As we traveled the interstate, it seemed like the longest three hours. For the most part, I was nervously numb, in disbelief and silently panicking.

We finally arrived in Kansas City, went straight to the hospital and I made a bee-line to my sister's room in ICU. I walked in and there she lay listless, flat on her back and unable to move, except for turning her head towards me. All I could see were the whites of her eyes. I don't think she recognized me. A closer look at her surroundings, I noticed she was wearing a large, white boot on her left leg. Her hands were wrapped in bandages up to her wrist, because she apparently underwent the surgery to remove the remaining decayed digits that had not fallen off. So she has no fingers and toes. And I just froze. I was overcome with tears yet I was relieved to be home.

It was a tense and traumatic experience for us as a family. I stayed in Kansas City for a couple of weeks during which time it was apparent I was needed at home to help out. So I decided to go back to K-State to get incomplete grades in all of my classes, leave before the end of the semester and return home.

The day before I actually left, I stopped by the local pharmacy. I had only $10 to my name. I did not have anything particular to buy but noticed a display at the end of an aisle with green-covered *Living Bibles* for sale. I picked up one, thumbed through it and was intrigued that it was easy-to-read, easy-to-understand. The Bible was $9 and some change. So with that last $10, I purchased it. Later on, that purchase would prove to be the best I ever made.

The next day I moved back home. I was uncertain about the days, unsure if I would be able to complete my college education at K-State. But certain that for now, I needed to be with my family.

Kathy was instrumental in helping me get a job working in the personnel department for the Kansas City School District. The office was located in the Board of Education Building on 12th & McGee. Kathy worked in the same department in insurance and benefits.

But it was tough on the family in many ways, financially included. Mother spent an inordinate amount of time at the hospital. I was the oldest sister at home. So I made another decision — take on a part-time job. It was the least I could do to help out.

The days seemed long. I woke up at six in the morning to get to work by eight o'clock, then leave at 4:30 that afternoon to catch a yellow school bus waiting just outside of the Board of Education Building to take workers to the baseball stadium to work during home games. That was my part-time gig, Royals concessions at Kauffman Stadium.

After the part-time shift, I got off work at 11 at night. I rode the school bus back downtown to catch The Metro's Swope Parkway bus at 11th & Grand. Around midnight, I stepped off The Metro bus at 56th & Swope Parkway, frantically made a mad dash down the hill of Friendship Village Townhomes. The split second I entered the front door, I was thankful I made it home unharmed.

Before going to bed, I picked up the Bible I purchased in Manhattan. I never knew where to start reading. I just thumbed through pages, read a few verses, said my prayers and turned off the light to go to sleep.

This was the weekly routine. On the first Wednesday in July, in the wee hours, something totally unexpected happened. It was what I now consider my first major turning point. Little did I know that it would set the stage for the life I now experience.

After getting off work from the night job and making the frantic sprint from the bus stop to our townhome, I was exhausted. I was also nervous from the fear of being out alone, in the dark and so late at night. Actually, I felt as though I was at the end of my rope. Nevertheless, I still picked up my Bible and somehow turned to Psalm 51. I read the first few words, "Oh loving and kind God..." I continued to read and the more I read, the more some of the words penned in this chapter seemed to address whatever was happening inside my heart. "You deserve honesty from the heart...Create in me a new, clean heart...Don't toss me aside..." These were the words I needed to express to God.

As I prayed, I repeated the words in the Scriptures as though I had committed them to memory; although I read these verses for the very first time. I remember ending the prayer with, "Lord, my sister is sick and I am sin sick, and I need you to come into my life." That was the blank I filled in. "...I need you (Lord) to come into my life."

When I turned off the light in my room and laid down, I closed my eyes and immediately a light shone in the room that was so bright until it was as though my eyes were open. Afterwards, I noticed a sense of peace in my spirit. This unusual calm was unlike a feeling of relaxation from fatigue. I was under unbearable pressure from the weight of responsibilities I had assumed, while also feeling tense over the possibility of encountering danger from being out and on foot late at night. Oddly though, I knew that whatever I was experiencing so immediately after I prayed, it had to be from God. My prayers were answered that very moment.

Up until then, I felt like a scared little girl, trying to help out financially around the home; trying to piece together what was going to become of me and this situation my family was experiencing. *Would I be able to return to K-State? Is Sharion going to pull out of this?* I tried to shield the fear, burden, anxiety and strain around others, but I carried these emotions on the inside. I was just so unsure about the future–just going through the motions trying to help out. Still, at times I wondered if perhaps I had taken on more than I could handle.

So July 1979 marked a new beginning for me, my first turning point. Although the situation was dramatic and the details beyond my ability to rationally describe, it was yet a decisive and defining moment.

In his message, *Opportunity Out of Chaos*, Bishop T.D. Jakes recalls a time when he was driving using his GPS (Global Positioning Satellite) and yet he still made a wrong turn.

Keep Turning: Lord, I Need You

For anyone who is challenged with directions while driving, having a GPS in your car is a welcomed piece of technology. There's no need to pretend as if you're a pro at knowing your way around the city. Husbands don't have to hear wives nag them to stop at the nearest gas station to ask for directions. Just let GPS talk you through the directions and take all the guesswork out of getting you to your destination.

But you have to be sure to pay attention. Otherwise, you will make a wrong turn as if no instructions were given.

When Bishop Jakes made that wrong turn, the GPS instructed him to make a U-turn "when possible," he recalled. He further explained that he still had to look for a turning point even though he had the benefit of the GPS. When he saw the place to turn, it "was at an intersection with a lot of traffic," he said. That meant he "had to get in the position and wait for the moment to make the turn in order to reverse" the mistake he previously made.

This is a profound analogy that I believe relates to life experiences. Consider this. The struggles, heartaches, pain and disappointments that affect us could also be viewed as "God's Positioning System" or GPS setting us up for unforeseen turning points to a greater, meaningful purpose. Nevertheless, we have to be open and willing to follow the directions God provides.

When I think about all of the turning points in my life, I now understand the importance of being in position or even repositioned to make "the one big turn" that will make the difference for a lifetime.

Looking back to July 1979 on a Wednesday around midnight, I was moved to pray a prayer I never imagined I needed to pray, "Lord, I need you to come into my life."

It was the first time I ever prayed out of a deep sense of knowing that something about Anita needed to change. Prior to this, I was a bundle of nerves and emotions, yet I managed to free myself from the inner turmoil long enough to get to God.

Allow me to pause at this point to encourage you in whatever you may be facing. If only you could muster up enough strength to get past your pain and confusion to simply pray, "Lord, I need you," then your help will come sooner than you think.

July 1979 was the first time I admitted my need of God, but it certainly was not the last. I have prayed that prayer countless times ever since. I know that I will be confronted with more situations that will prompt, if not drive, me to pray the same.

However, when I asked the Lord to come into my life, that was the pivotal turning point upon which hinged upon every situation I have experienced afterwards, and am still experiencing today.

I say this because the summer of 1979 I was "born again," a new Anita. A few weeks later, I learned this expression and its meaning from Jesus' response (John chapter three) to a religious leader named Nicodemus who privately asked Jesus its meaning. How can an adult re-enter the womb to experience a second birth?

By now, I had returned to K-State to resume my studies. Sharion was out of the woods, although still in the hospital. Mother encouraged me and insisted I go back. So I did and I made sure I had my *Living Bible* in tow. I enrolled carrying a full class load, plus there were assignments to complete in order to change the 'Incompletes" to grades. Additionally, I signed up with a work-study program. I needed to work to supplement my education and living expenses.

My schedule was jam-packed. However, I noticed that I was spending more time reading my Bible and passing up going out to weekend parties at the student union. It used to be my weekend partying pastime. As my chapter's dean of pledges, now I would only go out when the Deltas or all the Greek organizations on campus sponsored a party.

Even better, I became fascinated with reading the Bible, especially the Gospels. I understood what I read. *The Living Bible* cracked the King James Version's vocabulary codes of "hithers" and "thithers."

I knew a change had occurred in my life. I believed that Jesus had everything to do with that change, but I knew very little about Him. The Gospels were for me the most logical reference to Jesus' life because they were filled with red-letter print. Some may wonder, perhaps even chuckle, because I mention this. Back then, red-letter edition Bibles were a quick find to the life of Jesus. This type of print is commonly known as the words of Jesus. And the Book of John was perhaps the most red-lettered of all the Gospels. I first began learning about Jesus by reading this book of the Bible. It came across so personal, so heartfelt. I was drawn to it. I became increasingly devoted to reading.

My favorite verse was John 3:16, "God so loved the world that he gave his only begotten Son. Whosoever believes in Him will not perish but have everlasting life." Here was written proof that God loved me. God made good on His unconditional for us when He gave His only Son as a priceless gift. To think that all it takes is to start by believing Jesus is the Son of God.

Reading John's Gospel deepened my understanding about Jesus' death on the cross, the phenomena that occurred when He was raised from death and His promise to return to earth as He was taken away in the clouds. I could not put it down. *The Living Bible* read and flowed with ease, which helped me to quickly comprehended the reality of Biblical references such as Jesus sacrificing His life, His crucifixion, resurrection and ascension.

I heard these expressions from attending church with my family as a child and teenager. I was even baptized at age 12. We attended Emanuel Baptist Church. I remember Daddy serving as a deacon, while Mother was the church announcer for the live radio broadcast and during the church services. My sister, Kathy sang in the choir. What stuck out in my mind was seeing Daddy, Mother and Kathy out front. Regina, Tressa and I were restless girls with eyes occasionally peering up from the pews to make sure Mother couldn't see us getting into mischief.

One Sunday, I broke ranks from my sisters and proceeded towards the front of the church to the front-row pew, as a demonstration of my desire to be baptized. Eventually, that day came. About three weeks later one Sunday evening, I was baptized and I took communion for the first time.

Thus, the terminology previously mentioned was not totally foreign to me. And yet crucifixion, resurrection and ascension took on a new meaning and relevance in this new life I began living. Of my own initiative and from an inner commitment to read the Bible, over time I learned that "born again," "saved" and "Christian" all meant the same.

Throughout years of struggles, trials, disappointments, heartaches and pain my sense of self-worth, aspirations, optimism and desire to make something of myself often collided with doubts and questions about being a Christian. Many times I found myself going back to day-one when God answered the life-changing prayer that I prayed, "Lord, I need you..."

Since then, I have filled in the blanks with accounts of my life that, like this account, expose my genuine need for God. I needed His help in many areas of my life but mainly to live by faith. I also needed God's help in treasuring and maintaining close relationships. I highly value relationships and never wanted my friends and family to question where they stood with me. Obviously I needed the Lord to help me not only endure experiences of loss, but also to appreciate seasons of success.

These accounts have emerged as turning points that I am not ashamed or too proud to share as you keep turning the pages.

Everyday I find myself fighting for my freedom. Sometimes, it's a toe-to-toe, mean-mugging encounter. Other times, it's a hotly contested debate against the opponent. Then there are moments I have to put my foot down and stand my ground. And in some situations, I will ball up my fist and take a swing.

I am free and I cannot allow systems, people, situations and challenges to re-write my standing in life. In no way am I advocating violence. This freedom I am referring to is not in my race, gender, financial status or age. It has less to do with the accessibility that accommodates my physical disability.

This freedom is challenged to a daily sword-drawing duel because it is rooted in who I am in Christ based on God's word. Either somebody did not get the memo or tossed it in file 13, but I am free to be God's new, spiritual creation. I no longer have to be bogged down and bound to a flesh-controlled life that settles for a generic and general impression of Jesus.

He is free to intimately live His life through me. This intimacy awakens my spiritual sensitivity so that I can relate to God and tap into the greatest love I will ever experience. Based on this love, I am free to live as an overcomer against those stigmas that falsely define the real me.

Instinctively, I know who and whose I am and how God wants to use me. In Jesus, I clearly see my liberty which was secured when He died on the cross. For this reason, I cherish the cross. This emblem of suffering and shame represents the decisive blow needed to liberate me from my pre-existing sinful condition. Turn the pages for *Globe* articles on life, liberty and love through Jesus Christ.

'Oh Say, Can You See...' Your Liberty? Part I
Originally published July 16 - 22, 2009
Reprinted with permission from the
Kansas City Globe

It came and went so quickly until it's hard to believe this holiday was celebrated just two weeks ago. I'm referring to July 4th, a.k.a. Independence Day.

Every year on July 4, America celebrates its independence from Great Britain's government in 1776 which also signaled the birth of the United States starting with 13 colonies.

In general, we use this occasion to commemorate our freedom and formation as a country. It's a federal holiday so most people enjoy time off work to barbecue, have picnics and family reunions, shoot fireworks or go somewhere and watch as elaborate fireworks displays light up the sky...the whole nine.

Americans do this all in the name of freedom. There's nothing like it. Who wouldn't want to be free? Any volunteers to be slaves?

Most of the time when we think of the term slave, we immediately think of being oppressed, controlled and in a situation with an intense desire to be free, i.e. the Israelites under Egyptian bondage or our heritage as African-Americans.

From Biblical history and out of our tradition, many people readily look to leaders such as Moses and Harriet Tubman, a.k.a. "the Moses of her people." Both in their own right led people to freedom.

Believe it or not, though, slavery has not ended. *Oh, I*

know that, you may think. But before you hastily rush to the plight of a third world country or to some religious compound, you may want to take a closer look…right in the mirror.

Is this you? Do you attend church week after week, listen to sermons, sing songs and even share your finances? Do you also read the Bible, pray and maybe serve in an area of your church? While all of this is good, deep down inside; however, you know that it's only on the surface.

You may be one of countless Christians who ponder that there has to be more to it than this. Or you may feel that this is as good as it gets. So you continue to follow the routine, have settled into the mundane without a clue about what it means to experience genuine spiritual growth—just going through the motions of the same ol', same ol'.

You see, we're good at claiming our freedom. We'll shout it to the heavens. But truthfully too often the temptation to yield to wrongdoings is more intense than the test to say yes to the things of God.

It's difficult to see (let alone experience) liberty in Christ when the "old man's," ways (Colossians 3:5-10) can easily serve as comfort food that satisfies our fleshly appetites.

When this happens we only set ourselves up to be less than the person God desires and more like the person the Enemy demands.

Yes, it's true. Even as Christians we are subject to miss experiencing the full measure of liberty in Christ Jesus. God has always planned liberty for us.

When Jesus announced His public ministry in Luke 4:18, He read from the Book of Isaiah telling all who were assembled in the synagogue, "the Spirit of the Lord is upon me, because he anointed me to preach the gospel to the poor. He has sent me to proclaim release to the captives, and recovery of sight to the blind, to set free those who are oppressed."

Twice in this announcement, Jesus refers to freedom as part of His ministry – release the captives, set free the oppressed.

In addition, the word "Gospel" or good news is used for the first time in Scripture and its Greek translation literally means "good news from the battlefield."

Jesus' words were liberating for those in the synagogue whose lives never seemed to escape doubts, fears, heartaches and emotional scars. Life's battles kept them enslaved and struggling with seemingly no hope for freedom in sight. They could not see their liberty.

I believe the same is true today for many dedicated churchgoing Christians.

Nevertheless, God has willed that Christians walk in liberty. Next month, I will share more about what God has done to help us experience the freedom in Christ for which the ultimate sacrifice was made.

Until then, keep the faith.

'Oh Say, Can You See...' Your Liberty?, Part II

Originally printed September 24 - 30, 2009
Reprinted with permission from the
Kansas City Globe

Before I share this month's topic, humbly I feel indebted to you, the *Kansas City Globe* reader, and to Marion and Denise Jordon for recognizing me among the 100 Most Influential Kansas City African-Americans in my ministry and profession—media and marketing. Congratulations to all who were selected.

For me, it is the most meaningful recognition of my life. It came at a time when decisively my primary focus is to be used by God to make a difference in others' lives. Despite my own challenges, those opportunities seem to keep coming; those opportunities keep me going.

Furthermore, your feedback keeps me searching for topics to share that I pray will encourage you – topics such as the one this month.

In the last column, I ended, '*Oh Say, Can You See*'... *Your Liberty?* by stating that I would share what God has done to help us experience freedom in Christ.

To live in our society is to live in pursuit of as much freedom as humanly possible. From the moment we are old enough to realize it, our nature longs for, at times manipulates and often pushes the edge in its quest for independence. This quest begins at early childhood then carries over into adulthood.

We live to do what we want, whenever we want, with whomever we want, wherever we want. And should we act irresponsibly or without regard to obedience to God, we feel we should be free from any consequences.

Nevertheless, freedom costs. That's why freedom cries out for boundaries. Sounds like a contradiction? Actually it's not.

We have freedom of speech. Right? But listen to the increasingly negative commentary partly responsible for fueling intense and angry criticisms of politicians and the role of government.

The freedom of communicating through social media invites all sorts of predatory, criminal and unwholesome activity that prey upon the impressionable and naïve and are beyond the reach of regulatory safeguards.

How about this example: teens want freedom from parents; parents long for the day to be free from raising their children. So now society is plagued with higher than ever rates of teens dropping out of high school, violence, teen suicide, life-threatening STDs and youth incarcerations.

On another front, many who considered themselves free to spend however they chose now live within the bondage of debt, unable to make ends meet and the fear of collection agency calls.

There are so many examples I could share. But I think you get my point. Because we choose to abuse freedom, God in His infinite wisdom knows that freedom needs boundaries.

We mistakenly think we are free because we can choose our beliefs, habits and behaviors although they may contradict God's will.

According to Galatians 5:1, the basis for genuine freedom is in Christ. "It was for freedom that Christ set us free." This means that Christians are no longer bound to anything that opposes God and are free to pursue whatever God has planned for their lives. Christians are "called to be free." Yet we are "not to use that freedom to indulge the sinful nature; rather, serve one another in love," Galatians 5:13.

This alone is revolutionary because often times we don't view being the person God wants us to be as freedom. We erroneously believe the Christian way takes all of the zest and zeal out of life. Hence, we can't see our liberty.

Being the person God desires also means being free to learn and receive Biblical truth, John 8:31, 32. "To the Jews who had believed him, Jesus said, 'if you hold to my teaching, you are really my disciple. Then you will know the truth, and the truth will set you free'."

Jesus concludes this debate on freedom by setting the record straight, "I tell you the truth, everyone who sins is the slave to sin," John 8:34. "So if the Son sets you free, you will be free indeed," John 8:36.

Based on the above Scriptures, we can rest assured that in Christ we are not only free from sin but also from the bondage of insecurity, a guilt-ridden past, low self-esteem, the effects of rejection, the tendency to compromise – whatever robs us of the life God wants us to enjoy.

I hope you have been helped by this insight so that now your liberty is something you can see.

Until next month, keep the faith.

How's Your Love Life?
Originally published May 5 - 11, 2011
Reprinted with permission from the
Kansas City Globe

How would you respond if you were asked, "How's your love life?" Some would sarcastically respond, "What love life?" Others might awkwardly say, "Why would you ask a question like that?" Then again I wouldn't be surprised if some would immediately, euphorically answer, "It's faann-tas-tic!"

This is a question that is not asked daily, but maybe it should.

Now before you take this statement and run with it, let me clarify by saying I'm not referring to the love shared between spouses or significant others.

Many of us recall these lyrics, *What the world needs now is love, sweet love. It's the only thing that there's just too little of...No, not just for some but for everyone.*

The lyrics are so true. It's also true that the world has love. It's a love that is unconditional and difficult to comprehend. Nevertheless, it exists.

It's God's love and in its highest expression, His love has been given to us through His Son, Jesus Christ.

The central verse in John chapter three says, "For God so loved the world that He gave His only begotten Son. Whosoever believes in Him will not perish, but have eternal life," (v. 16).

God loves us unconditionally. Nowhere in this verse does Jesus offer a reason or rationale for God's love. He just loves. In choosing to love, God is simply being and expressing who He is – a loving God (I John 4:8).

However, knowing and experiencing that love in a personal and intimate way is another story. It is conditioned upon believing in Jesus as God's Son sent to be the Savior of the world.

Beyond that moment of salvation, there awaits a lifetime of intimacy with God that increasingly awakens our senses so that we are able to spiritually relate to Him; thus we tap into the greatest love we'll ever experience.

So the question is how's your love life?

Sadly many believers miss the genuine essence of God's love. They are so consumed with the things of this world and their cares of life. They actually do not know or have not considered the fact that each day God allows us to live, He also constantly reveals His love.

In Psalm 63, David describes an active pursuit of God that can only be the result of his insatiable love for the Lord. "O God, you are my God; earnestly I seek you; my soul thirsts for you; my flesh faints for you, as in a dry and weary land where there is no water," (Psalm 63:1).

These words are not the sentiments of what some may call "a love-sick puppy." Instead David describes a love for God that is so deep within until without it, there's an achy feeling. His life is unfulfilled – faint, dry and weary.

I recall the lyrics of a popular praise and worship song which says, *I'm chasing after you, no matter what I have to do. 'Cause I need you more and more.*

In human love relationships, especially those are that in the beginning stages, there exists a passionate desire for the other person.

In this Psalm, David affirms that same desire for God.

So again, how's your love life? How often can you say you've felt the same way?

In the same Psalm, David's love for God enabled him to see God as the God who was worthy of praise. "So I have looked upon you in the sanctuary, beholding your power and glory. Because your steadfast love is better than life, my lips will praise you," (Psalm 63:2, 3).

A book entitled, *The Five Love Languages* by Dr. Gary Chapman is credited for reviving relationships on the rocks. According to Chapman one of the love languages is a word of "Affirmation." He explains, "…unsolicited compliments mean the world to you. Hearing the words, 'I love you,' are important—hearing the reasons behind that love sends your spirits skyward. Insults can leave you shattered and are not easily forgotten." Thus, positive expressions will attract; negativity repels.

When our love prompts spontaneous or intentional affirmations of who God is and all He has done then expect the relationship to get closer. "I (God) have loved you with an everlasting love; I have drawn you with loving-kindness," (Jeremiah 31:3b, NIV).

Also in love relationships, there's the tendency to reflect especially during those quiet, private moments. It's automatic. Love can leave you vulnerable yet you're inspired as you revisit a parade of memorable moments. Merely thinking through those memories, one after another, can lift your spirits.

Consider how David was also consumed with his personal reflections of God. He wrote, "When I remember you upon my bed, and meditate on you in the watches of the night; for you have been my help, and in the shadow of your wings I will sing for joy," (Psalm 63:6, 7).

In your love life, how often do you recall the goodness of God? How much time do you allow for personal, private reflections that make you want to just burst with praise?

Like our human relationships, love expressions don't just happen and closeness isn't instantaneous.

The love relationship we have in God needs just as much our time and attention in order to experience love to the fullest.

So how's your love life? It's a question you should not shy away from. Instead, you should consider assessing your love relationship with the Lord. It may be worth pondering so that you can respond immediately, euphorically, "It's faann-tas-tic!"

Until next month, keep the faith.

Why 'Cherish the Old Rugged Cross?'
Originally published March 29, 2007 - April 4, 2007
Reprinted with permission from the
Kansas City Globe

There are things in life that we cherish. Often it's because the sentimental value, monetary worth or its expensive material composition makes it priceless. Or it inspires memories that we treasure. If it's tangible, it may have a special designated place stored away as a keepsake. Or it's in plain and public view for all to see.

If it's something you remember, you may not think of it often. But let an event, someone you know, a landmark or object cross your path; you'll make an instant connection so that what you cherish as memory appears during that moment as reality.

It's refreshing when we can cherish the good things, those good memories that leave us with a good feeling, a sense of calm and even hope.

If you're a believer reading this month's column, allow me to take you back in time as I attempt to answer the question presented in its title, "Why *Cherish the Old Rugged Cross?*"

In general, Christians appreciate the cross because as the traditional hymn proclaims it is *the emblem of suffering and shame*. Also, Jesus Christ "endured the cross, despising that shame" (Hebrews 12:2) when in fact, that should have been our punishment.

The crucifixion was an extremely graphic and dramatic form of public punishment and humiliation. Nails were driven through Jesus' flesh from point to head. The nails penetrated His hands and feet tightly securing Him to the cross' wood-splintered surface. His arms were extended the length of the cross until He hung so that the bones of His shoulders, arms, hands and pelvis were out of joint. No other part of His body was supported. Jesus already was intensely exhausted from being brutally beaten throughout the night just before He journeyed to Calvary. He perspired profusely. And as the blood flowed freely from His body, so did His life. The first part of Leviticus 17:11 says, "The life of the flesh is in the blood…"

I'm sure my feeble attempt to briefly capture what Jesus endured while on the cross faintly scratches the surface of what actually happened. But sometimes we get so caught up celebrating Jesus' dying in our stead, until we perhaps fail to consider the details of this punishment that justifiably should have been ours.

The cross' message tells us that Jesus sacrificed His life, accepted full and final punishment for the sins of the world and willingly allowed Himself to be the perfect substitute to pay the sin debt no man had enough righteousness to pay.

The means to accomplish this required the cruelest physical abuse. Even the prophet Isaiah foretold that "there were many who were appalled at him." Why? Because Jesus' "appearance was so disfigured beyond that of any man and his form marred beyond human likeness," (52:14). In other words, Jesus was so viciously beaten beyond recognition until it disgraced many to look at Him on the cross, dying a death that left the earth dark for three hours.

Psalms 22:14-16 prophetically depicts what happened that was fulfilled when Jesus was made a public spectacle during the crucifixion. "I am poured out like water, and all my bones are out of joint. My heart has turned to wax; it has melted away within me. My strength is dried up like a potsherd, and my tongue sticks to the roof of my mouth; you lay me in the dust of death. Dogs have surrounded me; a band of evil men has encircled me, they have pierced my hands and my feet." All of this took place while Jesus hung on the cross.

These are details that get away from us as we break out in jubilance, rejoicing over our sin-debt-paid-by-the-Savior celebrations.

And yet, the cross is to be cherished. Stained with the blood of Jesus, its value and worth go beyond sentiment to sacrifice. On the cross, the sinless Savior willingly endures the worst form of human sacrifice ever known.

It was not a cross made of gold, but it is nonetheless priceless. It lacked the brilliance that appeals to the naked eye. The cross was rugged.

Still, the cross was essential to God's plan to rescue our sinful selves, redeem us with the bloodshed of His only Son and give us opportunity to right relationship and eternal life with Him. God's plan should appeal to anyone in pursuit of a second chance at life.

And so, I encourage you in this season of the crucifixion and resurrection of our Lord and Savior, to cherish the cross reflecting on the verses to this meaningful hymn:

> On a hill far away stood an Old Rugged Cross,
> The emblem of suffering and shame;
> And I love that old cross where the dearest and best
> For a world of lost sinners was slain.
> Oh that Old Rugged Cross, so despised by the world,
> Has a wondrous attraction for me;
> For the dear Lamb of God left His glory above
> To bear it to dark Calvary.
> In that Old Rugged Cross, stained with blood so divine,
> A wondrous beauty I see,
> For 'twas on that old cross Jesus suffered and died,
> To pardon and sanctify me.
> To the Old Rugged Cross I will ever be true;
> Its shame and reproach gladly bear;
> Then He'll call me some day to my home far away,
> Where His glory forever I'll share.
> So I'll cherish the Old Rugged Cross,
> Till my trophies at last I lay down;
> I will cling to the Old Rugged Cross,
> And exchange it some day for a crown.

Until next month, keep the faith.

Everyone Has A Pre-Existing Condition

Originally published March 25 – 31, 2010
Reprinted with permission from the
Kansas City Globe

Within the past week, there emerged yet another one for the history books. Capitol Hill was a-buzz and a busy place. Eventually, it happened. President Barack Obama signed into law health care and insurer reforms that had eluded his predecessors for decades.

If you have been following the debate, you may recall some of the major provisions. Although controversy and opposition continues, there's a provision that is popular with American people, regardless of their political affiliations.

Earlier this week, a news segment on *Good Morning America*, told the story of a woman who although employed and recently diagnosed with cancer, was denied health coverage. The insurance provider used language in her policy to conclude that her cancer met the criteria for its pre-existing condition clause.

Simply stated, a pre-existing condition is a medical condition that existed before someone applies for or enrolls in a new health insurance policy. That can condition range from something as life-changing as cancer or a spinal cord injury to minor illnesses such as hay fever or asthma. Currently, 45 states allow insurers to deny individuals, charge higher premiums, and/or refuse to cover that particular medical condition.

Bottom line, it's estimated that of the more than 12 million non-elderly adults with pre-existing conditions, 36 percent were denied insurance coverage, one in 10 people with cancer could not buy insurance and another six percent lost their coverage.

Obviously, their collective personal stories make the case for health care and insurance reforms.

And yet in another sense, there remains a greater and more significant reality.

The truth is everyone has a pre-existing condition.

Not me, you may think. *I'm fit as a fiddle.*

The pre-existing condition to which I am referring is not in the physical sense, but the spiritual one.

So in this Lenten Season and as Christians worldwide are poised to remembering the sacrificial suffering, death and the glorious resurrection of the Savior Jesus Christ, I'm inspired to share this month, "Everyone Has A Pre-Existing Condition."

In Psalm 51:5, King David acknowledges his spiritual condition before God, "Surely I was sinful at birth, sinful from the time my mother conceived me," (NIV). His confession speaks for everyone born into the world.

The prophet Jeremiah describes the heart as "deceitful above all things and desperately wicked; who can know it," (Jeremiah 17:9)?

Centuries later in Mark 7:21-23, Jesus puts the MRI to the subject of sin. He taught that sinful actions come from within and are expressed in three forms – our nature, our minds and our hearts. He identifies 13 sins and further explains that "they all come from within and defile the man (individual)."

Let's take this a step further and consider ways in which we live:

To satisfy our physical longings, we tend to go after meeting the needs of misplaced desires. This often clouds our judgment which leads us to ignore or dismiss any spiritual or physical consequences of our actions. Indulgence is evidence that we lack spiritual growth and physical discipline.

The need for more power, prestige and possessions, no matter the cost, is so prevalent until even the church seems to have departed from its core identity as the body of Christ.

Motivated by a false sense of self-confidence and false humility, we are driven to succeed so that others will think well of us because of our achievements.

In the pursuit of happiness, it does not matter if our misguided ambitions lead to robbing others of their genuine joy and fulfillment in life.

Some of us have the mentality that others are obligated to do for us what we can and yet refuse to do for ourselves.

Then there's the attitude of ingratitude syndrome. As people give out of the goodness of their hearts, we feel that we are entitled.

Lastly and perhaps most of all, we're losing our grip on things we once upheld as sacred such as God, Jesus Christ, the Scriptures, the church and human life.

Without a doubt, sin is the condition of all human beings. But for many people, "enjoying the pleasures of sin" (Hebrews 11:25b) is more appealing than yielding to God to enjoy the fulfillment He offers through Jesus Christ. His shed blood as He died on the cross insures our freedom from sin, which is where I'll continue in part II next month.

Until then, keep the faith.

Chapter 4
Walk. By Faith.

After doing a muscle test on you, you should not be able to walk.
— Deanna, my physical therapist.

Oft times, the difference made in a person's life begins by simply making a decision. Of the many messages one could glean from *The Parable of the Prodigal Son* (Luke 15:11-32), there is one message that serves as a teachable moment for anyone in any situation. That message is the power of decision-making.

Unexpectedly one day, the younger son approached his father and demanded the inheritance due him. Afterwards, the son decided to leave the safety and security of his home. With his newfound freedom, he unwisely chose to live wildly, irresponsibly and without accountability.

Having squandered his wealth, he ended up in a famine-stricken region. Unfortunately his life spiraled downward and he reduced his worth to a livelihood of slopping pigs.

That is, until he came to his senses. Now this was not some light-bulb, "ah-ha" moment. He made a life-changing decision to return home, just like he made a life-changing decision to leave home. Either way, both decisions made a difference at different periods of his life.

While adapting to life as a paraplegic, I faced a number of challenges, some of which I chose not to talk about to others. Adapting seemed to constantly shine a light on new opportunities, but also emerging oppositions and obstacles. So instead of burdening others with one problem after another, my morning quiet times were also quality times for introspection about myself, my situations and spirituality. As I contemplated and sized up the challenges, those moments often prompted me to make sound decisions that affected my life.

In many ways I saw my life as this puzzle; it was in pieces. Although I believed God was primarily responsible for putting together the pieces that fit, I also believed I played a part.

This insight made faith all the more important and all-encompassing. So, I made up my mind that this faith-awakening could not be limited to just my physical health. Otherwise, I missed the bigger, meaningful picture of God's overall purpose for my life.

Allow me to reiterate. By faith, I believed God for physical healing in His way and in His own time. I had to drown out other voices in exchange for an eagerness to hear God speak to me about healing, because faith is usually celebrated when someone has overcome some type of sickness. However, every area of my life was affected by the accident. The day it dawned on me that I had somehow unconsciously believed God more for my health issues and ignored the other areas, I decided to be just as deliberate in exercising faith in all areas of my life – my spiritual well-being, relationships, needs, goals and ministries.

Indeed this felt like a risky, tall order. I knew that I was intentionally leaving myself wide open for whatever the Lord wants to do in my life. The measure of my faith in God for physical healing, though, was the catalyst.

In Christianity, much is preached, taught and testified about faith healing. I became more conscious of it during my youngest sister's (Sharion's) sickness. Based on the Scriptures, the principle simply teaches that God heals according to one's faith. Faith healing was stressed in the earlier days of my Christian upbringing. This is not a criticism, for we tend to rally around faith as the solution to sickness. But in reality, faith is a lifelong experience.

So I had to change my perspective and revolutionize my outlook on life. I decided that faith in God was going to be the sum total of who I am – a woman of faith. It would not be limited to my health and healing. We take for granted that we believe and trust God for every area of our lives. But do we? Naturally we like to think we do. On the surface, it's a sincere desire. However, trusting God all the time in every area of our lives does not come naturally. Trust and faith are learned disciplines, just like obedience.

It is no coincidence then that this chapter is titled "Walk. By Faith." Some readers may think I am referring to the physical act of walking while others may interpret the title as a reference to the spiritual experience. Actually, I am referring to both using "walk" as a command or something to do and "by faith" as a qualifier.

As the Spirit of God works in my life, I am more eager to learn to walk (also defined as live) according to my faith. As the power of God manifests the return of muscle activity, strength and endurance, I am more determined to learn how to use every ounce of return to physically walk.

Getting started with the physical rehabilitation became a form of faith-testing. My faith was at work (spiritually) as I worked (physically). Over time, some of my rehab experiences became personal parables–that is, profound teachable moments that cautioned me against frustrating the faith walk with preconceived notions about how God worked in my life. I chose two of those experiences to illustrate this point.

The first experience occurred on a Monday morning, the third week in June, while I was an inpatient at Mid-America Rehabilitation Hospital in Overland Park, Ks. My occupational therapist, Julie and physical therapist, Linda, entered my room. I had been bedridden since early May, when the accident occurred. In rehab, my hospital bed was equipped with an apparatus attached to it known as a "trapeze." It's a bar that was elevated at the center and attached to the length of the bed. It had a triangular-shaped ring hanging from a horizontal pole. Patients use the ring for pulling up the body. My paralysis was such that among other things, I lost muscle strength to physically sit up.

On this particular day, my therapists entered the room and happily announced this would be the first time for me to try to get myself out of bed. They gave me tips on how to sit up and swing my legs so that I end upright on the side of the bed. It looked so easy and I was ready. They told me they would help "but we want to see how much you can do."

So I pulled and pulled strenuously. To my dismay, I could not pull myself up to the full range at a 90-degree angle, let alone swing my legs. It was such a strain until my eager readiness soon turned to naïveté. The therapists kept coaching me, "Come on. Pull. You can do it. Come on. Pull." I was trying, perspiring and losing my breath but also thinking, *Okay you said you were going to help me. Can't you see I need help? Yet you're not helping me!*

I pulled as hard as I could, for as long as I could. All of a sudden, I lost my grip on the trapeze ring and since I had no trunk-muscle control, my back plopped onto the bed as I burst out in tears. I cried because number one, I couldn't do it. On the other hand, I'm mad because they wouldn't help me. While sobbing I looked at Julie and Linda who then turned their heads and looked away from me. They wouldn't even look at me.

I just knew after seeing the strenuous struggle, the plop to the bed, the fatigue and my emotional outburst, they would say, "That's it. Session's over." Not hardly. They turned around and one of them looked at me and calmly asked, "You ready to go again?"

I thought to myself, *Can't you see how this is affecting me, and you're asking me if I'm ready to go again?"* I had to contain my inner protest. After all, I couldn't tell them, "I'm not going to do this again." We had one hour to work together. I'm sure by this time, we were about 15 minutes into the session; about another 45 minutes remained, and they were going to put in their time.

I told myself, *They're not leaving. You have to get up and try this again. So just get it together*. I reached up for that trapeze ring again, and I pulled. I still could not reach the 90-degree range but I raised up high enough to get my therapists' help to end up sitting on the edge of the bed.

What is the life lesson behind this personal parable?

Along the way in our walk by faith, this lesson taught me that God knows when it is time to rise and go beyond whatever has confined and immobilized me. The strain and struggle are not to be misconstrued as signs to give up, because it is always too soon to quit. Obstacles often tempt us to jump to wrong conclusions. Or, we will just settle for second-guessing what God is doing.

I still live with physical struggles. I still live with pain. In fact, I don't know how it feels to experience a pain-free day. However, the pain, strain and struggles are in no way an indication that God has reneged on His healing promise in my life.

My being bedridden was not going to position me to experience God's promise of restored health; getting up and starting to move would. Julie and Linda weren't asking me to get out of bed by myself. They were challenging me to do

Keep Turning: Walk. By Faith.

what I could to get out of a bedridden state.

God will not allow us to miss that moment of truth when He knows we are ready to rise. Furthermore, He will provide much-needed help at the right time and be our number one coach encouraging us with, "Come on. You can do it!"

This was the first time I attempted moving on my own. Unknown to me, I was not expected to reach full range of motion or achieve maximum movement on the first try. You could say I was somewhat naïve; for I was expected to just move; get beyond my comfort level.

Thankfully, God has the patience to know we won't reach our full potential at the starting point. Yet He knows we have to rise up from ground zero in order to reach new heights awaiting us.

Months following in September, there was another instance. I am now in the outpatient program at Mid-America and my physical therapist Deanna introduced an exercise to slide my left leg forward while I am seated on the mat. She placed a towel on the floor to make it easy for my foot to guide my leg forward and back. Deanna instructed me to push my foot forward. I tried but there was no movement in my lower leg while I was in this position. She said, "Push, push, push. You can do it," but it would not move. It's five months since the accident and I was desperate for evidence this movement had returned. I wore myself out trying to slide my foot. I became disheartened, weary and disappointed because the foot would not move. Finally out of frustration I dropped my head and started to cry.

The next thing I remember was Deanna placing her face underneath mine, looking up at me as our eyes met. She sternly said to me, "Anita, you must work through the alphabet! You cannot jump from A to Z; it's A then B then C." Her voice grew forceful as she sounded each letter.

Deanna and I had worked together for weeks. She came highly recommended. She was in demand and I was fortunate to have her as my therapist. Prior to this session, she never addressed me in that tone of voice. I knew she wanted me to experience as much muscle return as possible. Yet in some ways, I needed a dose of reality in the proper perspective.

The personal parable from this therapy session resonated a lesson about an experience we seldom value. That experience is process. We tend to get so excited about God's promises until we sense an urgency to leap from where we are to where we want to be. Process, however, forces us to temper that excitement with patience and reevaluate whether we are genuinely committed to the journey that leads us to whatever God has promised.

God fulfills His promises most of the time through a process. We have to go from A, then to B to C, then to D.

We read about Biblical characters who encountered difficulties, sickness or loss, and within a matter of a few verses or two to three pages, God turned their situations around. We innocently get caught up in the euphoria of their deliverance, failing to understand there was a period of time or a window of opportunity when God worked to shape their perspectives, mature and prepare them for the next step.

Life is not always going to read on page 1, "I encountered a problem" then on page 2, "God fixed my problem." It could, but most of the time life's circumstances call for a process towards change. We have to work through our experiences. Psalm 23:4a says, "Yea though I walk through the valley of the shadow of death..." The operative phrase is "walk through." A valley experience is not like a revolving door that allows us to walk out as soon as we walk in. We have to go through.

Yes, I wanted to be able to go from A to Z quickly. I wanted that leg to just move.

To clarify, I clearly understand that having faith in God is a required channel for healing. God has instilled that testimony in me. I often talk about it. Just the faith conversation alone is invigorating, as it should be. Talking about seeing possibilities out of impossibilities, beating the odds and defying medical prognosis, Lord knows is the lift my spirit needs.

I also know now more than before, that faith in God requires a commitment to balance going the long haul with the expectancy of a fulfilled promise. Process should never be underestimated because in many unimaginable ways, the Spirit of God makes us stronger, wiser and better over time, if (and I do mean "if") we are willing to go through.

The timeframe that comes with process also comes with God's divine purpose. Here is where God works to draw the best out of us that would not have been uncovered, if our change came instantaneously without any struggle, heartache, brokenness or pain.

To put it simply, if change came quick, we are more prone to quit. We're subject to quit praying, quit reading, cease seeking or abandon following through with a closer, healthier relationship with God.

However, God knows that in the experience of process, we have a better chance for a deeper understanding of who He is, how He works, His will for our lives in Jesus Christ and how to be effective when reaching out and touching others' lives. Our relationship with God will become more intimate and our spirit more sensitive to His desires and direction. All of this I am learning and has evolved out of faith-based, grace-based experiences with an awesome God and the unexplainable yet life-affirming power of process.

In terms of my health, Deanna, my outpatient physical therapist at Mid-America Rehabilitation Hospital often tells me that she references my experience with other patients she treats, "I don't use your name but I tell my patients that according to your muscle tests you should not be walking." She adds to her observation the "amazing drive and fortitude" she witnessed in me to "use the muscles I have available."

What she is actually seeing in me is a resolve to live according to my faith. It is a faith that asserts that there is always something within us God can work with in spite of damage or loss. This is an encouraging spiritual principle for anyone who may have blown it or because of bad decisions. Nothing would please God more than if we allow Him to show us that there are remnants in our character- redeeming qualities at the core of our being that anxiously await a chance to spring forth and flourish. All we have to do is make the decision, come to senses right where we are like the prodigal son, even it that place is the pigpen.

Truthfully, when we don't have it all together we're in a better position more than we realize. Even when there has been brokenness and damage, there still remains something about us that is useful to God.

This is why we have to take the simple principle that God heals according to our faith, a step further. Many people have been discouraged or disillusioned by this principle when there has been prolonged illness. After all, who would not want to experience the one-touch or speak-the-word instantaneous healing Jesus often performed in His day? Be healed. Be on your way.

Nevertheless, faith challenged me to keep sharpening what I believed about God and His power to heal His way – either at any moment or over a period of time. The timing was up to Him. But, I still had to step up to the plate. I could not pray then do nothing. Just wait on the healing? God forbid.

Faith, therefore, became the bonafide driving force behind my responsibility to exercise discipline in following the prescribed medical requirements and rehabilitation plan. Most of all, it was imperative that I prayerfully stand on the promises that I believe God gave me based on His word. These were spiritual and physical decisions anchored in my faith. Without a doubt, faith in God emerged as a deliberate and daily reality.

I am in a different, more spiritually confident place than I was pre-accident. Now, much of the understanding and insight that I have emerged from aligning my experiences with God's word and prayer. I know what God has done. I know the role that His word and prayer played.

Out of all of this, God has proven His track record of faithfulness. I now have personal experiences as reference points for believing what God will do as I continue to live this life and walk by faith.

Did you know you have something of extraordinary worth to God?

That's right. The God whom Psalm 24:1 says the earth is His, the world and everything in it, values highly something you have.

And everyone has it, believers and non-believers alike. Everyday we use it. Frankly it is ours to use as we please because God generally will not intrude upon our choices.

"What is that something?" I'm glad you asked.

We have faith. It is so valuable until according to I Peter 1:7b, "...your faith—of greater worth than gold..." (NIV). However, we cannot know its worth based on God's perspective if we are unwilling to exercise faith in Him.

Everybody believes in something enough to trust its ability or capacity to provide whatever is needed or desired. Unfortunately for many people faith in God is often ignored, untapped or underutilized.

Some people feel they are incapable of relying upon God's trustworthiness and therefore lack confidence in where to begin. If this is you, you may need a faith lift. I am a living example that in lifting the level of your faith, you will see just how faithful God is.

It is worth the struggle to depend solely upon God. So why not start by consulting the written testimonies of Biblical personalities whose lives reveal lessons learned about faith.

Hebrews chapter 11 profiles the lives of ordinary persons who overcame obstacles and gained divine approval for their faith in God. I mention a few of those personalities in the *Globe* article *Lessons Learned About Faith*.

I delve deeper into an experience of the Apostle Paul, who by faith actually benefitted from the power of being weak.

Now that you have read my story in *Walk. By Faith.*, turn the pages. Check out their stories in the *Globe* articles.

I Need A Faith Lift
Originally published July 20 - 26, 2000
Reprinted with permission from the
Kansas City Globe

Sometimes if I think about it long and hard enough, it scares even me. It tends to take me down a mysterious, inquisitive path, showing me very little along the way. I could just stop dead in my tracks, wander off the beaten path and trade it in for a journey mapped out with specifics. But it's too intriguing to abandon so quickly.

So I choose to stay the course, and the result of that decision has been a life that has evolved to unimaginable heights.

I'm writing about the reality of living with an enduring faith. And trust me, I will just barely scratch the surface in this month's column.

I concluded last month's *Moving on With Milestones* column with the thought that milestones represent both an ending and beginning. In my rehabilitation, I had ended a weekly schedule of physical therapy that began three years ago. Now I am challenged to begin a program of regular physical strengthening and exercises on my own.

Spiritually, I am also challenged to live at a new level of faith. Faith that endures refuses to remain at ground level, scoffs at stagnation and most times leaves the quest for details to the ignorance of rationalizing. For faith boldly asserts itself as the proven and sole authority over human reasoning.

Without sounding bragadocious, I know the faith I have at this time in my life is not the same. Three years ago when the accident occurred, the faith that applied to this particular experience was a teeny, tiny seed. Yet that seed was ready to achieve the impossible in the face of the spinal cord injury I suffered, along with other health, financial, employment, mental, social and spiritual issues I would face.

Jesus talks about "mustard seed faith" in Matthew 17:14 to 20. From these Scriptures, I saw that I did not necessarily possess strong faith, nor a faith void of questions. Living within me, however, was a faith with the greatest potential to grow and ultimately reveal what God can and will do.

With this kind of faith I was driven to diligently search its record. Hence, the Scriptures – the word of God – spoke so intensely over and over again. What God said played a major part in establishing and shaping my beliefs.

For days that led to months and during my times of meditation, I would read the story of Jairus' daughter in the book of Mark, chapter 5; Lazarus' experience in John, chapter 11 and Tabitha in Acts, chapter 9. All three of these Biblical accounts are about persons who died and were brought back to life.

Based on these Scriptures and now three years since the accident, my faith in Jesus Christ says, "Lord, if you can bring full and complete life back to Jairus' daughter, Lazarus and Tabitha, I know you can bring life back to the muscles and nerves in my body that have yet to respond."

This is the level of faith I now possess.

It's a living reality and I am a living witness to the rewards of exercising Biblical faith against human reasoning and against the odds. I am still to this day experiencing progress. To some, the recovery may be slow. But to insist that a divine plan be accompanied by a human schedule, at best, promotes walking by sight and discourages living by faith.

Why take my word for it? Instead I encourage and challenge you to take God at His word. So in the next series of columns, we will explore the faith experiences of some Biblical personalities. Which ones, you may ask? You'll have to find out in upcoming issues of the *Globe*.

Until then, keep the faith.

Lessons Learned About Faith

Originally published in October 1999
Reprinted with permission from the
Kansas City Globe

Faith is a fascinating subject. More fascinating to me is the lineup of Biblical personalities in Hebrews chapter 11. This chapter profiles a list of ordinary persons who overcame obstacles and gained divine approval for their faith in God.

Several Scriptures in this chapter are introduced with the phrases, "by faith" or "through faith." Then the Scriptures offer some insight on the accomplishments that made these Biblical characters "so great a cloud of witnesses," Hebrews 12:1.

Most of the time when I hear sermons, read books or participate in Bible class on Hebrews 11, the minister, author or teacher has a lot to say about verses one, five or six. Recently, I found myself taking a closer look at verse three which reads, "By faith we understand that the universe was formed at God's command, so that what is seen was not made (accomplished - my interpretation) out of what was visible." Abraham, Sarah, Noah, Moses and more accomplished the extraordinary because they dared to trust God. They set their sights on accomplishing the impossible in the face of contradictory circumstances and seemingly shameful consequences.

Take Noah for instance. He prepared for the flood in every way God instructed. For years, he built the ark. In the meantime, there was no rain. In fact, 120 years passed before the floods came. He was ridiculed because to others he looked awfully ridiculous. If Noah were a contemporary, he would probably be scoffed at, "It's going to rain? Yeah. Right." Well, it rained and the floodwaters destroyed the earth and all its inhabitants, except Noah, his family and a pair of each animal.

Consider Joseph (verse 22). He didn't have much of a support system where his family was concerned. As a young teen, his brothers envied him. Their conspiracy to murder him didn't pan out. However, they threw him into a deep pit. Slave traders came along and the brothers sold him into slavery. Joseph, a 17-year-old slave, was wrongly accused and imprisoned on false allegations from the slave owner's wife. Eventually he rose to become the governor of Egypt. He was second in command to the Egyptian king. So from a despised brother, to 11 years a slave, to a two-year convict, to governor is obviously not your average career path. Nevertheless, Joseph remained faithful to God despite his troubles. And while in his troubles he made the most of his opportunities.

That is typical of Biblical faith. This faith audaciously bewilders, baffles and completely alters the outcome of events even when circumstances are threatening and consequences are unpredictable.

God's greatness is revealed when we put our faith in Him. We all have faith. That's not the issue. It is the object of our faith that matters. Without sounding judgmental, I'm afraid much of what we hear today concerning faith is a faith in what we already know. It is not the type of Biblical faith that is defined by the "hoped for substance" or "unseen evidence," (Hebrews 11:1). Instead, it is a faith that dares to frustrate, if not shatter the comfort level of any person or situation.

We are comfortable in what we know about God and what He will do based on past experiences. We have the evidence. When it comes to situations that we have yet to experience, we would rather fight and struggle our way back to where we are comfortable and to what we already know. We will go all out to maintain the level of faith we have; when we should at least view such experiences as opportunities to experience more of God and what He can and will do.

Jeremiah 33:3 is an invitation, promise and challenge with the kind of faith that yields results beyond familiar territory – "Call unto me (invitation) and I will answer you (promise) and show you great and unsearchable things that you do not know, " (promise and challenge).

In my case, I have been asked, "how long" it will be before I am able to walk on my own? Usually my response is, "I don't know, but I'm in this for the long haul." I've also been asked about the doctors' prognoses on my chances for recovery. I hear what the doctors say. Honestly, I pay attention to the medical prognoses.

However, I do so mainly to size up the odds that may be against me. Odds, mind you, are no match for God.

I've been told that I am "positive" and "optimistic" and therefore, "I'm going to make it." I appreciate these glowing remarks and recognize people are sincerely encouraging me through this difficult time in my life. But who am I kidding? For I know that deep within me, God is the one who has given the level of motivation and determination that others see in me.

By faith, I have endured two and one-half years of physical recovery and rehabilitation. Through faith, God has enabled me to experience the results of "hoped for substance" and "unseen evidence." About four weeks ago, I purchased my walking canes. I now practice using the canes at home. This week, I returned to a full-time work schedule and began driving again. I have come to terms with my fears about driving, despite the affects the accident has had on my life. I have resolved that, at best, I will not be emotionally defeated. So, I had to get behind the wheel of the car again. I continue to exercise the weak muscles in my legs and trunk. For my mobility, I am now about 80 percent walker-dependent. I rarely use the wheelchair. Moreover, I pray constantly as I anticipate experiencing more evidence of healing.

I have discovered something interesting. Each time I progress to another level of physical activity, I first start at ground zero to build up strength and endurance. Nevertheless, it is this type of diligence and Christ-centered faith that reaps God's rewards. For Hebrews

11:6 says that God "rewards those who diligently seek him."

Writing next month's column will be a real challenge. I vividly recall November two years ago. I had an experience that most would find it hard to believe happened to me. But it did and now I am ready to talk about it. I would clue you in, but I rather like the element of anticipation.

So until next month, keep the faith.

Is Your Faith Worth Its Weight in Gold?

Originally published July 11 - 17, 2002
Reprinted with permission from the
Kansas City Globe

Is your faith worth its weight in gold? "What kind of question is that," you may ask? It's a question worth considering. Think about what God's word says in I Peter 1:7, "These (trials) have come so that your faith – of greater worth than gold, which perishes even though refined by fire – may be proved genuine and may result in praise, glory and honor when Jesus Christ is revealed," (NIV).

Based on this, the question remains. How much worth do you place on your faith, especially when facing difficult situations?

Many people may remember the plight of Kansas missionaries who were held captive for about a year in a Philippine jungle by rebel soldiers. It's hard to imagine such an experience. But I will admit, I admire their steadfast demonstration of faith. And although the outcome may have been only part of what many desired (Martin Burnharm died; his wife Gracia was returned to the United States), the name of the Lord Jesus was honored and praised by Gracia the widow and others who personally knew the couple.

It is so easy to get caught up in our own troubling situations and totally disregard the amazing affect we could have on people around us who witness firsthand our response to difficulties. Our lives are faith stories in the works.

Faith is central to the Christian experience. We are "saved by grace through faith," (Ephesians 2:8). We "walk by faith, not by sight," (II Corinthians 5:7). "…the just shall live by faith," (Galatians 3:11). And we are to look to Jesus Christ, who is "the author and finisher of our faith," (Hebrews 12:2).

From the beginning of our Christian lives until we near the very end, faith in our Lord should flourish to its maximum potential.

Often when I am confronted by a difficult situation, I literally take myself through self-talk as far back as the day Jesus Christ died on the cross, to His resurrection and ascension and finally, to the day I received Him into my life. It is clear to me that faith in Him is the only way to wisely go through any good or bad experience. But when life deals a tough one, it becomes imperative that I turn to Him in faith. I find the validation I need when I go back in time to Christ's redemptive work and my personal acceptance of Him.

God gives us faith because He knows we need it. We do not or cannot earn faith. As a matter of fact, Christ only requires that we begin with faith comparable in size to a grain of mustard seed (Luke 17:6). Our faith simply needs to be placed in Him and no one or nothing else. Faith in our Lord is how mustard seed-size faith grows and becomes worth its weight in gold.

Furthermore, we can't manufacture or create a faith experience then await our chance to share a testimony, just because we think it will go over big with other believers. God's word says that genuinely proven faith "will result in praise, glory and honor when Christ is revealed." That response becomes the natural overflow when we have allowed faith in God to grow, despite situations that tempt us to do otherwise.

A major reason God allows the testing of faith is in order to prove its strength. Unproven, untried faith is worthless – not worth a penny, let alone its weight in gold. No matter what form our trials may take, we will never know in advance what we can handle without the testing of faith today.

So don't waste the potential worth your faith has. Let it be tried. Let it be proven to let the name of God be praised.

Until next month, keep the faith.

Profile of a 'Powerful Weakling'
Originally published April 6 - 12, 2006
Reprinted with permission from the
Kansas City Globe

It's a contraction in terms, an oxymoron. I recently heard a local pastor use the phrase "powerful weakling" in his sermon, and I asked myself, *What does a 'powerful weakling' look like?*

Then I recalled the Scripture that says, "For when I am weak, then I am strong" (II Corinthians 12:9). Thus, I've taken a snapshot attempting to profile a "powerful weakling."

The Apostle Paul possessed an inordinate amount of strength. He was boldly committed to penetrating regions with the Gospel of Jesus Christ, knowing he would likely face fierce opposition, (Acts 16 to 28).

He had an impressive list of credentials which dated back to his Jewish upbringing on into his adulthood (Philippians 3:4-6).

His timeless letters to the churches (Romans to Thessalonians Epistles) and to his protégés (Pastor Timothy, Titus and Philemon) address issues that if left unchecked, would threaten the health, power and witness of the Christian church.

In fact, Paul knew that he received "surpassingly great revelations" from God (II Corinthians 12:7). These observations of mine only scratch the surface and yet contradict the life of one who devoted the first 11 verses of II Corinthians, chapter 12 discussing his weaknesses. He specifically mentions having a physical weakness, although he was not specific about the nature of his condition. This ailment pressed him to plead with the Lord three times to remove it (II Corinthians 12:8).

Hence, a powerful weakling diligently seeks the Lord, while shamelessly allowing those raw and real emotions to run their course.

Paul didn't just politely ask. He persistently pleaded - an indication of how desperate he was. You may say that he only went to God three times. Well, that was all it took before God responded.

Too often, if God does not answer our prayers our way and in our time, we give up. We stop praying and will settle for things as they are. Could it be that as Christians, we are living way below our privileges to receive God's best? God gave him divine power despite Paul's physical weakness through the all-sufficient grace of Jesus Christ (II Corinthians 12:9).

The unearned favor of God rested upon Paul's life and though Paul was less than his physically healthy best, he still lived and ministered in that favor. God will also work in our lives in amazing and awesome ways.

Last week, in our Sunday School discussion on Job's experience, I asked the class, "How do you respond to tragedy?" One of our class members who is currently undergoing mobility challenges answered, "I just thank

God that I can work with what I've got." I can relate to her testimony. For that has been my prayer and attitude for some time, since losing some physical functions almost nine years ago.

A testimony like that flips the script on the Enemy's attempts to welcome you into his pity-party, where you can never wear out your welcome.

I shared with the class, the more I acknowledge God in my condition, the more I am in awe at what He enables me to do. I'm still a paraplegic, but more than that, I'm living by the power of His healing grace.

Secondly, a powerful weakling gladly surrenders that weakness to Jesus Christ. *Oh that's easy,* you say. Then why do you still rely upon your human wisdom and ingenuity to fix your situations?

The power of *you* will leave *you* disillusioned and discouraged because as humans, we possess the failure factor. When we fail ourselves, we further exacerbate the weakened state we're already experiencing.

The power of Christ, however, is life-changing. There is absolutely no failure in Him. Paul knows this. He alludes to a faith exchange, where he transfers faith in his circumstances to faith in Christ so that the Lord's power can rest on him.

Perhaps there were a lot of head-scratching people who wondered how Paul endured so many seasons of difficulties. Paul indicates joy in weaknesses because he delighted in boasting about the Lord.

The powerful weakling who yields to Christ will witness the presence, promise and provision of God at work and gain strength to keep going with a testimony to share.

And finally, the powerful weakling sees past the situation in order to see the salvation of the Lord for someone else.

What do I mean by this? Paul says in verse 10, "That is why for Christ's sake…" This phrase does not mean Christ depends on our weaknesses for His salvation. He is our Savior. However, our walking through tough times can lead to someone's salvation who does not know our crucified Christ as the sin-pardoning Lord who gives eternal life.

Just think. People can embrace God's power through our pain. While we're going through our weaknesses, others tend to read how we're handling the situation more than reading God's word. So why not let your powerful weakness be the word that witnesses to a wayward soul?

God has shown me much about Himself and me throughout my experiences. When I share with others what God can do, I'm not just talking about what I've read. I'm living it and loving it.

Paul suffered weaknesses, insults, many hardships, persecutions and difficulties. Make no mistake. The Enemy will try to intimidate, diminish and accuse you. Then he'll back off, but only for a season as he did with

Jesus (Luke 4:13). And he'll use whomever he can enlist to carry out his schemes uniquely crafted against you.

Paul said he delighted in those times. He experienced the blessed results in being weak enough to depend on and be saturated by the power of God.

Jesus says, "My grace is sufficient for you. For my power is made perfect in weakness."

Now that I have given you my snapshot profiling a powerful weakling; you get the picture, don't you?

Until next month, keep the faith.

Faithful Is Our God
Originally published April 25 – May 1, 2013
Reprinted with permission from the
Kansas City Globe

"Life happens." How many times have you heard or even made that comment?

Sometimes it comes from the mindset of one who has a blah-zay, blah-zay view of situations that take place. Other times, the statement serves as a dose of reality when disturbing circumstances catch us off guard.

The recent tragedy in Boston and the subsequent killing and capture of the suspects were headline newsmakers for a number of reasons – the loss of innocent young lives, the runners and spectators who were injured and those with amputated limbs, questions and speculations swirling around the threat of foreign or domestic terrorism, the bombs used in the explosions and the fact that they were strategically placed near the finish line.

Amid the casualties and chaos, the surviving Boston Marathon bombing suspect was seen on campus where he attended college two days following the incident. A fellow student reported that the two of them talked about the tragedy and the suspect's response was, "Tragedies happen."

It is true that life itself ushers in a series of circumstances that leave you scratching your head in bewilderment or shaking your head in shame. Yes, life happens. But for the most part, how we choose to respond is what makes the difference.

One morning this week while reading my devotional, I could not resist reflecting on the portion of Scripture from Deuteronomy 7:7-9, which states *God is faithful*. "Know therefore that the Lord your God is God; he is the faithful God, keeping his covenant of love to a thousand generations of those who love him and keep his commandments."

The passage has much to say about God's purpose for the Israelite's enslavement and liberation from the Egyptian King Pharoah. However, I zeroed in on the fact that God is faithful.

No matter what we may face, no matter how tough or intense, it is reassuring and comforting to know that almighty God is the one constant we need. The faithfulness of God means that His every intention is to see us through and ultimately deliver us from our troubles. Based on this, God will never risk making us feel as though we cannot count on Him. God's faithfulness is at stake.

Actually, God desires that we count on Him at all times, even if it means allowing difficulty and pain to be the catalyst. Know that in times of uncertainty, loss and tragedy, God is always in position, ready to offer us opportunities to depend upon Him and what He can do.

Our challenge (or for some, the problem) is our failure to draw from His faithfulness. Instead, our tendency is to be so self-reliant, until we are our own first responder to painful, difficult or uncomfortable situations. Yet our self-reliance can only go so far.

The Bible is filled with the happenings of life. God Himself knows life happens. He inspired the writing of incidents after they occurred, as they occurred as well as future occurrences. God remained true to His character, plan and promises.

God is also aware that our reactions to life's happenings are the best gauge for determining how we live. It stands to reason that most of us would prefer to go through life showing ourselves strong, composed and capable. That's our preference, not our reality.

So whenever we find ourselves vulnerable to our troubles, we should consider how faithful is our God.

The apostle Paul writes, "God is faithful, who has called you into fellowship with his Son, Jesus Christ our Lord." God is the one who initiated and opened the door for us to share in the life of His Son, Jesus. Ask yourself. Why would God do anything or allow anyone or any situation to break that fellowship?

God's faithfulness in this sense should give us the confidence to know that nothing "will be able to separate us from the love of God that is in Christ Jesus our Lord," (Romans 8:39).

Furthermore based on Psalm 145:6, we should be encouraged because, "The Lord is faithful to all His promises." Can you think of anything God has promised and yet failed to deliver? One of my favorite Scriptures is found in Numbers 23:19, "God is not a man, that he should lie; neither the son of man, that he should repent: hath he said, and shall he not do it? Or hath he spoken, and shall he not make it good?"

According to 1 Corinthians 10:13, whenever we are tempted beyond our ability to withstand, we can count on God to help us endure as He discloses His exit strategy. "There hath no temptation taken you but such as is common to man: but God is faithful, who will not suffer you to be tempted above that ye are able; but will with the temptation also make a way to escape, that ye may be able to bear it."

Temptations and troubles are part of life and life happens. But no matter how much life changes, our anchor is in God's faithfulness. We can count on it. We can count on God.

Until next month, keep the faith.

Chapter 5

I Lost My Job

Feeling "forsaken" and "begging bread," Psalm 37:5

I lost my job. But the loss was not a result of the automobile accident. This particular unemployment dates back 12 years prior; it was in 1985. Throughout my employment history, I have been out of work twice. Both times, I was off work two years. Obviously, the most recent unemployment was a medical leave resulting from the accident. However, the first time was because of corporate downsizing. Otherwise, I've always worked.

I landed my first job when I was 13 years old. One day Daddy was sitting at the dining room table. He appeared to be deep in thought but I interrupted anyway and asked Daddy if he would buy a pair of shoes I saw in a Sears catalog. To this day I remember his response. He said to me, "Girl, if you want to have all these things then you need to get a job."

I don't think Daddy realize what he did. It wasn't what he said but what he did. With that response, Daddy planted a seed and just like that, my focus was no longer on getting the shoes. Daddy got it right. I wanted "things" and I didn't want to be deprived if there was a chance I, on my own, could do something like work to get what I wanted.

I interpreted Daddy's response as a sort of dare, not a denial. Ok. So I didn't get the shoes. Better yet, I got a job. In my mind, Daddy's subtle laying down the law was a setup preparing me to venture out into the work world. A few weeks later I started my first summer job through a youth employment program sponsored by the City of Kansas City. It was called the Job Opportunities for Youth or JOY for short. The program offered teens a chance to work during the summer. And I worked each summer before I left KC to attend college.

My employment history began in my teen years – from JOY to college work-study to jobs during the summer and Christmas breaks to jobs right after graduating from college. I wanted to work.

By working I felt a sense of responsibility and pride. I can't explain why. Working was motivating and made me feel good about myself. I could put certain skills to use and discover skills I didn't know I had. In my tender teenage years, I knew I was not a professional; I was a potential. That is what working was about. Don't get me wrong, I enjoyed earning money but working meant more than making money to get things.

When I completed my undergraduate degree in Journalism and Mass Communications with an emphasis in Radio-Television Production & Broadcasting, I wanted to pursue a profession in broadcast news. However breaking into the broadcasting market in the KC area was virtually impossible for African-Americans. Minority hiring in television news seemed to be more quota-based, not talent-based. Once a TV station hired its one or two minorities, the door was shut to hiring more.

At that time, African-American journalism grads were among thousands of aspiring professionals who packed up and headed south to Atlanta, Ga., in hopes of jumpstarting their careers. Major cities in the south were known for being welcome mats to the door of opportunity for up and coming minority professionals and entrepreneurs.

As for me, I feared leaving KC. Atlanta was too far away and I was closely tied to home. Yet I was surrounded by college friends working in their respective careers. Some wore the corporate blue suits and carried briefcases.

I was still trying to figure out how to break into my profession. Living in KC just wasn't working out. Still I needed to get a job. With Kathy's help again, I was hired to work at the Board of Education Building, but this time as a substitute secretary.

As a "sub," I did not work a regular schedule so to earn extra money, I also worked part-time for Newsome Realty, a family owned real estate business. Delores, my roommate, put in a word for me to her brothers, Robert and Sterling, who hired me to help type home appraisals.

Now I am working part-time and subbing as a secretary. My eagerness to find work in my field was falling off my radar. I had to work; that was the immediate need. Then finally in 1983, the dream job came. That same year,

Delores and her fiancé Jeff got married and I found an apartment in Kansas City, Ks.

I was hired as a communications assistant for a building materials firm headquartered in KC. At last I had traded in my office skills for communications skills. I breathed a sigh of relief, thrilled to be full-time employed and working in my profession.

Work could not have gotten any better than this. I had finally joined the ranks of corporate America. I worked in the communications/marketing department and a whole new world in communications opened up, because the department was multifaceted–specializing in internal and external communications, newsletter writing and printing, corporate event planning, product promotions, advertising and media. It was fast-paced and kept me on my toes. I was still very green but determined to be a quick-study. Like a soaking wet sponge, I absorbed all I could as I observed professionals hard at work: Dale, the vice president of communications/marketing; Carolyn, the director; Karen, the manager; Megan, the staff writer and Ramona, the administrative assistant.

I was grateful to God because the work was not just limited to television news. I felt as though the Lord had blessed me beyond my desire to work as a broadcaster.

Unfortunately after working two years and gaining new skills, the company downsized and I was let go with a severance package worth three month's salary. It's the first time in my life I was out of work despite my desire to work.

It was also a letdown but I tried to keep myself together and not let my disappointment show. You know how it is – all smiles on the outside, all sadness on the inside.

On the surface it was, *Oh well. I'll get another job before my severance runs out.* So I thought. I exhausted that severance within three months, which made me eligible to apply for unemployment compensation. I had hoped to find work and head-off applying for unemployment – find something, perhaps secretary subbing again, but not this time. There were no vacancies. I had to apply for unemployment. Now my income is significantly less than the professional-level salary I had grown accustomed to in two short years. Obviously, I struggled financially. Added to the struggle was the schedule to start paying back school loans.

Believe me, the situation I found myself in did not square with my post-graduate plans. I lost my dream job. My future as a professional looked awfully bleak. I have an undergraduate degree but was out of work and not using the skills and education I worked hard to acquire. The weekly unemployment checks were not enough to cover rent, utilities, school loans, money for bus fare, groceries and other daily expenses. I am falling behind on paying my bills and can barely afford enough groceries for a decent meal. Occasionally, I reached out to family. However, I was so adamant I wanted to make it on my own.

All of this was compounded by my belief that I am a Christian and the Bible teaches that God takes care of His children. The testimony in Psalm 37:5 asserts, "I was young and now I am old, yet I have never seen the righteous forsaken or their children begging bread," (NIV).

I wondered, *Now who can honestly say that these days?* I felt forsaken and at least in my mind this child begged. I am struggling to find work, pay bills and take care of myself. Sometimes the struggle tried me to a point where it felt like begging, not simply asking God for help. Plus, I questioned whether I wasted time going to college to eventually land that professional dream job. There was something wrong with this faith picture.

Here is where I press the pause button in sharing my experience. I realize that unemployment was the turning point serving as a milestone test of my faith in God, during a time when I was still a "babe in Christ."

However, my experience addresses a broader and more common issue primarily for anyone who is either relatively new to the Christian faith or uncertain about faith's role in their lives. Since receiving Christ, joining the church or deciding to commit to a closer relationship with God, it may seem as if life no longer goes your way. Or you may see yourself as an easy target for adversity. Or perhaps you can't seem to get ahead, taking two steps forward followed by 10 steps backward.

The point is no matter where you are in your maturity as a believer, faith in God will and must be tested. In faith testing, God allows difficulties in our lives but by His grace He meets us where we are in order to accomplish what He has in mind.

Undoubtedly, it is always a good decision to move forward in an effort to become a better person. You've got your head on straight. An unexplained weight has been lifted. You're now experiencing a dramatic sense of freedom from whatever has held you back in your desires for the things of God. But don't make the mistake of misreading God when adversity strikes. It is not designed to work against you. On the contrary, by God's design adversity can and should work for you.

You may ask *how*? For the moment, like I was, you are feeling forsaken. You're begging bread and I am not only referring to food. "Bread" can mean anything tangible that you need, is within reach yet the need remains unmet. "Begging" can imply an outright pursuit or a burning desire waiting to erupt to get your needs met. Either way, you have an unmet need. And the timeframe to turn your situation around doesn't jive with God's schedule "to wait until your change comes," (Job 14:14).

Adversity confronts us with the reality that the faith walk is not a call to pursue the path of least resistance. In fact, sometimes those trying situations may worsen before getting better.

While struggling to make ends meet and feeling the pressure to repay the student loans, I decided to go the temp route. After all, I could always fall back on my office skills and work as a secretary or administrative assistant. Besides, a temp assignment could lead to permanent work. Although I preferred to not get locked into office work, it was better to be employed while seeking another job as opposed to being out of work.

I got an assignment within days of signing up with an agency. I was glad to be working. I could also pass on an assignment to go on job interviews. As the saying goes, "sounds like a plan." My game plan worked for about two weeks. Then I received a letter in the mail from the Division of Employment Security. To my dismay, the letter notified me of suspension of my unemployment benefits because the office received records of unreported income I had earned working a temp assignment.

The letter gave instructions to schedule a hearing and appeal; which I did. But ultimately the ruling resulted in loss of benefits.

Now my only income came from temporary jobs; however, I encountered another problem. There were no temporary assignments. I literally had no money coming in. On the job front, nothing is going according to plan. I have run out of options, no drawing board to go back to.

I had to turn to Daddy for financial help more than I wanted to since he lived closer to me in Kansas. Instead of allowing rent to go unpaid, I met with the landlord to explain my situation. I promised to pay whatever I could but no less than $75; rent was $230 monthly. Just think, for months I lived in a one-bedroom apartment paying only $75 a month. She could have started the eviction process but she did not. I know that it was none other than God who touched her heart and graciously made it possible to at least keep a roof over my head.

Still I was pinching pennies. There were some days when I saved the little money I had to take the bus job hunting and interviewing. I remember many days when my breakfast was chocolate covered peanuts because chocolate gave me energy to venture out. And lunch or dinner was McDonald's two small fries and a chocolate shake. The fries made me full and the shake was a kind of energy drink.

As I go through this trying time, my life is riddled with concerns – my daily needs, my quest to prove I can make it on my own, finances, finding work and whether I lost had ground and ambition breaking into my profession as a result of unemployment.

Praying to God, sometimes I pleaded; other times I protested. "God, you said in your word..." and I then proceeded to roll out a litany of the few Bible verses I knew verbatim, promises God made as encouragement that He takes care of His own. I wasn't being childish. I was God's child, new to the faith and yet struggling to understand why the shattered plans, roadblocks and setbacks under the weight of unmet needs and unfulfilled promises.

So where am I spiritually with all of this going on in my life? I am very active in my church, Macedonia Missionary Baptist Church, where my uncle and Daddy's twin brother Rev. O.L. Cobbins, Sr., pastored. My beloved uncle passed away in 2002; but being under his leadership and teachings tremendously helped me to get stable in my faith. It was here where I learned the importance of faith's foundation when a person is new to Christianity.

I faithfully attended Wednesday evening prayer services, Monday mission meetings, and Bible study sessions. I come from a musically gifted family so I sang in the choir and served as a choir director. In 1986, I was even elected as president of the young women's mission auxiliary for an association of affiliate churches in Missouri, Kansas and Nebraska. The leadership role afforded me the opportunity to lead about 75 young adult women in various mission projects. This role also opened the door for public speaking opportunities and leading workshops at various churches during my five-year tenure. Best of all, I was still devoted to personal Bible study, prayer and meditation.

I am attempting to give you an idea what faith in its infancy may look like. It was a struggle trying to reconcile spiritual principles with practical realities marked by trials and not condemn myself over the contradictions the two presented. I wrestled with the dilemma of feeling forsaken and begging bread while still loving and serving the God I depended on to supply my needs.

Nevertheless, I believe if we're sincere in our struggles, God permits us to question His ways and challenge Him to reveal Himself as we solicit His help. In the end, God knows what we will look like when the trial has passed. Starting out, though, it's difficult to see God's hand and tap into His heart past our own problems, negative thoughts, doubts, intensifying emotional pain and bewilderment.

All kinds of reactions that are not of God can be formidable foes threatening our sincerest desire to solely fix our "eyes on Jesus, the author and finisher of our (your) faith," (Hebrews 12:2b).

However, I kept going to God as an expression of my dependency upon Him. Early in my faith walk, that part of my relationship with God I took seriously. At the core and deeply anchored in my spirit are two qualities that I will not compromise—my love for the Lord Jesus Christ and my dependency upon Him. Although it appeared that God was not answering my prayers, I would not allow myself to believe the answers were in the hands of anyone other than the Lord's. How much sense does that make? It makes no sense at all — to keep reaching out to the Source who is also silent and unresponsive.

But that is the unexplainable dichotomy of spiritual faith–adversity working against us at the same time can work for us.

Pain kept pushing my limits until I realized my limits were powerless to turn my situation around. The more pain I experienced the more my desires for the things of God rose to the challenge. As hurtful as the situation was, it seemed that with each passing day I had a little more fight and determination left in me. I could not quit on God. To do so meant I also let myself down.

There were many moments I was low in spirit and short on strength. But if I sensed a trace of strength, not much, only a trace, I turned to God. In my weak times, I often asked the rhetorical question, *God, who else can I turn to?*

Consider Hannah's condition in I Samuel 1:6-8.

Because the Lord had closed Hannah's womb, her rival kept provoking her in order to irritate her. This went on year after year. Whenever Hannah went up to the house of the Lord, her rival provoked her until she wept and would not eat. Her husband Elkanah would say to her, "Hannah, why are you weeping? Why don't you eat? Why are you downhearted? Don't I mean more to you than 10 sons?"

Hannah endured years of shame because of her inability to bear a child. In her barrenness, she could not escape the one-up arrogance and taunting intimidations instigated daily by rival co-housewife Peninah. To make matters worse, her husband Elkanah's insensitivity proved that he was utterly clueless about what Hannah needed for her personal fulfillment.

When she went to the temple to pray, Hannah was an emotional wreck. Yet she had enough strength, despite her deep anguish to seek God and make her request to give birth to a child.

Clinging to a weakened faith and with only a trace of emotional strength, I was at a Sunday morning worship. I remember the youth choir singing, *Help is on the way. Help is on the way. So just keep the faith, day by day, and know that help is on the way. Just keep the faith and know help is on the way.*

I heard the singing. I joined the congregation in clapping and swaying to the music. Still something inside prompted me to pay closer attention to the words. At the time, I could not explain what I was feeling except that my spirit was uplifted. Not only that, but the heaviness I had carried for weeks seemed to ease. Those simple words put to music stayed with me the rest of the day even until I went to bed that night. I just knew I was on the verge of something.

The next day, the phone rang. Lo and behold, before the conversation ended I had scheduled a job interview for a secretarial position at the Pioneer Campus of Penn Valley Community College. That week, I was interviewed. That week, I was hired. It all happened so fast.

Help finally came my way. The year was 1987 and aside from the two-year medical leave which began in 1997, I have since been full-time employed.

The unemployment experience occurred in my early years as a Christian. I viewed it as the first time I learned to define and refine my understanding of exercising faith in God. One could say I was forced into this position because of my circumstances. It is easy to claim by faith "the Lord will provide" when you work and expect a paycheck in return. It is another thing to depend on provisions with no prior mutually agreed upon arrangement such as a day's work for a day's pay.

The ripple effect of loss that was precipitated by my unemployment included the following: I lost a comfortable level of income, a sense of stability handling my affairs and the ability to support myself.

As a result, my self-esteem took a hard hit, as I often

teetered-tottered back and forth from self-confidence to insecurity.

It was difficult reconciling living with the joy of the Lord, while also experiencing hunger, struggling financially to maintain utilities and running into roadblocks on my career path. As Christians, we often experience joy over the God who opens doors. Seldom do we consider the fact that God also closes not one, not two but multiple doors, one after the other.

Yet James 1:2-4 opens with a challenge to, "Consider it pure joy, my brothers and sisters, whenever you face trials of many kinds, because you know that the testing of your faith produces perseverance. Let perseverance finish its work so that you may be mature and complete, not lacking anything," (NIV).

"Count it all joy," James 1:1a (KJV)? Seriously? How on earth God expected me to react in joy amid my circumstances was beyond my ability to comprehend. We don't typically wake up daily welcoming God to test our faith. *Ok God. Here's my faith. Test away!*

Either God took away or allowed me to lose some of the "joys" of my life and in response, I was expected to consider my losses as something to be joyful about. I sometimes felt as though God was expecting a bit much. And perhaps He was. God never does anything without a purpose in mind. He may close multiple doors because He knows that it takes only one open door in return to prove His faithfulness to us and that God's outcome was best.

Still, the finished work of faith, according to James 1:4, should not be based on our circumstances but instead our ability to persevere. In other words, we will never know if we really possess the ability to keep going when the going gets tough unless and until we are faith-tested. Beyond the test and our perseverance awaits a maturity that we never knew we had. We are not to just *endure* trials, we are to *mature* in our trials.

When the trial has accomplished its purpose, God's goal is that we know firsthand that faith is dynamic. Faith was never meant to be dormant or dead, lazy or without life. Neither will faith passively accept life's circumstances as they are. When our faith is being exercised and we are willing to hang in there with God, then we will see God as the supplier of our needs (Philippians 4:19) and Jesus as "the way" (John 14:6) and not just a way.

God delights in seeing a lively faith—a dynamic faith that is always in position to prove it can finish its work and get the job done, while it is sifted through tests and trials.

God also knows that we have more to gain than we realize. We are in the best position ever to be "mature and complete, not lacking anything."

However, I must confess that these blessings that came from being faith-tested were far from view. While going through this testing, I did not realize what God was up to according to James 1:2-4. All that I could see was my problem-ridden immediate circumstances.

It was not until after the testing and over time, I discovered what I gained after experiencing loss.

I lost my job. But I gained a greater sense of purpose. Whether I worked as a secretary, in my communications profession or in the church, I discovered that God is the source and has use for the gifts, skills and abilities I possess. Therefore, there was no room for an inferiority complex. I repeatedly fought back the notion that I was less competent as an office worker than a college-educated, aspiring journalist. Over time, I realized the uniqueness in my character–the person whom God created me to be–complements my calling and career choice. The sum total of who I am requires that I give my all when opportunities come my way. This is a main reason why I am so resolute and focused when God sends those opportunities.

I lost my job. Thankfully I was humbled throughout this experience. While a teenager, my independence emerged from a simple conversation with Daddy over buying a pair of shoes. As I matured into adulthood, I lived by an on-my-own code of conduct. However, I encountered conflict keeping my independence in check so that it would not collide with dependency upon God. It is a difficult yet delicate balance and another dichotomy of the spiritual faith walk. It's true, as adults we are independent; as children of God, though, we are to be dependent upon Him. Many times, I thought I was following God's lead. I just knew that either I moved on cue or remained still when I was supposed to, only to discover I was self-directed. I had to constantly work at humbling myself because I desired two things from God: His grace (James 4:6) and to be in a better place than my present situation (I Peter 5:6).

I lost my job. Most of all, the adversity affirmed I made the best decision when I received Jesus Christ in the summer of 1979. In the midst of this seemingly prolonged season of trial, the Spirit of God was so in command of my life until the adversity became a catalyst to affirm and increase my faith. I evolved learning to accept the fact that through all of my problems, I was maturing into my truer self, the woman God saw from His eyes. It was as if God was saying, "Anita, this is who you are and not that person."

The experience grounded me in Christ. I know I can do nothing fulfilling apart from Him. So I am yet eager to pursue those worthwhile possibilities God has for my life.

During my early Christian years, I was a piece of work. I never doubted my decision to let God change my life. I was just clueless what I got myself into. It seemed as though more things were going wrong than going right.

There were moments when I felt conflicted. But I was determined to hang in there, confront my commitment and tackle the difficulties. I could not give up. Plus, there was no guarantee my life apart from Christ would get better.

When in 2006, I wrote a three-part series published in the *Globe* titled *I Told You So*, I wanted the readers to understand that even Jesus kept it real when teaching His disciples.

The Gospel writings are filled with His commands, warnings, instructions and illustrations. When exposed to His messages people brace themselves. They mistakenly presume that most of His teachings take the enjoyment out of life. I have discovered otherwise.

In John 14:29, Jesus said,
"I have told you...so that...you will believe," (NIV).

"I have told you this so that my joy may be in you...and complete," (John 15:11 NIV).

"All this I have told you so that you will not fall away," (John 16:1 NIV).

"I have told you this, so that when their time comes you will remember that I warned you..." (John 16:4 NIV).

"I have told you these things, so that in me you may have peace..." (John 16:33 NIV).

Jesus taught His disciples because they needed to be clear about following Him. Likewise, God knows that we need Jesus' messages to stand firm in our beliefs, live in the joy and peace Jesus gives and stay encouraged during opposition.

Keep this in mind as you turn the pages and continue reading the *Globe* articles.

"I Told You So..." Part I
Originally published June 15 - 21, 2006
Reprinted with permission from the
Kansas City Globe

"I'm not going to say, 'I told you so'." There have been times in my life when I cringed to hear those words. Equally as much, I quietly loathed at the notion that someone got the satisfaction of saying that to me. *"No she didn't,"* I'd think.

The phrase usually pits opposing views, perspectives or facts against each other. Like me, if you've ever been in this situation you just knew you were right; the other person was wrong. You stood your ground, but so did they. You had undeniable proof, and they did, too. Your position was valid, as was theirs. And after all had been said, you both walked away thinking you won the debate over the other person.

That's why, it about shatters our world when the situation is revisited and we have to hear the opposing side say (or watch as they gloat thinking), "I told you so."

For about six weeks leading up to this year's crucifixion/resurrection season, I read through the Gospel of John. It was my way of reacquainting myself with the life of Christ since John's Gospel was the first Biblical book I read when I became a Christian in 1978. At that time, I believed that since I was born again, I needed to get to know Jesus.

I reached the concluding chapters (13 to 21) during Passion Week. By the time I got to the 16th chapter, I made an amazing discovery. I had read a series of "I told you so's" from Jesus to His disciples.

So, for the next three months, I plan to devote the columns to our Lord's "I told you so's." And you'll probably want to have your Bible handy.

I'll begin by pointing out some general principles. First, I noticed that when Jesus interjected the "I told you so" phrase, it was mainly because He was stating the purpose for which He spoke. You'll see what I mean as I discuss each.

Contrasting my opening comments in this column, there were no debates taking place, maybe some doubt or confusion by His disciples— but a great debate? Not at all.

Secondly, Jesus' "I told you so's" were so that His disciples would be uplifted through His encouraging, reassuring words. Unlike us, Jesus was not interested in pulling a "one-up" over His disciples.

And thirdly, Jesus revealed promises His disciples could live by the rest of their lives.

I am so excited about this series and I pray it will bless you.

Now, let's explore the first "I told you so" passage for this month.

Most of us as Christians will agree on one of God's attributes — He is faithful. As a matter of principle, we believe God is the only constant who can be counted on no matter what we face.

However, here's the challenge — applying what we believe in principle so that it translates into our practical, daily experiences. We often keep God in the perpetual position of making believers out of us.

When we're faced with acting on our beliefs, we usually have to first get past the fear factor. Or, we have to deal with our doubts. Either way, we come up short exercising unwavering belief.

In John 14:28-31, Jesus reveals to His disciples the plans and promise to "go away" and return. He lets them in on what to expect so that they would believe. He wanted them to remain encouraged for He would be put to death, buried then resurrected.

Perhaps Jesus didn't want the disciples to second-guess or wrongly size up the events surrounding His suffering, death and burial. Since the "Father is greater than I," could have been Jesus' way of reassuring the disciples that God was in total control. Thus, He said, "I have told you now before it happens, so that when it does happen you will believe."

God's word is complete with promises, life's lessons, commands and personalities presented in a way to cultivate in us a spirit of belief that focuses on Him. That belief began when we accepted Jesus Christ, God's Son, personally as Savior and Lord. Yet for many of us, it's easier to believe God for our eternal destiny. But when it comes to our temporary daily situations? *Well...that's another story.*

Ask yourself, *since I believe God saved me the moment I confessed Christ, then why do I struggle to believe He can handle my adversities, disappointments and trials?*

In essence, Jesus' word is His way of saying, "I told you so" that you will believe — believe He can heal you emotionally, physically and mentally. Believe He will bring you out of financial, employment and business struggles. Can He help you reconcile that strained, estranged relationship? What about your sins, weaknesses and shortcomings? Can He deliver you from hurts you have so deeply internalized until it's impossible to get past? Can He counsel and direct you when you don't know what to do?

The answer to all of this and more is an absolute yes. But don't just take my word for it. Get in God's word and let Him tell you so that you will believe.

Next month, I'll discuss two more of Jesus' "I told you so's"

Until then, keep the faith.

"I Told You So..." Part II
Originally published July 27–August 3, 2006
Reprinted with permission from the
Kansas City Globe

"If you rejoice in the God of your salvation and the finished work of Jesus Christ, you have put your joy in a place that cannot be compromised," said Bishop T.D. Jakes in his message titled, *The Blood Speaks*.

Joy. Who wouldn't want to experience all they can? Yet, joy often seems to elude believers who find themselves going through one struggle after another.

This is the second in a series I introduced last month titled, *I Told You So*. I began by discussing why "I told you so" is an expression we prefer not to hear. Usually, it's in response to proving us wrong about something or some facts we previously upheld as truth.

However when Jesus expressed this phrase throughout chapters 14 to 16 in the Gospel of John, it was not to prove anyone right or wrong. He was intimately sharing final farewell discussions with the disciples just before His arrest, brutal beating, crucifixion and death.

Thus in John 15:11, Jesus says, "I have told you this so that my joy may be in you and your joy might be complete."

Here's proof that Jesus commits Himself to our living with sustaining, fulfilling joy. He knows that life is not a steady stream of euphoric celebrations, mountaintop, or sitting-on-top-of-the-world experiences.

We will often journey through the wilderness. We'll climb mountain highs, plunge to valley lows. We will run into roadblocks and detours. We seldom travel paths of least resistance.

All the more reason to struggle as much as possible to let the joy Jesus imparts accomplish what God desires as we go through difficulties.

Think of joy as your spiritual firewall, protecting you from being defeated by doubt, worry, hopelessness, sin and failures.

The real truth is that none of these are a match against the joy Jesus gives. But in reality, the Enemy works tirelessly to deceive us into thinking otherwise. He's usually un-phased when we express joy.

For instance, he'll even step back and watch our worship - uplifted hands, thunderous claps, shouts of amen, the music, the dance, the jubilant atmosphere – they all make up the event of worship. To him, though, it's a setup. Because after the *event of worship*, he knows we're prone to returning to the *experience of worry*.

Jesus gives His joy as an expression of experiences, not events.

But the Enemy knows that usually all we want is a momentary good feeling and we're good to go.

I remember my infantile Christian days. As a young adult woman in my mid-20's, boy, I struggled. The trials just kept coming as I tried to better myself.

The struggles drove me to doubt my salvation and question, *How can God who claims to love me make me suffer so much?*

I never really wanted to quit the faith, but I sure questioned it. This went on for years. And although my life seemed complicated, I kept reading Scriptures, kept praying, kept attending and serving in the church, kept myself open to learning.

Eventually as I matured, I questioned less as the Spirit of God confirmed more. I would vividly recall the day, hour, the setting and situation surrounding my born-again experience. It was on a Wednesday, at midnight in July. I prayed and asked God to come into my heart and heal my sin-sickness. I laid down, closed my eyes to sleep. And with my eyes shut, I saw a light so bright. I knew God had answered my prayer. This along with recalling John 3:16 and imagining Jesus dying while giving His life to save mine became continual confirmation that I was saved.

There were no shortages of situations teaching me to surrender doubts and anxieties to the joy that would not be compromised by trials and tribulations.

Instead, when we surrender to the joy of the Lord, it's strengthening. And God keeps us when we would have otherwise given up. I believe that's what Nehemiah meant when he acknowledged, "the joy of the Lord is your strength," (Nehemiah 8:10).

Now back to Jesus' discussion with His disciples. He gave them assurance in the joy He gives. Prior to John 15:11, Jesus also revealed that their lives would flourish as long as they remained in active fellowship with Him (John 15:1-6).

Union with Christ would also result in the privilege of asking God whatever they wished (John 15:7).

And finally, Jesus wanted the disciples to know that their pleasing God, based on His unconditional love for them, is the greatest witness that proves they were His followers (John 15:8-10).

Fellowship with Him, answered prayers and loving obedience all come full circle to form the basis for living a joyful life that God wants to be fully matured in us.

Situations hit us sometimes like a ton of bricks. We can easily get knocked off balance. The Enemy catches us on the blind side. If it weren't for Jesus' joy within, we would lose all sense of reason.

Am I suggesting that you shouldn't be sad? Am I admonishing you to keep smiling even when you're hurting? Not at all. I've learned that joy does not dismiss or demean the pain we feel. Joy is not insensitive. Joy is well aware that we have natural emotions.

The Joy Jesus gives is an empowering emotion that meets you where you are in fears, sorrow, heartache, discouragement and despondency.

As you pray, joy speaks and lovingly whispers, "Trust God." Joy strengthens your resolve so that you'll know for certain God will meet your needs. He wants to help you and He alone has all that's needed to address your situation.

But again, don't take my word for it. Get in God's word in John 15:1-11 and let Him tell you so.

Until next month, keep the faith.

"I Told You So..." Part III

Originally published September 14 - 20, 2006
Reprint published by permission from the
Kansas City Globe

What if you could get a glimpse of your future – a sneak peak of what lies ahead? You could probably pattern your life to avoid society's snares and personal pitfalls. Right? Not necessarily.

The Bible is filled with revelations of the future that sometimes warned of the trying times of this world. Life will not always be characterized by a steady stream of euphoric experiences and good times.

Why? Because we live in a fallen world with established systems that actively oppose the ways and people of God. And yet, ironically this sin-cursed world manages to present Christians with enough appeal and allure to cause many to stray.

Jesus was careful to warn His disciples about the world in which they lived. He was concerned enough to reveal specifics of what they would face as they lived committed to Him.

The column you're reading is the last in a series I began in June titled, *I Told You So...*, which is a phrase that usually pits conflicting viewpoints or facts against each other. Some people love to use it on others. Others hate hearing it.

Recall how I was inspired to write this series. It started with my reading John's Gospel as part of my devotion during Lenten season. As I read, I discovered that Jesus shared several "I told you so's" with His disciples to state the purpose for which He spoke. In the Scriptures, John 14:29, Jesus said, "I told you...so (that) you will believe" and John 15:11, "I told you this so my joy might remain in you...and be complete."

Now we come to John 16:1, 4 and 35. Take time to read these verses along with John 15:18-27 and 16:29-33. Notice that Jesus' emphasis is how the world would react as the disciples upheld their belief in Him.

In a nutshell, the world would respond aggressively out of hatred. The disciples would be persecution targets. But not only that, they would also experience tribulations. Obviously, Jesus didn't mince words or try to sugar coat the future they faced. Persecutions. Tribulations. Their view of their future. It's difficult to imagine what they were thinking. Did it ever cross their minds to wave bye-bye and just walk away? Forget this persecution business altogether? Or were His disciples confident they could go through tribulations so that life as an overcomer would be their reality?

My pastor, from a recent trip overseas to Turkey, shared with the congregation their visit in Ephesus. As part of the tour, the group was taken to a lion's den located eight stories below the earth's surface. Pastor recalled how he could sense the faithfulness of the early Christians when they were persecuted.

"They gave their lives, thrown into amphitheaters," he explained, "where people paid to come and watch lions tear them limb from limb, all because they refused to proclaim, "Caesar is Lord."

What about believers today? We all know someone who is no longer living the Christian life; that person no longer attends church. There also are people who have issues stemming from controversies in the church. Some left after being disillusioned by Christians who compromised their lifestyles. Or because of unfair treatment by a church member, the straying began when they first resigned themselves to just being a "bench member," then ultimately no member at any church at all.

Perhaps they strayed because they just could not let go of the pleasures of the world. Maybe the world's cares lured them away. Or, trials that came "to make them strong" instead made them stray.

If Jesus warned His disciples (John 16:4) about persecution and then encouraged them to remain committed by saying in John 16:1, "All this I have told you so that you will not go astray," then don't you think this same desire applies to us, no matter the situation?

Our Heavenly Father, through Jesus Christ, desires an intimate, fulfilling relationship with us that lasts a lifetime. When we stray from Him, we are in a sense giving a compliment to Satan that says his influence is more appealing, to say the least, and his way is better, at best.

Last week in Sunday School, I talked about the need to encourage ourselves. We need to have conscious conversations with the Lord and reinforce what He says about us based on His word, not so that we come across as scholarly and neither to prepare for a time in the public spotlight. But instead, we will appreciate and value living by the power of God's word.

We cross paths daily with entirely too many influences, planting seeds that if cleverly and cunningly cultivated by the Enemy, will discourage us from the faith. We risk devastating spiritual consequences just from the seeds of gradual, continual discouragement.

Yet when we focus on "...the author and finisher of our faith" (Hebrews 12:2, 3), we can resolve to go through whatever we experience in this world.

But don't take my word for it. In John 16:33, Jesus said, "I have told you this so that you might have peace (resolve). In this world you will have tribulation. But be of good cheer. I have overcome the world."

Until next month, keep the faith.

God Knows Our Needs Before We Ask

Originally published April 23 - 29, 2009
Reprinted with permission from the
Kansas City Globe

They were gripped with grief. Some may have struggled with unshakable guilt. Still others sensed an unsettling fear. However they may have felt, it's certain that there was no cause for celebration.

What just happened? How did this happen, they may have wondered?

For three years, Jesus' disciples were awed by the way Jesus changed lives performing one miracle after another. They were captivated by the wisdom of His authoritative teachings and His profound preaching. They saw firsthand multitudes on multiple occasions flock to Him. He spoke and calmed a raging storm. He spoke and cut off a fig tree from any future signs of life. On command, miles away and in the same hour, Jesus healed the centurion's paralyzed servant.

They witnessed Jesus resolutely focused on His oneness with God and commitment to accomplish God's will. They may have even been attracted to the strong possibility that as the Jews' Messiah, Jesus was poised to lead an unprecedented political revolution. And they were privileged to be intimately connected to Him and His ministry.

Nevertheless, nothing could have prepared them to witness the intense suffering, widespread rejection, brutality, near-riotous sentencing and ultimately Jesus' crucifixion. As close as they were to Him, nothing could have set the stage for the loneliness they faced in the aftermath of His death.

Beforehand, it was difficult to fathom life without Jesus. When He disclosed His sufferings, being killed and raised to new life (Matthew 16:21), Peter reacted with rebuke, "Never Lord...this will never happened to you," (v. 22).

In John 14, Jesus further attempted to assure them, "Do not let your heart be troubled...I go to prepare a place for you. If I go to prepare a place for you, I will come again and receive you to Myself, that where I am, there you may be also."

The darkest moment in human history shined a light on the irreversible void in the disciples' hearts. Jesus knew that the disciples eventually would experience loneliness as a direct result of His brief absence from their lives. That time came immediately after Jesus' death and burial. The loss was too great. They were overcome with unanswered questions. Without Jesus, what would become of them?

But God had already begun making provisions to meet their need with promises such as the one in John chapter 14. Herein lies a lesson worth noting when we're facing unmet needs.

The comforting side is this. No matter how much or how little time exists waiting on God, we can begin to fill that gap with promises from the Scriptures.

We all have needs. Simply put, but profoundly true. Besides the more obvious basic needs such as financial stability, food, health, insurance coverage, clothing and shelter; some people may need an affirmed self-worth. Others need peace of mind. Some need to overcome insecurities, while others need freedom from enslaving behaviors taking them down a destructive path.

Based on God's very nature of unfailing love, His proven track record of providential and compassionate care and His inexhaustible resources, God has always been the best source for meeting needs, in spite of ourselves. He knows our needs even before we ask (Matt. 6:32).

The disciples had their issues and character flaws. Jesus knew Peter would deny Him, Judas would betray Him and others would abandon Him. Yet in His final discourse (John chapters 14 to 17) the week Jesus triumphantly rode into Jerusalem, He still promised, "believe in God, believe also in me...I go to prepare a place for you."

So you're still unemployed, without health insurance and barely making it from day-to-day. Or you just can't seem to beat that drug use thing. Problems with your spouse have robbed you of everything you imagined a committed relationship would bring.

Whatever the case, whatever the need one thing is certain, that need remains unmet. Most of all, God has a promise that can at least help you see your situation from His perspective and strengthen you through the days until your change comes.

Why not let God be the first one who hears from you. If you don't, it's natural to frustrate the process of getting your needs met by drifting into self-effort, independent of God's guidance and the resources He can provide.

It's true. God wants us involved in the process. However, His greatest desire is that we trust Him and resist the temptation to depend upon ourselves and other deceptive and bogus approaches that lead to nowhere fast.

Getting back to the grief-stricken, guilt-ridden disciples, relatively speaking their loneliness was short-lived. In due time, God raised Jesus from the dead. Last week, Christians worldwide celebrated His glorious resurrection.

When He appeared to His disciples, they were no longer overwhelmed, but overjoyed, as Jesus reassured them of God's greater purpose, (John 20:19-30).

The needs Jesus meets on our behalf have a greater purpose than what's on the surface. They are wrapped up in promises waiting to be revealed in God's own time, at the right time.

Until next month, keep the faith.

Chapter 6

I Lost My Joy

"...weeping may endure for a night..." (Psalm 30:5b)

It had become my routine. The alarm loudly goes off, six o'clock in the morning. It's already time to get up after a restless, sleepless night.

C'mon, Nita. Stretch those muscles. You need to work up the strength to transfer out of the bed and onto your wheelchair. I had to literally talk myself through getting up to start my day, because I simply was not feeling it—not starting out, that is.

As the day progressed, I sensed perhaps a trace of motivation. But at this point in my life, I struggled to perk up, get motivated and rearing to go.

Instead, I was numb. I felt less energetic and just going through the motions of my ho-hum morning routine. The atmosphere was dark and quiet as I wheeled myself from my bedroom through the living room, dining area to the kitchen. I pushed myself to the kitchen table where my Bible laid.

I opened my Bible to read. I can hardly see the words from the tears in my eyes. The blurred print ran together. *Plop* goes a tear from my eye to the page of my Bible, then another tear and another. Suddenly the drops turn into streams then more drops so frequent until what followed was a steady stream. I'm no longer reading. I have slumped onto the table, sobbing like a baby.

This became an every morning scenario for about three weeks. It started sometime late October. After breakfast, the next order of the day was take a shower, get dressed, stretch out on the floor to watch TV until lunchtime, then wait for the Mid-America Rehab van to pick me up for outpatient OT and PT. In between the routine activities the phone would ring – mom, dad, stepmom or one of the sisters, most of the time.

Some days I could carry on the conversations as though everything was fine. Other days I faked my way through, never letting on that I started my day feeling deeply down in the dumps.

To make matters worse, I began to experience one of the most challenging side effects of my paralysis. I was living with severe spasticity, commonly known as muscle spasms.

I was on medication to relax the muscles, the highest dosage allowed for oral use. At times, however, the pain hit so strongly until I would jerk out of my wheelchair onto the floor. My only other recourse was to lay flat on my back on the floor. So that is what I did most of the day. *What a life?*

The afternoons typically were devoted to therapies. I was working towards a goal to return to work walking on a cane by January 1998, which meant I needed to be out of the wheelchair by November progressing towards using a walker in December. The goal was my motivation to work as hard as I could during the five days of therapy. While at home I decided to be more determined to apply, whenever I could and as best I could, the OT and PT exercises and maneuvers to routine activities.

Thanksgiving Day 1997, the family gathering was at Mother's. I just knew it was going to be a Thanksgiving to remember. Mother's Day weekend, I lost my ability to walk. Six months later, Thanksgiving Day 1997, God turned the situation around and I am upright, on my feet and using a walker. As an act of my faith, I believed my healing would happen just like that. But... I am still in my wheelchair, still wheelchair-dependent and not even close to balancing myself using a walker. In my mind, I was glad to be around family, enjoying Mom's appetizing home cooking and the usual sibling and in-law camaraderie. My spirit, however, was a different story.

It was as if two people showed up in one body for Thanksgiving dinner. When I realized this, I found myself yielding to the thoughts in my spirit: *You're still in this chair. You're not going to make that goal. Maybe that Jeremiah 30:17 promise is not for you. You're going to end up being a burden. Why not end it all?*

Then I asked myself, *How would I end my life? What would I do?* This continued for a while, at least long enough to make ending my life a justifiable option.

After all, I had serious doubts about being able to walk again which meant I would be paralyzed the rest of my life.

I was so preoccupied and deep in my thoughts, when gradually my attention started to turn towards the little people in Mom's apartment.

They were my toddler- and elementary school-age nieces and nephews: Dominique, CJ, Chrissy, Cherish and L'il Marques. I started to pay close attention to what they were doing. *Look at them; they are so carefree.*

Mom's apartment was somewhat small but they didn't notice. They found room to run around, tag each other, fall to the floor, roll around even if it meant on top of each other, get back up and tag each other again. They laughed. They screamed. I heard one scream, "I got you!" Another loudly answered, "Uh. Uuuhhh!" They looked as if they were getting tired yet they kept going. And the more I watched them the more I tuned out those dark thoughts in my spirit.

However, the defining moment in all of their frolicking and fun was when Chrissy and Cherish stopped for a moment, panting so hard until their chests pulsated expanding and contracting as they tried to catch their breaths. They paused long enough to put their arms around each other's shoulders for a moment of tender, affectionate embrace. It was so natural, so pure and innocent. The bond and embrace seemed to simply flow out of several minutes of boundless, playful energy.

I remember this as if it was a Kodak moment and I snapped the picture at the right time.

For me, this priceless picture served as the wake-up call I needed to come out of those deep and disturbingly dark thoughts of putting myself out of my misery. How *would* I do this was not the question. How *could* I do this? That was the question.

How could I end my life and leave adult family members with the responsibility of explaining and making sense of what I did to my young and innocent nieces and nephews? How could I leave my loving, caring and devoted family feeling as though they fell short and were incapable of doing enough to help me? How could I let them down and countless others who were following my faith lead, anticipating an outcome of healing that only God can bring? In the beginning, I put myself out there to be God's vessel of faith. How could I turn on God to become a victim of failure?

It was this moment when I realized I was in serious trouble; I needed help. My face trembled. I fought back the tears as I went around and around in self-interrogation. I did not want the kids to see my fluttering face while crying and emotionally struggling.

Yet I was relieved that this wake-up call was the turning point that drove me to admit I needed help. It was a pivotal moment and the first step.

Thankfully that day, in Dominique, CJ, Chrissy, Cherish and L'il Marques, God showed me six worthwhile reasons to dismiss suicidal thoughts and confess my need for help.

But again...that was the first step. There is more.

Fast forward to the following Tuesday. Ironically, the morning routine had not noticeably changed even after the Thanksgiving Day experience. The nights prior were still restless and sleepless. The morning atmosphere was still dark. The devotional time in the kitchen was just as tearful. The only difference was I am aware of my problem and I tried to deal with it the best way I knew how – through communion with God in prayer and His word.

I finished breakfast. I showered and got dressed.

Around 10:30, the phone rang. It was Rev. Donald Ford, pastor of Second Missionary Baptist Church of Grandview. At the time, Kathy and Larry were active members at the church. Rev. Ford called regularly to check on my progress and pray for me.

I knew a number of pastors and ministers throughout the city from their relationships and associations with my family and me. I am part of a large family, a ministering and music family. I am grateful that these pastors and ministers reached out to me and were, in a way, an extended support system for my family.

When Rev. Ford called on this particular Tuesday, he started by asking, "How are you doing?" I told him I was fine aside from not being able to sleep at night because of the muscle spasms. He then proceeded to inquire about my therapy sessions. He also continued to encourage me to work on my exercises outside of therapy sessions and to stay focused on my goals to return to work and ministry, as a testimony to the power of God working in my life.

As Pastor Ford talked, I responded with the typical affirmations, "Yes sir. Um hm. I appreciate that. I will." Eventually, Pastor Ford concluded the conversation with a prayer on my behalf. I recall in the prayer he asked God to grant a restful night's sleep. After the amens and goodbyes, as soon as I hung up the phone I said to myself, *I just lied to that man. I'm NOT fine. I'm depressed.*

That was the deep, dark hole where I found myself. Week after week, day in and day out, I was suffering from depression, struggling with despondency and at an all-time emotional low.

I did it. I finally got to a place where I could no longer deny that I had lost my joy. The painful muscle spasms, sleepless nights, the struggles to get out of bed, morning darkness and the constant emotional meltdowns during what should have been uplifting devotional moments with God, all added up to a gradual, inevitable plunge into the abyss of depression.

Now I know why I needed help. I could not overcome let alone shake off what I felt. The darkness was too heavy, the low too deep.

I was helpless to help myself and the Enemy knew it.

After the conversation with Pastor Ford, I had only about an hour before lunchtime and the arrival of the Mid-America Rehab van that picked me up for my afternoon therapies. The atmosphere was strange. On the one hand I was sort of relieved confessing to myself my need for help to deal with the depression. But I was still sort of somber, in a dark quietness trying to process it all. *How did I get here? What happened? What should I do?*

Furthermore, an avoidable conflict surfaced. How on earth can I claim to have so much faith in God and His promises and yet suffer depression? *You, Anita?* The Anita whom people were drawn to for her healing conviction that would come by God's power? That Anita? The Anita who is part of a seemingly strong family of believers – the family that God has graced to be pastors, preachers and church leaders in their own right? That Anita whom many enjoyed visiting in the hospital and rehab because upon entering her room, they could not get past the door from being met with her excitement, a bright smile and an exuberant, "Hi. Come on in!"? That Anita? That strong woman of faith? I'm afraid so – that Anita.

Then it dawned on me that I not only had lost my joy but also I failed the faith test. I let myself down way before I considered the affect disclosing my depression would have on others. *What would they think of me?*

Eventually that day, I arrived for therapy. I wheeled myself into the gym, found a mat and transferred onto it from my wheelchair. Deanna came out of the office, all perky, bubbly and rearing to get started. As for me? I could not look her in the face. The gym was filled with other patients and therapists. But one would have thought I was the only patient in the gym.

With my head down, the tears began to drop from my eyes. I was too consumed with grief and discouragement to feel ashamed about the open display of emotions. Deanna immediately shifted to consoling me. I could hardly get my words together to tell her what was wrong. That was okay. She knew. She put her arms around me and allowed me to just pour out as she said, "Anita it's ok. This was bound to happen. I am surprised it has taken this long because you are doing so well." I answered, "I'm having a hard time – the pain, the spasms and sleepless nights. It's all too much to handle emotionally." Deanna goes on to say, "Anita you are a phenomenal woman. You work so hard. I brag about you to my other patients. But this happens. Would you like me to recommend additional help?" I appreciated the offer but answered with, "Let me see what I can do first. If I need more help, I'll let you know."

We got through the PT exercises. Afterwards the van took me back to my apartment. I began a repeat and replay of those conflicting questions that surfaced before I left for afternoon therapy.

Depression. Although it may not be the silent killer for most people, it is still the cleverly silent tormentor. We often fraternize with this enemy because we keep it bottled up inside for fear of exposure. We want everyone within our circles of interaction, connections and influence to view us as having it all together.

Whenever I was out with family and friends, I could effortlessly set aside my depressed mood to at least appear to be going along with the fun flow. I managed to mask my depression in exchange for masquerading as if the joy of the Lord truly was my strength. However, as soon as I returned home – switch! It was back to the darkness, the emptiness and the Enemy's grip. It was so instantaneous.

Oftentimes, it seemed as though the Enemy happily showed me the door and waved goodbye as I left my apartment. Depression flaunted a confidence that was so sure I would return, "Go ahead and enjoy yourself. Have a good time. I'll be here when you get back. 'And I'm telling you, I ain't going nowhere'." So the minute I returned home and the key unlocked the door, depression met me, welcomed me in, wrapped me in its arms and smothered me with its spirit as it whispered, "See. I told you I would be here when you came home."

However, this "shocking" story is about much more than my depression and suicidal thoughts. In a real and broader sense, I am attempting to expose an experience that is all too common among people, even believers. Too many times, many of us fall victim to living our lives in contradictions.

Beneath the veneer of all those smiling faces, among the energizing atmosphere of hallelujahs, amens and praise the Lords, powerful pulpit preaching and music that lifts one's spirit to heights never before experienced lies a silent and somber condition, that can be overwhelmingly deceptive and too shameful to admit. Depression caves in so deeply until a believer easily struggles to come to terms with professing a belief in God, yet living as though God exists to help everyone except him or her.

This does not only apply to depression. What is true of this emotion is also true of other emotional challenges believers face such as fear, insecurity, doubts, paranoia, shallowness, an inferiority complex, loneliness, heartache, callousness, low self-esteem, co-dependency and more. Having it all together can be an appearance that more than meets the eye.

We have mastered the art of shielding "the tears of a clown when there's no one around." Some of us are old enough to remember this line sung by Motown legend Smokey Robinson. Portions of the lyrics say, *Now if there's a smile on my face. It's only there trying to fool the public....Now if I appear to be carefree. It's only to camouflage my sadness. And honey to shield my pride I try to cover this hurt with a show of gladness.*

In a sense, my being outgoing was a distraction or an escape from imprisonment in my own home. Depression held me captive. In another sense, my outgoing activities were a cover-up that something deep down inside was wrong with me. To cover up was not something I trained for. To cover up was simply a decision I made. It was how I chose to outwardly deal with my inner turmoil.

However after awhile, covering up got old and I got nowhere living with this contradiction.

Thankfully, I finally got to a point in my life where I could confront putting on a front. I was fed up. I knew I needed help and I had admitted to myself and my therapist that I was suffering from depression. I was at a critical point to either go down in defeat or rise up in deliverance. I chose the latter.

Deep within, I longed to be free but that freedom was not going to be handed to me. I was in for a battle. There were things I needed to do. To remain passive when I should be actively engaged in the battle meant that I conceded defeat before the battle began. It also meant that I had given up the ground and weakened in my core belief that victory in Christ is imminent and always available.

I had to do something. "Do something. (emphasis) Do something," said Dr. Charles Stanley of *InTouch Ministries*. To this very day, I can still hear those words and the firm tone in his voice as he shared a message during a Sunday television broadcast. On this particular Sunday morning, I tuned in as I did each week. Only God could have orchestrated the timing for me to hear Dr. Stanley's message on depression based on Psalm 42. I quickly grabbed my Bible so that I could follow along and take in as much as I could. Dr. Stanley had my undivided attention and I recall consciously being grateful to God for sending His word to help me.

Verse five of that Psalm reads, "Why, my soul, are you downcast? Why so disturbed within me? Put your hope in God, for I will yet praise him, my Savior and my God." I could relate to living with a downcast and disturbed soul. The constant weeping during devotion and at breakfast made it seem as though my tears poured out as seasoning onto my food (Psalm 42:3a). At times, I thought God had forgotten about me (verse 9b).

In the message, Dr. Stanley stressed that God is with us in our darkest moments. We can rest assured God is intimately involved in the affairs of our lives and that He always has our best interests at heart. Yet God has a purpose even during the dark times so that ultimately we will be effective in service.

For me, these were not new principles of my faith. However, they were effectively presented as a sort of segue into his emphasis that the person who is suffering from depression should get up and do something – allow the Spirit of God to give the strength needed to just do something. I pondered, *What could I do?* I was willing. I just needed to know what to do.

The next morning, the answer came. I got myself out of bed and the first thing I did was open the blinds in my living room and turn on the lights. The wheelchair push through the living room, then the dining area and into the kitchen this time was not going to be a journey in the dark.

Something as simple as brightening the atmosphere in my apartment made a huge difference.

Next up. Devotion time. I turned to the passage of Scripture in Jeremiah 30:17. Every morning in my devotional time, I started with this verse even during my meltdowns. It's evident because the page in my Bible that contains this verse is wrinkled with permanent tear-stains.

Ironically whenever I open my Bible, it opens to that page. This page now has personal significance which I will reveal farther into my story. This is also why I chose to display this page in my Bible as the cover for *Keep Turning the Pages*.

So I continued with my morning devotions; that did not change. It may seem strange but even while depressed; I simply could not give up on God's word. With each passing morning, reading Jeremiah 30:17 which says, "'But I will restore you to health and heal your wounds,' declares the Lord..." led to another Scripture...

Exodus 15:26, "...for I am the Lord, who heals you," and another...

Jeremiah 33:5, "Call to me and I will answer you and tell you great and unsearchable things you do not know," and another...

Isaiah 40:29-31, "He gives strength to the weary and increases the power of the weak...but those who hope in the Lord will renew their strength. They will soar on wings like eagles; they will run and not grow weary, they will walk and not be faint," then another...

Numbers 23:19, "God is not human, that he should lie, nor a human being, that he should change his mind. Does he speak and then not act? Does he promise and not fulfill?" and another...

Mark 5:34, "He said to her, 'Daughter, your faith has healed you. Go in peace and be freed from your suffering'," and still another...

Ephesians 3:20, "Now to him who is able to do immeasurably more than all we ask or imagine, according to his power that is at work within us," and another...

Hebrews 11:6, "And without faith it is impossible to please God, because anyone who comes to him must believe that he exists and that he rewards those who earnestly seek him."

These verses in my New International Version (NIV) Bible became my anchor, as I gradually discovered renewed strength and encouragement motivating me to get back up from a faith fall.

Still, the peace of mind and release that I gained from allowing God's word to minister to my spirit wasn't enough. I needed answers to those gnawing, nagging questions. *How did I get here in the first place? How did I lapse into depression when my every intention and heart's desire was to flourish in my faith?*

Now don't get me wrong. I'm not a psycho-analytic. I just wanted answers to use as ammunition against the Enemy's potential for a repeat of the same.

Here is where I have a greater appreciation for God's compassionate, disciplinary love. God revealed to me where I went wrong. He showed me a naïve side of my faith.

Pay attention as I elaborate. I had no problems with talking faith and God's ability to heal my paralysis. Just the thought of a miraculous healing motivated me to be open to that possibility, while doing my best to make responsible

use of the resources God provided.

I worked hard in therapies. When the therapist suggested I do one more rep, I did five. When the therapist instructed me to walk a certain distance, I extended the goal line. I was disciplined in my mealtimes and medication program. I had a schedule to progress from the wheelchair to the walker to canes so that I could return to work. The schedule called for this "miracle" to occur over the course of three months–November, December, January. That was my highly anticipated window of opportunity with no time to waste, procrastinate or squander. No doubt, this was an ambitious goal but this is Anita you're talking about. And people knew me as "a determined woman, driven by her strong faith."

Unfortunately, all of this worked together to serve as my downfall. Allow me to explain it this way. To exercise Biblical faith means that God has impressed upon one's spirit a promise specific to that situation. I believed God gave me a promise based on Jeremiah 30:17. I took Him at His word. Nothing was more encouraging than being on the receiving end of a blessing that trumped this tragedy in my life.

I had faith God was going to spring into action and heal my paralysis in three months just as He promised. There was only one problem. God never told me He would make good on His promise in three months. You see, I imposed *my* schedule on *His* promise; then I had the nerve to flaunt that as faith in God. Yes, I did. Me...Anita.

Ephesians 3:20, "Now to him who is able to do immeasurably more than all we ask or imagine, according to his power that is at work within us," and another...

Hebrews 11:6, "And without faith it is impossible to please God, because anyone who comes to him must believe that he exists and that he rewards those who earnestly seek him."

These verses in my New International Version (NIV) Bible became my anchor, as I gradually discovered renewed strength and encouragement motivating me to get back up from a faith fall.

Still, the peace of mind and release that I gained from allowing God's word to minister to my spirit wasn't enough. I needed answers to those gnawing, nagging questions. *How did I get here in the first place? How did I lapse into depression when my every intention and heart's desire was to flourish in my faith?*

Now don't get me wrong. I'm not a psycho-analytic. I just wanted answers to use as ammunition against the Enemy's potential for a repeat of the same.

Here is where I have a greater appreciation for God's compassionate, disciplinary love. God revealed to me where I went wrong. He showed me a naïve side of my faith.

Pay attention as I elaborate. I had no problems with talking faith and God's ability to heal my paralysis. Just the thought of a miraculous healing motivated me to be open to that possibility, while doing my best to make responsible

use of the resources God provided.

I worked hard in therapies. When the therapist suggested I do one more rep, I did five. When the therapist instructed me to walk a certain distance, I extended the goal line. I was disciplined in my mealtimes and medication program. I had a schedule to progress from the wheelchair to the walker to canes so that I could return to work. The schedule called for this "miracle" to occur over the course of three months–November, December, January. That was my highly anticipated window of opportunity with no time to waste, procrastinate or squander. No doubt, this was an ambitious goal but this is Anita you're talking about. And people knew me as "a determined woman, driven by her strong faith."

Unfortunately, all of this worked together to serve as my downfall. Allow me to explain it this way. To exercise Biblical faith means that God has impressed upon one's spirit a promise specific to that situation. I believed God gave me a promise based on Jeremiah 30:17. I took Him at His word. Nothing was more encouraging than being on the receiving end of a blessing that trumped this tragedy in my life.

I had faith God was going to spring into action and heal my paralysis in three months just as He promised. There was only one problem. God never told me He would make good on His promise in three months. You see, I imposed *my* schedule on *His* promise; then I had the nerve to flaunt that as faith in God. Yes, I did. Me...Anita.

Ephesians 3:20, "Now to him who is able to do immeasurably more than all we ask or imagine, according to his power that is at work within us," and another…

Hebrews 11:6, "And without faith it is impossible to please God, because anyone who comes to him must believe that he exists and that he rewards those who earnestly seek him."

These verses in my New International Version (NIV) Bible became my anchor, as I gradually discovered renewed strength and encouragement motivating me to get back up from a faith fall.

Still, the peace of mind and release that I gained from allowing God's word to minister to my spirit wasn't enough. I needed answers to those gnawing, nagging questions. *How did I get here in the first place? How did I lapse into depression when my every intention and heart's desire was to flourish in my faith?*

Now don't get me wrong. I'm not a psycho-analytic. I just wanted answers to use as ammunition against the Enemy's potential for a repeat of the same.

Here is where I have a greater appreciation for God's compassionate, disciplinary love. God revealed to me where I went wrong. He showed me a naïve side of my faith.

Pay attention as I elaborate. I had no problems with talking faith and God's ability to heal my paralysis. Just the thought of a miraculous healing motivated me to be open to that possibility, while doing my best to make responsible

use of the resources God provided.

I worked hard in therapies. When the therapist suggested I do one more rep, I did five. When the therapist instructed me to walk a certain distance, I extended the goal line. I was disciplined in my mealtimes and medication program. I had a schedule to progress from the wheelchair to the walker to canes so that I could return to work. The schedule called for this "miracle" to occur over the course of three months–November, December, January. That was my highly anticipated window of opportunity with no time to waste, procrastinate or squander. No doubt, this was an ambitious goal but this is Anita you're talking about. And people knew me as "a determined woman, driven by her strong faith."

Unfortunately, all of this worked together to serve as my downfall. Allow me to explain it this way. To exercise Biblical faith means that God has impressed upon one's spirit a promise specific to that situation. I believed God gave me a promise based on Jeremiah 30:17. I took Him at His word. Nothing was more encouraging than being on the receiving end of a blessing that trumped this tragedy in my life.

I had faith God was going to spring into action and heal my paralysis in three months just as He promised. There was only one problem. God never told me He would make good on His promise in three months. You see, I imposed *my* schedule on *His* promise; then I had the nerve to flaunt that as faith in God. Yes, I did. Me...Anita.

I unconsciously had more faith in my schedule than in God's spoken promise. Much of what I did was wrapped up in the goal to return to work by January, which was an unrealistic expectation that was never part of God's plan.

I remember the morning God revealed to me that I had been openly talking faith and acknowledging God's ability to heal my body. But *I* gave Him *my* schedule and demanded that God divinely rubber stamp it. "Lord, I know what you promised. Here is my schedule. Now bless it."

When He did not, the slow yet downward spiral in despondency, disappointment and disillusionment began. The more I thought about the fear of not being able to walk when I wanted to, the more I unconsciously pushed these unhealthy emotions into my faith energy. The negative emotions overwhelmed and overpowered as I continued to see the clock ticking fast towards a self-made goal that was far within reach.

I did not joyously enter Mom's apartment Thanksgiving Day using a walker. My mobility was still dependent upon the aid of a wheelchair, 24/7. Disturbingly, my miraculous comeback was in jeopardy.

I made the mistake trying to live by faith and force a timeframe on God. Faith doesn't work that way. In a sense what I passed off as faith was presumption. I presumed that God would do what He promised when I wanted Him to and yet I failed to get God to commit to my schedule.

I got the message. It rang loud and clear. God showed me that His perfect plan includes His perfect schedule.

At this point my only response was to repent and confess my fault to God; which I did. I hurt Anita and I was so sorry. It may seem confusing but I felt broken yet at the same time liberated.

I was desperate for answers and God helped me to see where I went wrong in my faith. Now I have a new perspective on Psalm 30:5b, "...weeping may endure for a night but joy comes in the morning." My weeping in a season of depression, the dark moments when I cried my eyes out lasted so long until it seemed like there was no end in sight.

But the end came. Finally the joy returned as the Holy Spirit did exactly what Jesus promised according to John 8:32, "Then you will know the truth, and the truth will set you free," and John 16:13, "But when he, the Spirit of truth, comes, he will guide you into all the truth."

I was guided and set free as I meditated daily on all of those Biblical truths listed in the previous paragraphs. The verses came across in a fresh, freeing and invigorating way. I didn't just read them. I pondered and contemplated their respective messages in relations to the condition of my sincere and sorrowful heart.

I was too preoccupied and anxious about the unattained goal, but all that changed. I allowed myself to engage in quality time, quiet time with God through prayer and meditation, instead of cramming words from pages in my Bible into my anxiety-ridden, shortened attention span.

Time spent with God is the key. We benefit the least

from God's word when we read it on the run as if we're grabbing a breakfast Pop Tart before heading out the door. Having taken responsibility for putting myself on the pathway to depression, I had to take the initiative for deliberate and disciplined contemplation of God's word during quiet, intimate times.

With that, my outlook gradually emerged brighter. It was a process but I learned so much. The main lesson was how faith, as a powerful spiritual discipline, can yet be subject to misapplication and vulnerable to our blind side. My faith grew stronger. Those verses built my testimony as evidenced almost a year later when I was afforded the opportunity to publicly share my new level of faith.

November 5, 1998, the *Kansas City Globe* headline read, "Church Community Honors a Faithful Servant." The week prior, my church's fellowship hall was filled to capacity as over 300 well-wishers attended a recognition banquet in my honor. *The Globe* covered the event.

An evening of encouraging words and inspiring singers, the program featured a lineup of tributes from family members, area pastors and ministers, community leaders and personal friends, as well as women with whom I was privileged to work alongside while serving as president of the Sunshine District Junior Mission.

The banquet speaker was the 2nd Vice President of the National Baptist Convention of America, Inc., and my pastor Rev. Wallace S. Hartsfield, Sr.

It was an experience where I, along with my parents and siblings, felt humbled yet honored. Here are excerpts from *The Globe* article's recap of that event:

> *Anita Cobbins defies medical odds. Since the accident, she has been on disability and unable to work. But Cobbins is not a quitter. Despite medical predictions to the contrary, she has made miraculous progress in her rehabilitation program and plans to return to work soon, on a part-time basis. Her goal is to walk again.*
>
> *And those who know her believe she will walk again. Take the Rev. Wallace S. Hartsfield, for instance. Hartsfield, Anita's pastor, was the banquet speaker.*
>
> *As he rose to give the banquet message, a visibly choked up Hartsfield looked at Cobbins seated in her wheelchair to the right of the speaker's platform and said, "I have witnessed a lot of things in my lifetime and this has to be one of the greatest." He was referring to weeks ago when Cobbins surprised the congregation, got up out of her wheelchair and walked down the aisle with the assistance of a walker. (Daddy's Devotion chapter).*
>
> *Hartsfield's message centered on Isaiah 40:28 and Psalm 137. The texts speak to the historical experience of the people of Israel when they were in captivity in Babylon. Hartsfield said everyone will go through an exile experience in their lifetime.*
>
> *Being in exile simply means being in a place you*

would rather not be...'To be paralyzed, to look at feet that have no life, is exile,' Hartsfield said...

Because of her determination and enduring faith in God, Cobbins is seeing miraculous success.

Reciting Isaiah 40:31, Hartsfield shouted, 'But they that wait upon the Lord, shall renew their strength, they shall mount up with wings as eagles, they shall run and not be weary, they shall walk and not faint.'

He concluded, 'Now Anita, the feet that could not walk, can move again, the hands that could not feel, can feel again and those legs that could not move can move again.'

Following Hartsfield's message, presentations to Cobbins were made by Chester and Oneita Walker, including a check for $5,200—proceeds raised from the banquet. Remarks were made by (Deacon Maynard) Harvey and the Rev. C.L. Cobbins (Anita's father).

(Anita) Cobbins then thanked her family, friends, the church and the audience. And in her own sermonic way, she testified about how God's word has guided her through trying times. To shouts of 'Amen!,' Cobbins motivated the audience from her wheelchair, reciting scriptures she had obviously hid in her heart: Jeremiah 30:17; Hebrews 11:6; Exodus 15:26; Ephesians 3:20; Numbers 23:19...And on that note, Hartsfield gave the benediction.

Seeing all of the support from so many well-wishers was a definite turning point in how I viewed my experience. I so appreciate receiving a beautiful bouquet of roses, a plaque and the monetary gift. However, the greatest gift I received that night is summed up in one word – love. Despite all of the pain, discouragement and the depth of emotional despair, that banquet hall was filled with reasons to get up from a faith fall and stand tall.

Out of all the chapters in *Keep Turning the Pages*, the experience I shared in this chapter had the most profound impact on my life.

Contemplating suicide was never on my radar until I reached a point when I began to question why I should keep living.

However, I am not sharing this testimony to drum up sympathy. The message behind this story is victory. Whether God causes or allows weeping to endure for a night, it is not His intention, desire or goal that we wander aimlessly in the doldrums or settle for defeat. This was not God's destiny for me, which is why I am comfortable with breaking my silence without any reservations whatsoever.

The Lord has given me the strength to freely be transparent, real and raw about this area where I struggled emotionally to the point of even contemplating suicide.

By the power of God's word; however, the joy of my salvation was restored and my faith renewed. The full measure of faith in action means that I am done with coming up with my own schedules. Instead I strive to remain committed to God's timing in all areas of my life.

And as for God's promise to heal my body? I still believe God has yet to reveal the full manifestation of my physical healing. I will continue to believe the promise unless God shows me otherwise.

It is a matter of time, His time and in due time. I am committed and in it for the long haul.

I had to take several deep breaths. Opening up and pouring my heart out in the previous chapter caused me to question how readers would react. I had to come clean and reveal the experience when I contemplated suicide.

Thankfully, God gave me the courage to share and now I'm feeling liberated. With this revelation, my sincerest prayer is that you, too, will stop allowing the Enemy to sift you through those deep, dark inner struggles as though there is no hope for *your* deliverance.

See from my story how much God is concerned about your emotional well-being. If you are living in dark moments, pray. Do that much as a first step. This may be God's time to break you towards your blessing. You do know that beyond brokenness God has a blessing uniquely for you?

Brokenness is part of the faith journey. It's a journey filled with highs and lows. Even if your faith fails; it can make a comeback. Just ask Peter (Luke 22:31-32).

Like Job, your faith may be tested against the backdrop of troubling circumstances that hit too close to home (Job 1). Nevertheless, God can turn your life around so that your latter days emerge better than your former days (Job 42:12).

Throughout the book that bears his name, Job's anguish is obvious and justified. Where is God when Job needed Him? Martha and Mary challenged Jesus with the same (John 11:21, 32). Be careful, however, not to frown upon them because in anger, anguish or anxiety you may have asked the same, "God, where are you when I need you!?"

Bottom line is whenever God shows up – better late than never. Now turn the pages. There is a message for you somewhere in these *Globe* articles.

Praying In The Dark
Originally published December 12 - 20, 2002
Reprinted with permission from the
Kansas City Globe

Do you know what it's like to pray in the dark? I'm not referring to praying with your eyes closed or while in a room with the lights out.

I'm talking about seeking God through prayer and His word when you are experiencing the dark times of life, when it seems as though there is no end in sight and no light at the end of the tunnel.

For instance, when you lose someone very close to you or a close relationship takes a turn for the worse. Or, how about when you are told you've been diagnosed with a serious illness? These types of situations and more can thrust even the most admirable believer in God into endless dark days.

Remember the words God used to describe Job in His conversation with Satan? He said, "...there is no one like him; he's blameless and upright, a man who fears God and shuns evil," Job 1:8.

But when you keep reading from verse 13 to the end of the second chapter of Job, you find that at the hands of Satan, God allowed a string of dark circumstances to invade Job's life – loss of wealth, family, health and spousal loyalty.

Job experienced incredible sufferings and was in the dark as to why. Only God and Satan knew what was up.

There is a saying, "Desperate times call for desperate measures." At times, we are desperate for the dark times to move quickly. If we can find a smidgen of an opportunity to control that situation, our first priority is usually to move the darkness. It's too scary. Darkness leaves us vulnerable, dismantles our composure and can threaten our sense of security.

But God did not create us with the capacity to put an end to the dark circumstances we encounter. Only He can do that, because by His very nature He is light and "in him is no darkness at all," I John 1:5.

In a practical sense, we can rest assured that God who is in all places at all times, is also always ready to operate on our behalf out of His all-seeing eyes and divine wisdom.

The Enemy has the audacity to flaunt darkness in an effort to hide the essence of our trials from us. He cannot do that with God. Psalm 139:12 declares that "the darkness and the light are both alike to thee" (God).

And if that's not convincing enough, read Psalm 42:8. The psalmist testifies that in the midst of deep darkness, he still experiences the love of God even in the "night" which motivates him to pray.

God wants us to come to Him even more when we are in the dark. So, go right ahead. Pray in the dark. It's OK. As long as you're praying to the God who is light.

The One who is able to turn our "darkness into light," Psalm 18:28.

Until next month, keep the faith.

Be Broken, Be Blessed

Originally published February 13 - 19, 2003
Reprinted with permission from the
Kansas City Globe

"The Lord is close to the brokenhearted
and saves those who are crushed in spirit,"
– Psalms 34:18.

In the hymn writer's reference to the Lord, this Scripture is an encouragement. However, in terms of individuals, a Scripture such as this one will make a person cringe. A broken heart and a crushed spirit are often covered up by the façade or false composure of having everything together.

That's why the Lord engages in a process that often meets us at a point of resistance and rebellion. That process is called brokenness. It is God's strategy set in motion to free us from pride, stubbornness and the relentless tendency to have our own way. It is so uplifting to know that God gives and makes good on a multitude of promises revealed in the Bible. But nowhere in the Bible does God promise or even hint at blessing rebellion.

It is His desire and in a sense His obligation, to bless obedience. "If you are willing and obedient," He says, "you will eat the good of the land," Isaiah 1:19.

Believe it or not, in order to get in a position to be blessed, there will be times when you and I must first be broken. And if you've ever been broken, then you know that our Heavenly Father has been known to arrange or allow circumstances to try us in areas He knows are blessing blockers.

Or, sometimes God will break us in preparation for ministry so that we become committed to fulfilling His purpose and not our own. Consider the words of Jesus at a broken and low moment in His life. Facing death, Jesus opened up to His disciples and confessed, "Now my heart is troubled, and what shall I say? Father, save me from this hour? No, it is for this very reason, I come to this hour. Father, glorify your name," St. John 12:27.

Another example was when Jesus agonized in the Garden of Gethsemane. Closer to facing the reality of death and eventual momentary separation from God, Jesus told His disciples that His "soul was exceedingly sorrowful even unto death," Matthew 26:38. Later He prayed that God would allow this "cup" or suffering to pass. Then, He prayerfully resolved, "Nevertheless, not my will. Thine will be done," verse 39.

In these instances, in His brokenness, Jesus turned to the proper purpose and perspective for His suffering and death. In principle, two blessings are guaranteed results of being broken. 1) Like our Savior, we discover or recommit ourselves to a God-given purpose and 2) we're able to sort out our feelings as we go through difficult circumstances and place our experiences in the proper perspective.

Jesus' battered and bruised body hanging on a tree redeemed the world of sin. His brokenness brings wholeness that can only be applied to our lives when we, too, are willing to be broken.

Let's go back to John 12:25 where Jesus says, "A man who loves his life will lose it, while the man who hates his life in this world will keep it for eternal life."

There are those who will fight to the death, refusing to allow situations to break them. They believe that there's too much at stake, too much to lose – pride being numero uno. Yet, anyone who loosens his or her grip on life actually allows the process of being broken to be the ultimate pathway to being blessed.

Until next month, keep the faith.

Faith, Don't Fail Me Now

Originally published May 29 - June 4, 2008
Reprint publish by permission from the
Kansas City Globe

A recent headline read, *Clinton Campaign: Feet Don't Fail Me Now*. The news article was published the day after the North Carolina and Indiana primaries where Sen. Hillary Clinton lost big time in North Carolina and narrowly won in Indiana.

These election results prompted a chorus of calls from political pundits and some leading Democrats for Clinton to gracefully exit her aspirations and bid for the Democratic nomination.

After loaning her campaign millions of dollars and determined to stay in the race and see the primary process through, camp Clinton defied the notion that candidate Clinton was strategically working her way out. The camp played up Sen. Clinton's appeal among White voters, the progress recently made in a recent primary and big states and the belief that she is the best fit for an election matchup against Sen. John McCain.

According to the article, "The loan is a sign of Sen. Clinton's commitment to the race, commitment to the process and a commitment to stay competitive with Sen. Obama."

Now before you conclude that this article is all about politics, read on.

Keep Turning: Faith, Don't Fail Me Now

Earlier this week, I was talking with a friend and brother in the Lord. I wanted to get an update on his efforts to secure a job that required passing a written test. It was his second attempt at taking the test and unfortunately, he informed me that he did not pass.

He was confident and excited at the possibility that the outcome would end in his favor. And for a brief moment, it took me back to the times when I just knew something that I desired deeply and worked hard to hopefully achieve would work out. But it didn't.

I quickly turned my attention back to listening to him, how he felt and sized up the situation.

Then he confessed something that was so true, yet the comment struck me by surprise coming from him. Circumstantially, he failed the required test – not once, but twice. His heart was dead set on working for the company; the employer had to let him go. He was again out of work and now in a position to begin job hunting. But he realized that beneath the surface, what he was experiencing was a matter of testing his faith in God more than anything else.

So borrowing from the headline in the news article and the topic of discussion my brother and I were engaged in, this month's focus is, "Faith, Don't Fail Me Now." And I'm going right to the Scripture that inspired this month's column.

In Luke 22:31-32, Jesus says to Peter the disciple, "Satan has demanded permission to sift you like wheat;

but I have prayed for you, that your faith may not fail; and you, when once you have turned again, strengthen your brothers."

Think about it. Our faith, like Peter's, is an attribute Satan desires to prey upon and Jesus needs to pray for. There is something so powerful about the potential that lies within our faith until Satan is in hot pursuit to break us down, separating the good from the bad (to sift) so that strategically the bad prevails over the good. And in many instances, that is the case.

The Scripture in Luke 22 says the Enemy "demanded permission" of God. Imagine that. It's the same audacity recorded in Job chapter one, where Satan challenges Job's commitment before God. "'Does Job fear God for nothing,' Satan replied? '...But stretch out your hand and strike everything he has, and he will surely curse you to your face'," (verses 9-11).

Those of us who are familiar with Job's experience, know that his latter days ended better than his former days. But again, for many of us today, that is not the case. Under the pressures of life seemingly gone awry, we allow our faith to, at a minimum, fade. And for some be;ievers, faith fails.

If you get nothing else out of what I'm sharing, receive this as truth – God never intends for the final judgment of our faith to be stamped "failed." And if you can get another truth out of this column, understand that more than your possessions, finances, health, relationships, jobs, etc., Satan's main target is your faith.

Keep Turning: Faith, Don't Fail Me Now

True, the faith journey will have its highs and lows. At times it will seem as if faith will struggle to bounce back from insurmountable, crushing blows. But the good news is that faith can and will make a comeback. Jesus told Peter, "Satan has demanded…but I have prayed for you." Then Jesus shared something personal and prophetic, "…when once you have turned again, strengthen your brothers."

Just think. When Jesus, the great high priest who can sympathize with our weaknesses, (Hebrews 4:15) puts Himself in the same position and prays for us, the script is flipped on Satan, and failure is no longer final.

But, like camp Clinton, we have to be committed to seeing our strengths through God's eyes and not our failures through others' and our own eyes. We also may need to reinforce our faith by demonstrating that commitment in practical ways.

Our strengths will propel us to look and move forward, gaining greater strength and preparing us to help others along the way.

On the other hand, focusing on failures will only keep us on a path of failing faith.

And we don't want faith to fail us. Now do we?

Until next month, keep the faith.

Better Late Than Never

Originally published September 22 - 28, 2011
Reprinted with permission from the
Kansas City Globe

All of us have faith. The Bible says we all have "a measure of faith." Even if we don't have faith in God, we still have faith. When you woke up this morning you believed that you would accomplish at least some of your plans for the day. That's faith.

Before you end the day today, you will have done something to prepare for tomorrow – whether it's work, or school, whatever comes to mind; you are exercising faith.

So it's not a question whether or not we have faith. But the first question is what or who is the object of our faith? And the second question for believers is how far are you willing to believe God and what He has the power to do?

That's an important question because in some instances, we believe God to the max. We believe God is a healer. We believe God will provide food to eat. Some people choose to believe God for employment or that promotion on the job, despite the lingering economic downturn.

When it's something that we want bad enough, doubt is not an option. We can unleash our faith and hold on until our change comes. However, when the Bible says, "the just shall live by faith" (Habakkuk 2:4), that is broad and all-encompassing. It's not an every-now-and-then faith.

John chapter 11 is an eye-opening, powerful account that circumstantially centers on the death of Lazarus and his sisters', Mary's and Martha's responses. More importantly, it is a chapter about faith even though faith is not mentioned one time, which makes it eye-opening. However, faith is strongly represented. It is so crystal clear until it could provoke one to ask, "how far am I willing to believe God for whatever I'm facing or will face in my life?"

John chapter 11 also opens detailing a sorrowing situation. From all indications, Lazarus, Jesus' close friend, was deathly ill. A messenger was sent to deliver the sad news to Jesus. In turn, Jesus sent the messenger back with the encouraging response that Lazarus' sickness would not end in death, but it was for God's glory and so that Jesus would be glorified through it.

That is one of the challenges of faith because most of the time when we are going through, we are more preoccupied with what we're going to get out of our situations. It's so difficult to see our troubles as a way for God to get the glory, as a means for Jesus to be more real in our lives.

You know you're growing in the Lord when you can avow, "God, I may be sick, have financial struggles, be unemployed or be hurting from insults and offensive attacks. Nevertheless, God, you will get the glory."

When Jesus finally heads for Bethany four days after being informed of Lazarus' critical illness, Lazarus had died.

In verse 21, Martha gets right to it, "Lord, if you had been here my brother would not have died. But I know that even now God will give you whatever you ask." That's faith.

The conversation continues with Jesus telling her that her brother would rise again and Martha makes another statement of faith, "I know he will rise again at the resurrection." Martha expressed a faith based on confidence in the future. She believed in the teachings on the resurrection of the dead. She believed in that promise from God.

But, there is a problem with that kind of faith. I'll share that with you later.

Now it's Mary's turn. Like Martha, she too, said, "Lord, if you had been here, my brother would not have died." Mary appears to be the sensitive one who is taking Lazarus' death and Jesus delay harder than Martha. But recall Mary was also the devoted one (Luke 10:38-42). And in the midst of her mournful tears, she demonstrates a faith that is content with accepting what has happened.

It's a good thing to have that kind of faith – content with the present. It's a faith that says what has happened has happened, yet I still believe that God is in control. But there was a problem with that type of faith.

Martha's faith showed confidence in the future. Mary's faith showed contentment with the present. They both had shared a common problem with their faith statements. They told Jesus he was too late to do anything about the situation now, "Lord if you had been here my brother would not have died."

How many times have we written off our blessings, deliverance and answers from God too soon because Jesus didn't show up when we thought He should have.

Truthfully, whenever Jesus arrives on scene, it's better late than never. Wouldn't you rather that Jesus be a Johnny-come-lately than a no-show?

Time will always test our faith. We'll be tempted to doubt. But that doesn't mean God is not working. Do you have the faith to believe that?

Never did Martha or Mary imagine Jesus would restore life to their brother after being dead, stinking and in a tomb for not one, not two, not three but four days.

After all, Lazarus was irrevocably dead and a smelly corpse. From all indications, it was all over for Lazarus. However, remember the words of Jesus. He said Lazarus' sickness would not end in death.

Mary and Martha had the faith to believe Jesus' presence would have prevented Lazarus from dying. Since he came on the scene too late to prevent death, then Martha's faith took a leap into the distant future. Mary's faith accepted what took place in the present.

Yet, "it's not over until God says it's over." Jesus still had a miracle to perform that very moment.

If only we could cease protesting whenever we think God has gone past our deadlines, our faith could soar to unimaginable heights.

God is never off-the-clock, never too late. And there are times when He desires that we demonstrate the faith that believes He will deliver on a promise right now and not sometime in the ambiguous, distant future.

Perhaps you've come to the wrong conclusion and given up too soon.

Let God resurrect your dreams and desires from the tomb. Unwrap and loose them from the grave clothes of doubt, disappointment and disillusionment.

By faith, trust God and His timing because whenever He shows up, it's better late than never.

Until next month, keep the faith.

Chapter 7

Sisters by Heart Roles to Model

( )

One evening I watched with interest a program that airs on Oprah Winfrey's cable network OWN. The show title bears the host's name, *Iyanla VanZant: Fix My Life.*

The program's title is rather straightforward. Each week features Vanzant counseling and coaching guests to navigate their way through relationships in crisis to some level of reconciliation. In this particular segment VanZant responded to a request to help six women who reside in the Windy City, Chicago.

The segment, "Fix My Backstabbing Friends," does not keep the viewer guessing. Obviously, friendships between these women have deteriorated and VanZant was on a mission to try and help them heal and mend their broken relationships.

The show's promo sets up the episode describing "The Six Brown Chicks" as savvy bloggers who wanted to help other women. As a result, their unique partnership became newsworthy. This group of women was spotlighted by the local media, webisodes were produced and a television show was in discussion.

Yet in a matter of six short months, the show's promo

posts, "the partnership crumbled due to jealousy, anger and backstabbing. Now, there is no television show, the blog is stalled, and their relationships are torn apart."

As in previous shows, VanZant spends time asking probing questions and offering an assessment of character traits and behaviors in an effort to get at the root cause of the breakdown. During the show, the women shared their versions how their relationships began to unravel. At times, some of their words and actions were disturbing and downright disrespectful. Furthermore, some of the women reacted as though they could care less. I could not believe I was watching adult, professional women carry on like the actresses characterized on the Bravo channel's, *The Real Housewives of...*programs.

As I watched I wondered, *What on earth could have gone wrong so terribly until these women chunked their relationships?* I admired the fact that at the outset, they had a common purpose–to do good for other women. By pooling together their resources, skill sets and strengths, these women could have been a force to reckon with.

They lost an invaluable opportunity to showcase their relationships before others who could have benefitted from their unique story – so much for the good they intended for other women.

Also as I watched, it became irresistible to think about the relationship I share with five other women. You could say we're "six chicks," too. And because we met within the greater Kansas City area, we could be considered the "Show

Keep Turning: Sisters By Heart

-Me-State version of six brown chicks."

Now I recognize friendships between women are formed all over the universe. I also recognize that relationships between women can be dime a dozen. Women more than men will come and go so quickly and without warning, until it can cause you to question whether that relationship was worth the time and effort you put into it. Many women, including myself, have experienced friends who have done just that; they came and went.

But not the women in this chapter of *Keep Turning the Pages*. For me, these women represent the epitome of friendship, love, grace and commitment, to name a few.

They have taught me that good, genuine and solid friends can be assets in one's life, not in the sense of seeing what they can do for me but instead; what I can do to affirm who they are and how much they mean to me.

I write this story with a deep sense of emotion and rock-solid love that I have for these women. As they have stood by me, our relationships have withstood the test of time. I tend to thrive on healthy, wholesome relationships. And I have no qualms about closely guarding the bonds of genuine friendships.

The six of us began making each other's acquaintances in the early 1980s. One of the sisters and I met when an advertisement for a "Christian female roommate" caught my attention. It was handwritten on a hot pink large index card and posted on a bulletin board in the student union at the University of Missouri-Kansas City. It literally stuck out like a sore thumb.

I was prayerfully, desperately searching for a place to live because my rental arrangement was set to end that week. I took the card off the bulletin board. I didn't just write down the number and leave the card; I took it.

Eventually, I called the number. The next day we met and by the end of the week, Delores and I became roommates.

From our initial conversation, we discovered we had some things in common. Besides being Christian women, we were from families of faith. We were from large families (although she surpasses me on the siblings count). We were both taking college courses. Delores was studying for a degree in engineering. I had to complete three additional credits from the semester I had to return home and take 'Incompletes.' (See the chapter *Lord, I Need You*.)

Delores was an active member of the Stephen Baptist Church, along with Brenette, Jenette, Diann and Ann. They knew each other. Over time, Delores would invite me to join the ladies for social outings and so began the framework for a friendship in the making that has now spanned more than 30 years.

Who are we by name? Delores. Diann. Ann. Anita. Jenette. Brenette. Notice the phonetic rhythm when pronouncing our names in that order.

The more we spent time with each other, the more our personalities blossomed. And blossomed they did. But I can honestly say that I never detected nor witnessed a hint of one-upmanship, or a spirit to "take a sistah down a notch" – not among these ladies.

There have never been times when our communications were punctuated with vicious words or mean-spirited attitudes. There have never existed any green-eyed monsters or sabotaging schemers incognito within our friendship. No one ever pretended to applaud or contended to work against each other's successes or the pursuit of individual achievements.

Throughout the years of our relationships, we gelled so naturally until we could easily celebrate and rise to give each other standing ovations for our respective goals and successes. But we were not bent on self-promotion. We were just friends sharing our dreams and accomplishments during ordinary phone conversations and regular girlfriend get-togethers.

And if I'm starting to sound like a broken record, I don't apologize.

I feel like shouting to the rooftops how I value and treasure my friends. Although they never knowingly signed up for the job, these ladies have taught me how to define and be a genuine friend. They allowed their lights to shine, without advertising or boasting about their qualities. Yet, I did not have to look long, hard or far to see the profound goodness in their characters.

However, I point out the aforementioned negative qualities I saw while watching the Six Brown Chicks because, in general–whether real or perceived–feelings of insecurity, suspicion and jealousy are common among women. This is not an indictment but a fact.

That feuding spirit portrayed by the Six Brown Chicks, *Basketball Wives* and *Real Housewives* (of wherever) is not only limited to today's women living in the Windy City, Los Angeles, Orange County, New Jersey, New York or Atlanta. That feuding spirit has become commonplace. It will make you and your gal pals candidates for a reality TV show, played out while having lunch, hosting a party or during a night out on the town.

Fractured, phony and superficial relationships among women have unfortunately been our struggles, usually rooted in deeper emotions that often go unaddressed.

In her book titled, *Black Women Redefined: Dispelling Myths and Discovering Fulfillment in the Age of Michelle Obama*, author Sophia Nelson writes about "the everyday sister heroes of generations past" who "understood the virtues of loyalty, respect and sacrifice." Nelson points out, "These women understood that pettiness had too high a price and that bitterness, envy, strife and jealousy are the natural enemies of love, peace, joy and lasting friendships."

So my sister I want you to know that you were not attacked because of what "she heard that you said." You were attacked because *she* was suspicious.

Do you ever wonder why your character is constantly on trial or forced to line up along the firing squad's wall to face execution? Maybe it is because that green-eyed monster in *her* raised its ugly head and can't stand seeing your success and confidence that is not forced, but naturally flows from your personality.

If you have been robbed of opportunities to put your best foot forward by another woman who relishes using *her* authority to keep your capable, creative and assertive light hidden under a bushel; that was unfortunate. But the lost opportunity was not your fault.

Attempts at reconciliation often takes a back seat when a disagreement between two women is complicated by opposing alliances formed because other women take sides. This sets up a vicious cycle rooted in personalities that are comfortable with evening instead of settling the score.

Ladies, the character assassins, the cold-shoulder syndrome and the tendency to overtly give another woman the silent treatment as the two of you pass each other are prevalent because some women refuse to get a grip and confront the real issues.

Negative emotions left unchecked and unconfessed are the root cause of broken, irreparable relationships. It is so natural to flow into a fight with another woman than to take the fight into the ring where it originated–within yourself. That's where the conflict started, not with the other person but within you. Have you ever noticed how natural it is for some women to take another down a notch, flaunt that nice-nasty disposition or flirt with ways to throw another sister under the bus?

As Nelson observes, "Clearly, sisters, there is something very wrong in the sisterhood. You see it in the blogs, on social networking sites, in the sororities and even in church organizations: beautiful, smart, accomplished sisters feeling angered by other sisters." Although some may choose to engage in meaningless spats and squabbles face-to-face or on Facebook, you don't get to choose the consequences or control the fallout.

Until we stop denying and ignoring the emotional issues that are often at the core of our dislikes, criticisms and undermining of other women, we will continue to lose ground experiencing healthy and genuine relationships.

Now that I got that off my chest, it's back to my friends who are the subjects of this chapter.

One wintry Friday evening in early March, Delores, Diann, Ann, Brenette and I met after work for a girlfriend get-together. We gathered at a small, quaint restaurant and we were seated in a private section, making the atmosphere relatively intimate. While eating dinner, I bubbled over with unbridled appreciation as I reflected on the countless times we have taken time to spend quality time with each other – over 30 years and counting.

As we finished eating, I got the idea to ask each lady, "Give three words to describe each other." Overall, it was a fun exercise. Most of all, it spoke volumes about how we viewed each other, accept one another and the chemistry within our individual personalities that keeps us bonded as friends and women of God.

I am letting you in on the conversations around the table, as we took turns sharing our impressions of one another. But I added something else. Hopefully, the ladies will be pleasantly surprised as they read this chapter. For I also see in each lady a character trait which reminds me of certain women of the Bible. I admire my friends for the qualities they possess and I aspire to pattern my life after their examples because they are passing on roles to model.

BRENETTE STICKS TO THE SCRIPT.

Brenette was the soft-spoken one in the bunch. Each time I asked her to describe one of us, Brenette (unlike the rest) followed instructions to the 'T', stuck to the script and gave answers without the need to clarify her responses.

To **Brenette:** *Ann is a sassy lady...witty...and fun.*

As she searched for words to describe Delores, I interrupted her train of thought and spoke up.

Anita: *Delores is articulate.*

Brenette: *Yeah* (she agreed).

Then Brenette proceeded to put me in check.

Brenette: *But you use your own words.*

After an outburst of laughter all that I could do was apologize for trying to put words in Brenette's mouth.

Anita: *Sorry, Brenette,* I said (embarrassingly).

Brenette: *But Delores is articulate* (she conceded).

Delores: *Is that the word you want to put down for me?*

Anita: *Well...*(as I wondered how to respond) *Yeah.*

Then Brenette continued...

Brenette: (Delores is) *an organizer, particular and sincere.*

By now you will note that the three-word rule has been thrown out. Throughout the evening, the ladies answered in phrases and at times, more than three words. That was fine with me, because their cooperation and spontaneous responses made this impromptu experience all the more unpretentious and enjoyable.

Brenette: *I see Diann as a hard worker, business-minded and studious.*

In describing me, Brenette did not hesitate.

Brenette: *You are pow-wer-ful* (she said forcefully).

This description along with Brenette's emphasis took me by surprise.

Anita: *Ewww. That's a scary one.*

Still it wasn't half as scary as the next description. Brenette also viewed me as a "peacemaker."

Brenette: *Anita is good at keeping us together.*

With that, Ann leaned towards me to whisper and call me a "trouble maker," while Brenette sincerely continued sharing her comments. The sidebar between Ann and me led to snickering as we whispered, "Dr. Jekyll. Mr. Hyde. Peacemaker. Troublemaker. That's who she is. That's what she said about me."

Brenette: *Nooo. Did I say that?* (she asked).

A puzzled Brenette saw Ann and me at the other end of the table misbehaving like a couple miscreants up to no good. So Diann stepped in to reassure Brenette.

Diann: *No. You didn't. Ann said Anita was a 'troublemaker.'*

Brenette: *See. You (Ann) made me forget what I was going to say* (she whined).

Ann: *Ooohhh, I'm sorry.*

(Ann makes a sound as if she's erasing an audio tape).

Ann: *I erased that. Sorry.*

All the while it's Diann who is hilariously snickering.

Lastly, Brenette described me as "longsuffering."

Although I never saw myself as "powerful" or a "peacemaker," I understood why Brenette witnessed that side of me that is "longsuffering." The ladies have been right there with me, supporting me while observing the manner in which I handle the multiple challenges in my life.

BRENETTE AS A ROLE TO MODEL

Brenette impresses me because she works (often behind the scenes) to bring out the best in others. Frankly, in her soft-spoken, unassuming manner she sort of hounded, nudged and needled me for years to get started on this book. And rightly so. Brenette is the first among us to publish a book that gives her personal account on her struggles to fulfill a God-inspired dream. God revealed to Brenette an opportunity to tell her story and how to hit the ground running to accomplish her dreams. Her husband and daughters supported her every step of the way.

Brenette also enjoys working with at-risk, urban teenagers. She founded a program that helps them discover ways to be their best even in their formative years, partly by pairing them with adult mentors in a chosen profession.

When I think of Brenette, I think of the humble Hebrew slave girl in a valiant army commander's household, II Kings 5:1-19. The commander's name was Naaman who also was plagued with leprosy. This slave girl was the first voice of encouragement that ultimately led to Naaman's healing. Despite the loss of her freedoms while serving as a slave, she looked past her circumstance and used her faith mixed with sincere intercession to point the way. At first, Naaman had some misgivings. Eventually he experienced God's healing.

Likewise, to know Brenette is to appreciate her sincerity as she pushes you to live up to your potential and to pursue God's plan for your life. An excerpt from her book gives a clearer example. Brenette's brother passed away from cancer in 2004. However, his health challenges date back to his high school days when an injury during a football game rendered him quadriplegic. In her book, Brenette writes:

> *About three years ago I started telling my brother that he had a story to tell. At least three to four times a year I would send him an email message reminding him to get started. The message would simply say, "It's time to tell your story."*

Brenette had concluded that her brother's challenges—living with paralysis and cancer—were the basis for his story that would help others. Sounds familiar? It is Brenette being true to who she is. She often encouraged me with "how's that book project coming?" Anyone who dares to dream, has a story or goals would do well to make Brenette's acquaintance. Otherwise, there is the risk of an unfulfilled dream, untold story or unmet goal. Brenette's behind-the-scene encouragement is a role to model and one of the reasons I highly admire her.

Diann was full of mischief

On Diann's first chance, she cheated. In fact, Diann's mischief continued throughout the evening. For starters, she piggybacked on Brenette's descriptions for Ann.

Diann: *Ditto. Those are my words, too, after Brenette described Ann as a sassy lady...witty...and fun.*

Yet Diann chose her own words to describe Delores.

Diann: *Delores is very opinionated...faithful...and attractive.*

Diann sees Brenette as "faithful, too."

Anita: *It sort of runs in the family, doesn't it?*

When Diann pointed out that Brenette is "inquisitive," Delores chimed in under her breath...

Delores: *That's a nice way of saying nosy.*

We burst out with laughter until once again, we needed a moment to settle down so that Diann could end by describing Brenette as "creative."

When it was my turn..

Diann: *Anita is funny. I'll say funny because I don't want to use witty again. Anita is very classy, as well. She's also faithful. But I have to come up with another word.*

Diann paused a few seconds before concluding...

Diann: *Anita is very creative. And I say this in terms of her writing.*

Diann as a Role to Model

Diann, hands down, is businesswoman par excellence. She is a pharmacist and co-entrepreneur working alongside her husband at a nationally known, franchise-owned restaurant. She is also active in one of the most prominent African-American sororities and no telling what else. Whatever the situation, Diann is driven to take care of business. "Miss Diann" is always on the go, fun-loving, down-to-earth and still manages to consistently carry herself with grace and dignity; while juggling the demands of her family, work, spiritual and social lives. With all that she has accomplished, Diann has never flaunted or compelled any of us to feel as though we had to "keep up with the Joneses." Whether an individual or organization, Diann lives to give back, devoted to sharing her time and talent. That is her purpose, her passion.

Diann reminds me of Lydia of the Bible. From Acts 16:12-15, it is apparent that Lydia was a well-known seller of purple or in layman's terms, fabrics dyed in purple. In four short verses, we learn that Lydia was just as much engaged in the spiritual as she was in the secular. Oftentimes, businesspeople are so engrossed in their affairs they make little to no time for the spiritual. Lydia worshipped God effortlessly. She did not have to force time with God into her schedule.

In one short verse, I can compare the Lydia of the Bible with the Diann whom I know today. That verse is Romans 12:11, "Not slothful in business, fervent in spirit, serving the Lord." Diann, like Lydia, is keenly aware that God places no premium on being idle or slothful. Diann, like Lydia, balances her time so that her secular demands do not compromise her deeper spiritual pursuits. And Diann, like Lydia, is a conscientious businesswoman who believes in pouring her resources into areas of service to others.

What more can I say about my friend who has made such an impression upon my life, until I see her in a role I aspire to model?

DELORES, "THE SUSPENSE IS KILLING US."

When the sharing began, Delores was the first one to reach for a pen and paper to write her responses. Classic Delores. Leave it to Diann to object...

Diann: *Delores, you can't write them down.*

Anita: *Yes she can. Remember? She's organized.*

Brenette: *And that's a gift.*

Anita: *Yes it is. So Delores, how would you describe Ann?*

Delores: *Witty is one* (she answered).

Ann: *I thought witty meant funny?*

Diann: *It means very funny* (she explained).

Ann: *Oh. I understand.*

Meanwhile, Delores paused. She appeared to drift into deep thought searching for more words to describe Ann.

Diann: *She (Ann) can be serious..*

Delores: *I know.*

Delores agreed with Diann before pausing again...this time longer. The room was so quiet until the suspense was killing us. Finally, Ann broke the moment of silence.

Ann: *DELORES, YOU'RE TAKING TOO LONG. You're making me nervous!*

(Another laughter outburst.) While Delores was still thinking, I tried to nudge her by saying...

Anita: *One more.*

Delores: *We need three?*

Anita: *Yeah.*

Diann attempted to smooth things over so that we could move on past Delores' pauses.

Diann: *She has three more to come.*

Delores: *Yeah. I'm gonna have to pray about it.*

Ann: *Oooh Lord* (she said impatiently and tapping her pen onto the table).

(Outburst of laughter).

The laughter continued and I tried once more with a bit of psychology to get Delores to wrap it up.

Anita: *Real quick because your (Delores') turn is next.*

Stop the drum roll! At last, more words suddenly rolled off her tongue.

Delores: (Finally) *Ann is passionate, caring, faithful and a hard church-worker.*

With that, there was consensus around the table. All of us know that Ann is an extremely ardent church-worker.

In describing Brenette, Delores still took her time, just not as much time as she did for Ann.

Delores: *Uummm...intentional...*

Anita: *Intentional. Yes, she is* (I agreed).

Delores: *Focused...*

Anita: *Yes. Brenette is very focused.*

Delores: *And I want to say goal-oriented but it's like saying the same word.*

Then, it happened. *Oh no,* I thought to myself. *Delores has backslidden. Those long pauses. Oh my. This doesn't look good. She's still thinking. Waaiitt for iitt.. Whew. Finally...*

Delores: *I'll just go with intentional, focused, goal-oriented until I think of something else.*

Anita: (relieved) *Well, I think those are good* (trying to reassure Delores).

Then Delores had the nerve to throw us a curve. In describing Diann, Delores' words were quick and decisive. Surprisingly, she didn't ponder or trail off in deep thoughts. Instead Delores enunciated her words with rhythmic staccato.

Delores: *(Diann is) in-telli-gent...com-peti-tive...clas-sy.*

When Delores finished I wanted to stand at attention and respectfully give Diann the salute!

But as for me, there was suspenseful silence again, long pauses again. So this time, I decided to time Delores. It literally took about 10 seconds between her "umms" before Delores came up with the first phrase to describe me.

Delores: *Ummm...strong in faith...*(silence for 10 seconds) *creative...*(silence for another 10 seconds).

Each time it was as if Delores took us with her on this journey in search of the right words. As she drifted into silence, so did we until we could almost hear a pin drop. Again, the suspense was killing us. The room was quiet and still. Ssshhhh. Then finally, mischievous Diann to the rescue.

Diann: *Excuse me, ma'am* (to Delores.) *Those were my two words* (referring to the words Delores just used to describe me.)

That did it! Praise the Lord! The silence and suspense

were broken as we burst out in laughter.

Delores: *Great minds think alike.* (was Delores' swift, witty comeback).

Anita: *Wooo. Great minds,* (I instigated). *If that's the case then Diann wants you to keep talkin'. Keep talkin'.*

Once we settled down from this round of laughter, Delores had one final sentiment concerning me.

Delores: *I also see Anita as a caring person.*

DELORES AS A ROLE TO MODEL

One of the strengths I admire in Delores is her spirit of hospitality that spotlights her ability to plan and organize. I think it is accurate to acknowledge that Delores is mostly responsible for our frequent girlfriend get-togethers. Since the beginning of our friendships, Delores has always been at the forefront planning, initiating communications and organizing. I can imagine Delores serving notice on those devils in the details as she patiently and meticulously masters making arrangements, that also accommodate the quirks, can'ts and dislikes of our individual personalities. Delores makes it appear easy and worth the effort, all the while she is un-phased when changes arise.

On a number of occasions, Delores has invited me to her family's reunions and holiday dinners with her family members and friends. Delores and her husband are naturals at being gracious hosts. Strangers quickly and comfortably become acquaintances as guests who do not know each other immediately get introduced.

While waiting to gather around the dinner table, I often observed Delores putting all of her energy into making final preparations and putting on the finishing touches. I might add that Delores is an excellent cook. I have several food allergies–no breads, cheeses or seafood–and it may seem that I am a picky eater. Not a problem for Delores, though. She can whip out and mix up just the right menu for anyone with a limited diet to enjoy.

Not to mention no gathering is complete without social interaction through fun and games. I will never forget one year after a delicious Christmas dinner, it was game time. Card tables were set up but oddly not one deck of cards in sight. Well perhaps, we were going to play dominoes or some other board game. Nope. Not those games either. Delores instead whipped out a bag and announced that we were going to go back in time for a friendly game of Jacks!

That's right. Jacks! Remember? The object of the game calls for tossing a miniature rubber ball in the air and using the same hand to pick up metal jacks in groups of one to 10 as the ball bounces onto the table. The winner is whoever can pick up their jacks from 'onesies' to 'tensies,' without touching other jacks or losing control of the ball. The game of Jacks is a lost pastime. (Maybe someone should revive it. Can you imagine a Jacks tournament with sweet sixteen, elite eight, final four eliminations to the championship)?

Back to Delores. She personifies Martha of the Bible, Mary's and Lazarus' older sister. Most of the time when

Martha is the subject of discussion, she is remembered for her protest to Jesus concerning her sister, Mary. To Martha, Mary was negligent choosing to get in some "me-time" with Jesus, while Martha was busy organizing and slaving away around the house. In response, Jesus chastised Martha for complaining. And here is where we use Jesus' response as our basis for giving Martha a bad rap; when we should fasten our seat belts.

Within the context of Luke 10:38-41, Martha's priorities were misplaced. But Martha's overall sense of hospitality and organization are to be commended. For Jesus visited their home in Bethany on several occasions. Martha never needed to apologize for an untidy, neglected household lacking in the necessary provisions to minister to Jesus' weary soul.

Delores, like Martha, knows how to graciously "use hospitality (to one another) without grudging," I Peter 3:9. Delores can be counted on to set things in order, tackle the details and make arrangements that accommodates our wants, needs and yes, even our hang-ups.

When Delores shows hospitality she may not realize the powerful message her actions send. Hospitality is an encouraging way to demonstrate acceptance and belonging. Hospitality says the time invested is worth it. Occasions that call for bringing people together to mix, mingle and fellowship need a Martha-spirit in the mix—one who humbly embraces the role as host and organizer, willing to do whatever is necessary. I thank God that spirit stands out in Delores and represents a role I would love to model.

ANN HAD A LOT OF EXPLAINING TO DO

We were only a few minutes into sharing our responses when Ann caught a light-bulb moment. She realized...

Ann: *I had better put a positive spin on this...*

We laughed as though we knew we were busted. Leave it to Ann to blow our cover.

Ann: *All this KIND stuff being said* (she continued).

Perhaps the love language and warm sentiments were a bit much. So Ann had no other choice but to join the "nice-fest" confessing...

Ann: *I already wrote Delores is organized. And she is confident and matter-of-fact.*

Diann: *What does that mean?*

Ann: *Just straight...GET to the point!*

That's it. Show's over. No more "miss nice gals" for Ann. The *real* Ann has entered the building. We were loudly into our laughter until I hardly caught Ann's last description when she said Delores is "impatient." Actually, Ann said the first syllable so fast. I thought I heard her say "and patient." Quickly, I stood corrected as she stressed...

Ann: *IM...IM...She's IM...patient* (Outburst of laughter).

Anita: *Now Delores wants to modify her words to describe you, Ann.* (I jokingly instigated).

As we settled down, Diann philosophically weighed in with an interesting, opposite viewpoint.

Diann: *For me, I think she's patient because every time I ask her something or need something, she tries to...*

And before Diann could finish her point, Ann interrupted to clarify what she meant by "impatient."

Ann: *...in a teaching, structural way* (she backtracked). *Ok. So I'll take off impatient and stick with matter-of-fact.*

Finally, after all the discussion surrounding her, Delores breaks her silence.

Delores: *That's alright. It was your opinion anyway.*

Ann: *No, but Diann has a point. So I'll change impatient and say Delores is committed.*

That was a relatively lengthy round concerning Delores, so Ann raced through her words for Brenette.

Ann: *Brenette is gentle...focused...and kind.*

Diann: *Why are you rolling your eyes?*

Ann: *I did? No. I didn't. I simply just wrote that you (to Diann) are sophisticated...and secure...and observant.*

And finally, Ann did not hesitate when the time came to describe me.

Ann: *Gifted/talented...bossy...and determined.*

To which the term "bossy" I boastfully responded...

Anita: *There ya go. And I wear it as a badge of honor.*

ANN AS A ROLE MODEL

In an earlier paragraph, I referred to our consensus when Delores described Ann as a hard church-worker. However, it is not Ann alone; she and her husband serve as a team. They are a committed, faithful couple whose hearts beat as one in Christian service. At times, scheduling our time together as friends is often subject to Ann's availability. From serving as a deacon and deaconess, in music ministry, teaching, mission service, marriage enrichment ministry to hospital and nursing home visits, duty calls; and this couple answers. They are inseparable.

Their relationship reminds me of another couple in the Bible who also served as one ministering, teaching and sharing the Gospel of Jesus Christ. That couple is none other than Priscilla and Aquila and the Bible gives snapshots of their lives in Acts chapter 18.

Together, they were one in their secular occupations as tentmakers. Together, they taught the full message of the Gospel. Priscilla and Aquila opened their homes for church services, worship and teaching since physical buildings were few and far in-between in those days. In fact, all of the biblical references to Priscilla and Aquila name them as a couple, not separate individuals.

So am I implying that Ann has no identity apart from her husband? Hardly. Ann's career is in the medical profession. She is a natural at assisting hospice patients with coping emotionally and spiritually with their health challenges. She prepared herself for the path her life has currently taken, persevering for almost 10 years to complete her education and training as a nurse. Countless times Ann rallied us to pray as she struggled with exam anxiety and juggled her schedule to study, while coping with personal problems that seemed to relentlessly confront her at every turn. Through it all, Ann never wavered in her faith. Through it all Ann "learned to trust in Jesus" and "depend upon His word."

Based on her experiences, Ann has a strong sense of compassion and empathy towards others and their struggles. Relating to their pain opens the door for Ann to share Jesus Christ and the ways in which He can make a difference in their lives. She manages to see beyond her own problems and pain, fully aware that God allows them for a greater purpose.

Together, Ann and her husband possess a zeal for Christian service. They complement each other. They don't compete against each other. In the truest sense, they use the strength of their personal experiences with Christ to make the most out of their lives as a ministering team.

Ann is a natural at witnessing for Christ. I am inspired by the boldness, compassion and empathy Ann exemplifies as she unashamedly shares God's goodness and dedicates her life to easing others' pains.

JENETTE, OUR CLOSE FRIEND "AWAY FROM HOME"

Several years ago, Jenette, her husband who is also a dear brother and pastor; and their children relocated from Kansas City to Rockford, IL., then recently to Detroit, MI.

However not to be left out, we went around the table to capture the essence of who she is based on our experiences with her.

Anita: *Alright she's not here but three words for Jenette. Who wants to go first?*

Ann immediately jumped in.

Ann: *Bossy. With a capital 'B.'*

A puzzled Diann asked...

Diann: *Is she, really?*

Ann: *Yeah.*

Diann: *I never experienced that with her* (Diann noted).

Ann: *But Jenette is one of the reasons I am back in the church* (Ann confessed). *I will always be grateful to her.*

Diann: *So you can use that word* (bossy) *for her?*

Anita: *How 'bout saying she's insistent?*

Ann: *She's also consistent.*

To refresh her comments, I asked Ann...

Anita: *Insistent. Consistent. What else?*

Ann thought for a moment then complimented Jenette.

Ann: *Jenette can also be supportive.*

To Delores, Jenette is...

Delores: *faithful...ummm gee...confident.*

Ann: *Confident. Now that's true.*

Delores: *Jenette is also one who is proud.*

Again, Brenette stuck with the rules of the game and gave three quick answers.

Brenette: *Jenette is serious...structured...and talented.*

Diann was next. True to form, she tried to pull an earlier trick wanting to use someone else's descriptions. This time she wanted to "duplicate" (as she put it) Ann's responses.

Diann: *I gave mine with Ann.*

Anita: *No, you can't 'duplicate' Ann's.*

Ann: *Just say ditto. Or as we say in church, "And the people of God said 'Amen'."*

Again, Diann who was up to her mischievous chuckle needed a moment to pull herself together. Eventually, she began to think of words and managed to admirably share...

Diann: *Jenette is strong in faith, open and she's trustworthy.*

As for me...

Anita: *Jenette is my rebel sister. My 'Say it loud. I'm Black and I'm proud' sistah.*

Don't get me wrong; Jenette is not a radical, ready to strike out at every injustice. She strongly believes in living our heritage as African-Americans. She will stand up for our history, she confronts our struggles and has the ability to trace contemporary issues and events to their historical context. She challenges us to dig deeper and consider the spiritual, practical and historical perspectives, interrelated and woven together.

With that, I concluded by describing Jenette as...

Anita: *Contemplative and very analytical.*

JENETTE, AS A ROLE TO MODEL

People are often turned off or intimidated by African-American women who exude strength, confidence and assertiveness. These women are often misunderstood and mislabeled as angry, with chips on their shoulders–women who tend to subject people to walking on eggshells.

However, our friend Jenette, unapologetically is a woman who is comfortable in her own skin. Admirably, she can carry herself so that she is always approachable. She won't compromise her principles yet she can make people feel comfortable being in her presence.

There is another quality Jenette has that stands out. Of all of the ladies, Jenette is perhaps the most forgiving of the flaws, faults and even downfalls of African-Americans. She is usually the first to see those redeeming qualities that are often pleading with cynics and critics to give offenders the grace of a second chance and not rush to judgment. After all, "A word of encouragement during a failure is worth more than an hour of praise after success," writes an author unknown.

Jenette is loyal to the African-American heritage, which is why the Biblical personality Esther comes to mind.

Keep Turning: Sisters By Heart

Loyalty is a trait that is obscure or seldom seen. However, when it shows up, it is usually at critical junctures, during dark times or crisis moments.

Esther's fascinating story unfolds in 10 chapters of the Biblical book that bears her name. Esther was the name given to her which means "hidden." And yet her loyalty, grace and commitment to her people were in plain sight.

Although a Persian queen, Esther is known for her Jewish patriotism as ultimately evidenced by her sacrifice to save her people from genocide. That sacrifice was set in motion by a strategy that, in part, required her requesting time with King Ahasuerus.

This was risky and serves as the basis for the familiar verse in Esther 4:15b, where Esther resolves, "Then I will go to the king, though it is against the law. And if I perish, I perish."

Although Jenette has not been called to the same caliber of loyalty and sacrifice as Esther, absolutely nothing will sway Jenette from soberly owning her heritage and taking advantage of opportunities that favor African-American causes. Similarly, she knows how to exercise her sense of clear judgment.

Often during our "deep" and serious discussions, Jenette will challenge and provoke us to reset and reconsider. She is the one who encourages us to just try and envision unparalleled opportunities that await, if only we would get past and get over what may be misperceptions, wrong opinions, foggy notions and misjudgments.

Yes, that is our friend Jenette, loyal to the bone and capable of holding her own. I love being in her presence and experiencing this type of role to model.

After sharing our thoughts concerning Jenette, we noticed we were the only patrons in the restaurant. The hour was late. It was closing time–time to part ways, but not until my thoughts veered off to anxiously anticipate the next time I would spend time with my friends, my sisters, my role models.

That evening, we spent the majority of our time sharing our words and impressions of each other. However, words are inadequate to express my relationship with the women God has blessed to be in my life.

So, perhaps the inscription in this plaque Delores gave us years ago captures the essence of our lifelong, rock-solid relationship:

Sisters by Heart

We've shared so much laugher
Shared so many tears.
We've spiritual kinship
That grows stronger each year.
We're not sisters by birth
But we knew from the start.
God put us together
To be sisters by heart.

Now more than ever, women and men alike are challenged to find balance when juggling the daily demands of multiple, simultaneous responsibilities. If we are not careful, the balancing act alone can leave us feeling as if we accomplished little in our attempts to tackle, address and resolve everything that needs our attention.

Over the years in conversations with my dear friends featured in the previous chapter, I could tell yet still admire how they seem to manage home, work, church, social and recreational activities without complaint. At times these ladies could also tap into that sixth sense nudging them to pull back, adjust and re-evaluate how they were using their time.

Next to their relationship with God, my friends unwaveringly demonstrated the priorities they placed on their relationships with their spouses, children, grandchildren and other family members. In other words, faith and family were foundations they were unwilling to compromise against other activities.

From my observations, they live with balance. They are real housewives. And I have no doubt that my sister friends could share countless experiences of God's grace orchestrating situations and enabling them to accomplish whatever mattered most in their lives.

God did the same for Biblical role models such as prayerful Hannah, courageous Queen Esther, committed Anna and the bold witness of Joanna.

Turn the pages to the *Globe* articles and discover God's grace working in their lives and for more on the blessings of a balanced life.

Friends As Sisters

Originally published September 30 - October 6, 2010
Reprinted with permission from the
Kansas City Globe

How do you know when you've found a genuine friend? Or better yet, are you a true friend? Try measuring your friendship experiences against Proverbs 17:17, "a friend loveth at all times."

I have been graciously and richly blessed to be part of a friendship with five loving and trusting Christian women. For me, they represent a support system that comes full circle as I live through the daily challenges.

In the March column, I mentioned church friend, Shelia C. who inspired me to write about faith, family and friends. Shelia signed a book she gave me with these words, "Some folks would agree that the best of love can be found in the three F's: faith, family and friends. What a wonderful healing and trilogy?" I devoted subsequent columns on how I began this journey of faith. Last month, I paid tribute to my family. This month's column is dedicated to some special friends.

However, the support list does not end. There are many other relatives, friends, church members, classmates, sorority sisters, co-workers and colleagues who keep in touch and whose encouragement I'll admit, I need and appreciate.

But I singled out these friends because together the six of us share a unique and inseparable bond that has spanned nearly two decades. I laugh to myself at times for even our names phonetically bear a certain rhyme and rhythm – Delores, Diann, Ann, Anita, Jenette, Brenette. (See what I mean)?

I have always felt I was fortunate to have these sisters in my life. But for the past two years as I physically recover, their selfless actions have enabled me to maintain a lifestyle that promotes my mental, social and spiritual well-being, despite my condition.

I admire these dear friends. They are women of principles, committed wives and mothers who are involved in the lives of their spouses, as well as their teenage and adult children. They are leaders in church groups, active in sororities and other community organizations. They are exemplary in their professions, challenged by the demand of their careers - two are engineers, two are in health care and one is an educator. Nevertheless, they do a remarkable job juggling their schedules to make time for me.

Two years into my recovery one, some or they all could have gone their way - not these ladies. They will spend time with people and put their energies into activities that matter most to them. For this, I am humbly fortunate.

In fact, these sistahs keep my social calendar busy; and I love it. When we get together at times the atmosphere is so intellectually stimulating as we discuss our professions and current events. We can just as well engage in conversations regarding the Christian faith. Praise the Lord!

There are also times when we can be as giddy as girls in high school. That's cool, too. Any way you slice it, as the popular saying goes, "It's all good."

I have always treasured our time together, which didn't start as a result of the automobile accident. However since the accident, I believe we've grown to have a deeper level of appreciation for one another and spending quality time.

A few weeks ago during church service, the youth choir sang *Lean On Me*, a song by gospel artist Kirk Franklin and Nu Nation. It seemed as though each time the choir sang, "Friends will be there to catch you when you fall," I thought about these women. *Yes*, I thought to myself, *friends will be there to catch you* – not to put you down but to stick by and not abandon, to challenge but not compete and to promote your best interests, sometimes above their own.

These ladies have taught me that fostering lasting and trusting friendships require mutual respect and commitment. Friends who stick close can also unselfishly give you your space. Friends who are secure in their relationships will let you be yourself because they value being themselves. They don't seek to change you by the works of their hands. Yet, they live in such a way that the potential and power of being a confidante and genuine friend can be life-changing.

For almost 20 years, our relationship has been characterized by unconditional acceptance of and esteeming each other in whatever drives our individual passions. They epitomize class yet they are so down-to-earth. They personify grace and humility.

What can I say? They got it going on.

Until next month, keep the faith.

Real Housewives of God's Grace, (Reality Series I)

Originally published September 30 - October 6, 2010
Reprinted with permission from the
Kansas City Globe

We are living in the age of reality TV. Each season for about eight weeks, the Bravo channel crisscrosses the country to bring its viewers a look inside the lives of housewives in the ATL, New Jersey, DC and Orange County.

All of the housewives are portrayed as well-off and outgoing, often traveling in the same social circles.

And yet, each week they churn out the drama and ramp up enough tension in their relationships to keep millions of viewers glued to the tube and anxious for next week's drama.

It's hard to imagine women of such status lead their lives in the manner that is portrayed in Bravo's *Real Housewives of Atlanta, Real Housewives of New Jersey, Real Housewives of DC and Real Housewives of Orange County*. But, that's reality TV.

So I decided to flip the script and call the roll on a few housewives myself. However, these housewives represent a reality unlike the ones on the cable Bravo channel.

The housewives that will be shared this month and next are women whom by God's grace turned their dramas into opportunities for life-changing experiences for themselves and others.

I was inspired to title this month's column, *Real Housewives of God's Grace, (Reality Series I)*, because you will discover God's favor at work in each of their lives. But first, the introductions.

Meet Hannah (I Samuel 1, 2). Although at one time she was childless, she was never prayer-less. She enveloped the pain of not being able to have children in the power of prayer. Her silent, yet heartfelt prayers emerged to become the strength that sustained her, until ultimately she was no longer barren.

Next up is Queen Esther (The Book of Esther). Her natural beauty may have been the determining factor that caught the eye of the king to name her successor to Queen Vashti; but there was no flaunting her beauty. She was brought into the palace and eventually rose to prominence to "perish" (Esther 4:16), if need be, but for sure "for such a time as this" (Esther 4:14).

Anna (Luke 2:36-38) lost her earthly love after a brief seven-year marriage. Yet she did not bury her hopes in the grave. Instead she literally dwelled "in the house of the Lord" (Psalm 23:5), serving for 84 years. Anna grew old in the service of the sanctuary until she witnessed God's salvation – the long-awaited, promised Messiah at only eight days old.

Joanna (Luke 8:1-3, 23:55. 24:10) isn't a household name among women in the Bible. It's doubtful that she is a major character among women's bible studies. You probably read right past her name in Sunday School. In fact, this may be the first you've read about her.

So who is she? you may wonder. Like Esther, Joanna, too, was familiar with life in the palace. Joanna is identified as the wife of Chuza, the house steward of Herod, the tetrarch. Most of all, however, she's mentioned "among the women." She was among the women "Jesus healed of certain evil spirits and infirmities" (Luke 8:2). She was among the women whose early morning visit to Jesus' burial site resulted in the first discovery of the empty tomb and subsequently among the first to proclaim the Lord's resurrection (Luke 24:10).

Ironically, in the Hebrew setting the names Anna, Hanna and Joanna also share the common meaning of "grace" or "favor." More specifically, Joanna means "The Lord has shown favor."

So this is my shortlist of "Real Housewives of God's Grace." There are many more whose experiences are just as compelling.

Each of these women has as a testimony, examples where the grace or favor of God guided them through their personal yet public dramas. All the while God was orchestrating their circumstances to accomplish His will in their lives.

So powerful are their stories until through Hannah, we learn the value of being steadfast in prayer even when suffering the deepest emotional abuse and hurts.

Queen Esther's life offers one instance of teachable moments after another when faced with risks where others stand to benefit.

In three brief verses, Anna shows us how to remain on the lookout for the manifestation of God's promises, no matter how long it takes.

Joanna's motivation, initiative and energy to preach Christ, minister to Him and remain loyal despite open opposition are admirably qualities to emulate whenever God delivers us from any situation.

If any part of Hannah's, Queen Esther's, Anna's or Joanna's "dramas" or realities crisscross situations you are experiencing, then you'll want to get ready for next month's column, "Series II." We'll take a closer look inside and see God's awesome grace at work in the lives of these housewives.

Until then, keep the faith.

Real Housewives of God's Grace, (Reality Series II)

Originally published January 27 - February 2, 2011
Reprinted with permission from
Kansas City Globe

I introduced this column several months ago. Part I began with my thoughts on the Bravo channel's reality TV programs that crisscross the country to give viewers a look inside the lives of well-off, outgoing socialites known as "The Real Housewives of..." Whether the episode airs from the ATL, Beverly Hills, New Jersey, DC or Orange County, each week and for each season the format and themes are similar – in a word or three – intense, senseless "drama."

In the previous column I wrote that millions of viewers stayed glued to the tube, weighing in on the petty back-and-forth, near-juvenile spats these women seem all too eager to expose to TV viewers.

From a survey of the Scriptures, I discovered a few "real housewives myself." I introduced them in the previous column and indicated that these housewives represent a notable reality unlike the ones on the Bravo channel. Thank God.

I called them "Real Housewives of God's Grace": Hannah (I Samuel 1, 2), Queen Esther (The Book of Esther), Anna (Luke 2:36-38) and Joanna (Luke 8:1-3, 23:55, 24:10).

They all were married women whom God chose to show favor and use in extraordinary ways.

However, their stories were not shielded from their own public dramas. Nevertheless, God intervened and answered their prayers.

Much can be learned and applied to our lives from these real housewives...

Each of these women has as a testimony, examples where the grace or favor of God guided them through their unique situations. All the while the God of all grace (I Peter 5:10) orchestrated their circumstances to accomplish His will in their lives. Their willingness to surrender to Him and His plan was the disposition that placed them on the receiving end of God's blessings.

Hannah's drama? She was barren and had to endure living under the same roof with her husband Elkanah's second wife, Peninah. As the rival wife, Peninah gave Elkanah children but was sorely jealous and taunted Hannah something fierce. Hannah had Elkanah's heart and he proved it on more than one occasion. Still that did not stop Hannah from feeling sorrowful, anguished and abandoned by God. While in the temple, she acted upon her longing for a child by praying in a peculiar way – without external speech, lips moving and no sound. She gave Eli the priest the impression that she was drunk with wine. Nothing could have been further from the truth. She clarified and stood up for her innocence by pouring out her heart to the priest. Eventually, Eli pronounced a blessing upon Hannah and prophesied

God would grant the petition Hannah asked of Him. Although this is not the end of the story. The point is God answered her prayer and gave Hannah a son.

She became Queen of the palace partly because of her beauty and following her predecessor's defiance of the King, Ahasuerus. Queen Vashti was out; Queen Esther was in. But her reign came with a hefty price. Someone had to get to and influence the king to spare the lives of her fellow Jews from genocide. There were all sorts of twists and turns to this drama. To appreciate it in its fullness, you would have to read the entire Book of Esther. But suffice it to say, Queen Esther relied on God's providence, dared to risk death and ultimately won a great deliverance and salvation for her nation.

Anna's short story tells of a long-term widow. She lost her earthly love after a brief seven-year marriage and became a devout temple servant and worshipper. When the infant Jesus was presented in the temple, Anna was privileged, rewarded and is now distinguished as the first female to herald the incarnation of the Israel's redeemer and the world's Savior.

The last real housewife, Joanna was also a resident of the palace by virtue of the fact that her husband, Chuza was a guardian for King Herod. Joanna had already had an encounter with Jesus that resulted in her being healed of evil spirits and infirmities. She witnessed in the palace among the royals and servants, alike. She was the upper class, in the palace under King Herod who, by the way, orchestrated the beheading of John the Baptist.

Tradition has it that Chuza lost his position in the palace. His wife's courage and witness to the servants were more than the king was willing to tolerate.

But Scriptures reveal Joanna's deliverance at the hand of Christ was far too powerful and real. She became a follower of Jesus Christ. She was loyal to Christ's ministry and present at Calvary to watch with her very eyes the cruel punishment Jesus endured before He died. She was among the sorrow-stricken women who gathered early in the morning at the tomb where Jesus was buried and eventually had risen from the dead.

So what did she do? Joanna ran and told it along with the other women. Joanna went from possessing an evil spirit to being one among the first to witness Jesus' death, to enter an empty, neatly-organized tomb and to proclaim that the Lord—the lover of her soul—had risen from the dead.

These are powerful stories.

Through Hannah, we learn the value of being steadfast in prayer even when suffering the deepest emotional abuse and hurts.

Queen Esther's life offers one instance of teachable moments after another when faced with risks where others stand to benefit.

In three brief verses, Anna shows us how to remain on the lookout for the manifestation of God's promises, no matter how long it takes.

Joanna's motivation and energy to preach Christ, minister to Him and remain loyal despite open opposition is something to emulate whenever God delivers us from any situation.

These are realities that are well worth a closer look as you search the Scriptures.

So take time to do just that. When you're finished, no doubt you will join me in saying "Bravo. Bravo!"

Until then, keep the faith.

I'm Balanced Not Imbalanced, Part I

Originally published August 23 - 29, 2012
Reprinted with permission from the
Kansas City Globe

Hello *Globe* readers. Now raise your hand if you're like me. I never have enough time to do what I need to do, let alone what I want to do. Is your hand up? Good, then I'm not alone.

On the one hand, time is so precious. But it can get away from you — too many times. Nevertheless, we should not always blame time. Cease with the finger pointing unless we're going to acknowledge the three fingers that are pointing back at us. You see, the problem or challenge with not having enough time is having too much jam-packed in our schedules.

Most of us remember back in the day when we relied on our rolodex, Franklin Day Planner, pocket calendar or PDA to get through the scheduling demands of the day. Nowadays, if we leave home without our iPad or iPhone or cell phone or Blackberry, we feel out of sorts and unable to function.

It's funny that regardless of the advances in technology designed to keep us organized and up to speed, by and large we are still a stressed, overwhelmed and overworked society. We are a busy, imbalanced bunch. Some of us are so busy until most of our energy is fueled just trying to stay organized. And when that happens then at best our lives become nothing more than a revolving door of hits and misses.

In other words, we have just enough time to hit this over here, but not enough time so we miss that over there.

Now once again, raise your hand if you're like me. Sometimes all it takes is one "yes" too many before your schedule screams, "YOU'VE GOT TOO MUCH ON YOUR PLATE!" Is your hand up again? Come on, now. Tell the truth; shame the devil. Our schedules next to our bodies are the triggers that tell us when we're imbalanced.

For many, busyness is a by-word for importance. Having so much to do helps us stick out our chests and hold high our heads. Let's not fool ourselves, because busyness can be an overstated status symbol and an understated indicator or a shaky self-image.

Busyness can also breed and cultivate the pursuit of blind ambitions or cause us to crash from burnout. Yet, there are so many who believe their lives are more meaningful as they churn through the daily grind of being on the go. Some of us wear busyness as a badge of honor. That is, until we encounter a traumatic and unexpected experience that stops us dead in our tracks and leaves us numb with unanswered questions.

Or, we spend so much time on the treadmill of endless activities until when we finally get off; we wonder how we got off track from accomplishing the most important responsibilities.

So how do we achieve a semblance of balance in our lives? How can we be more consistent with refraining from over committing our time and overextending our energies? One way is by referring to what took place in the home of Mary and Martha one day while Jesus was visiting. Their story is told briefly in three verses, Luke 10:38-41.

Martha was busy but "distracted." Jesus told her she was "worried and upset." Yet she was the one engrossed in preparation as a result of Jesus' visit. In her mind, she was serving the Lord. She was stressed all because of her busyness with absolutely no help from her sister, Mary.

Earlier this week while on my way to work, I listened intently to *And That's My Truth,* a commentary by journalist Jeff Johnson that is featured weekly on the *Tom Joyner Morning Show.* Johnson shared insightful and thought-provoking principles on the causes and signs of stress and ways to manage it.

Johnson points out that stress will never go anywhere, "In the world we live in," Johnson observes "there will always be demands.

You will always have bills to pay, errands to run and people that need your emotional availability. There is one thing that we have to remind ourselves of when the tasks of life begin to overwhelm us. We are in control.

And how we manage our lives is a direct reflection of not how much we have to do, but how much stress is involved in getting it done," Johnson concludes.

Although Martha's stress may have been typical and expected, perhaps it could have been better managed. It certainly did not help her cause when she solicited Jesus' assistance in trying to guilt-trip Mary into getting up and getting busy.

When Jesus opted to do otherwise, the refusal spoke volumes about how one should choose to prioritize and relatively set aside time for the things that matter.

Nevertheless, when it comes to the issue of time, there are credible points to be made favoring both Martha and Mary. Although opposites in their respective responses to Jesus' visit, together their actions reveal a message about balance and time.

That message will be explored next month and prayerfully will help you evaluate whether "I'm balanced or imbalanced" with time.

Until then, keep the faith.

I'm Balanced, Not Imbalanced Part II

Originally published October 4 – 10, 2012
Reprinted with permission from the
Kansas City Globe

Some Biblical personalities often get a back rap. After we read or hear about their stories we tend to "smh" (shake my head) in shame or be the first in line to cast the first stone. Usually, we are quick to point out with hindsight in full view what they woulda, coulda, shoulda done.

Take Martha, for instance. Most Bible readers are familiar with the story surrounding her complaint to Jesus about her sister, Mary, giving Him undivided attention instead of helping out with unattended household chores, (Luke 10:38-41). In response, Jesus commended Mary for giving her time and attention to the more needful thing, but in the grand scheme His subtle rebuke pointed to the fact that Mary did what was necessary *at that time*.

Herein lies the underlying issue when it comes to balance and busyness. In some circles, it's called the art of time management. Too often, we complain about not enough time in a day or we feel the pressure of too much on our plates. For some of us the moment we hit the alarm clock in the morning, we're off and running the proverbial race against time in a day jam-packed with demands.

Are you someone who is driven to fulfilling a desire to always be in demand? Are you secretly and ambitiously coddling an unspoken need to be needed? When Paul claims, "I can do all things through Christ who strengthens me," (Philippians 4:13) that's not to be misinterpreted to claim, "I can do everything everybody puts before me."

Bottom line, we need more balance in our day-to-day responsibilities in order to be able to claim "I'm balanced and not imbalanced."

If you're one who is all over the place, wearing yourself out and running yourself down to a point of exhaustion, with only a foggy notion of what you've accomplished…then SLOW DOWN.

You need balance! You are anxious for a plan that teaches you to do what matters.

To Martha's credit, she was responsible and "given to hospitality" (Romans 12:13). Jesus was always welcomed where Martha, Mary and Lazarus resided. On one occasion He said that the Son of Man had nowhere to lay His head (Luke 9:58). Not so when He visited Bethany. Martha was always on cue to serve the Lord. He was sure to find a loving, hospitable home for His lonely heart and weary spirit mainly because of Martha. She is shown throughout Scripture as one who was sensitive to meeting physical needs.

To Mary's credit, she knew the affairs of her day could not be attended to if she neglected quality time in

Jesus' presence. She believed in being spiritually nurtured. Her spiritual well-being was of paramount importance. The "good part" Mary chose and Jesus acknowledged was making time for undistracted communion with Him, hearing His words and learning from Him. She meditated on the messages and contemplated whatever Jesus communicated. It was time well spent and worth her effort to maintain.

The words to a song that touches my heart say, *I miss my time with you – those moments together. I need to be with you each day and it hurts me when you say, 'You're too busy; busy trying to serve me.' But how can you serve me when your spirit's empty. There's a longing in my heart. I want more than just a part of you. It's true. I miss my time with you.*

Mary was unwilling to let time in God's presence escape her or be ignored. It is natural to anticipate the rhythm and flow of our daily frenzy, reassigning time with God for the next day. For some of us the time never comes because on the next day, it's the same ol', same ol'. Same busyness. Same neglect. Same missed opportunity.

While it is easy to use this story to bracket Mary and Martha together as rival siblings, both women can stand on their own and teach us lessons about time and priorities. Instead of turning these sisters on each other, let's give credit where it's due. Martha was inclined to take time preparing the feast – in other words, tending to physical and material affairs. She was responsible and assertive. Mary was inclined to take time to be fed, not forsaking spiritual needs. She was humble and just as responsible for meeting the needs within her soul. In a given day, both are needful things at a certain time.

A busy lifestyle which involves serving the Lord is not an excuse for a neglectful spiritual life. Likewise, we cannot use our spirituality as justification or a substitute for putting off handling our business.

Busyness is not a bad thing unless and until it becomes the culprit the drives you to overcommit yourself and neglect time with God.

However, you're all the better whenever you're balanced.

Until next month, keep the faith.

Chapter 8

Family Matters

I prayed for them perhaps more than I prayed for myself,
—Anita

Strike up a conversation with me about my family and two reactions will surely occur–one will be visibly evident; the other not as noticeable. My face will light up and my smile will widen whenever my family is the topic of discussion. That, you will see. Most of all, when I speak of my family I wish you could see what happens inside of me. The love that flows deep within is stirred. It swells and seems to pulsate with every beat of my heart. In fact, the smile on the outside is actually a mere reflection of the love within my heart. The love spills over; it is just that strong.

I have no doubt that some of the best outcomes from the accident and subsequently my life as a paraplegic are the strength and support of my family. For many people this statement may be easier to express than experience. But if you have ever been in situations where the weight of your dependency rests and relies upon your family, then you can relate to this point.

So here they are–my immediate family. Meet them by name: my parents Rev. Cle Otis Cobbins, Sr. (deceased) and Essie (Cobbins) Prince; Kathleen (Kathy) and her husband Larry; Regina; Tressa and her husband James; Cleotis, Jr. (Jr.) and his wife Pamela (Pam); Sharion and Carlton (my sisters, brothers and in-laws). Add to this clan are my nieces, nephews and their spouses: Shonte, her husband Marques and their son L'il Marques (Scooter); Janel and her husband Malcolm; Earnestine (Steen); Brandon; Dominique; Cleotis, III (CJ); Christian (Chrissy) and Cherish.

It has been said that we choose our friends but we don't get the privilege of choosing our family. That is true for the most part; there are some exceptions.

Still, I view my family as a gift from God. And it pained me to think that gift was hurting all because someone irresponsibly decided to get behind the wheel of a car, drive impaired from substance use causing him to collide head-on with my car.

At times, while alone in my hospital room I wrestled with taking it all in. Although the alone moments were rare with the constant care of medical staff, the ongoing assistance of my caseworker, meal times, visits and phone calls, I was concerned about my family. I wanted to wrap them in my arms, bring them close and comfort them as much as they rallied to comfort me.

I prayed for them perhaps more than I prayed for myself. That is how much my family matters to me. I often contemplated how my family must have felt and reacted when they each got the disturbing news.

So I reached out to my family and asked them to share their thoughts and reactions – the call, the wait, the news of my injuries, whatever they could remember and were comfortable to share.

As a different twist, I was inspired to take their comments and frame them as if I were a talk show host featuring family members as my guests. They opened up and shared their stories about the night they received the news. I begin with Regina's story.

Me. *Tell me what was it like for you the night of the accident.*

Regina. *Tressa and I rode to the hospital together.*

Me. *What was the ride like?*

Regina. *There wasn't much conversation. It was sort of quiet.*

Me. *Two sisters having small talk?*

Regina. *Yeah. You could say that. I was sort of scared but I couldn't let myself believe it was that bad. I kept thinking, "Hold on Nit-Nit* (one of my nicknames pronounced Neet-Neet). *We're on the way."*

Me. *So you get to the hospital. Then what?*

Regina. *I knew it was bad when I saw the trail of blood that led to where you were in the emergency room. It made me angry. I wanted to know who did this? Who did this to you?*

It didn't surprise me Regina reacted this way. She was always the protective sister. During my upbringing, I mainly grew up with Regina, Kathy and Tressa, and Regina was considered the tomboy – the one the school and neighborhood kids feared.

Don't get me wrong, she wasn't a bully. She didn't go looking for trouble but don't cross her. The few problems I encountered at school were quickly resolved whenever I dropped Regina's name as my sister.

Kathy on the other hand was boy-crazy. And Tressa? Well, one could say that she could care less about boys.

In case you are wondering about me and where I fit within this circle of sisters? Well, the answer is simple. My fit depended on which sister I was with. When I was around Regina, I thought I was tough, too. With Kathy, it was easy to fantasize an interest in boys. (Although, I couldn't think of any boy who was interested in me). Around Tressa? Well let's just say boys weren't even a topic of discussion.

So Regina's protective nature demanded wanting to know who was responsible? She felt what happened to me was so wrong, so unfair.

Regina. *But as the days went by, I noticed you asking about the driver and the other passenger in the car that hit you.*

Me. *Although I knew I suffered the greater injury, I still wanted them to be alright.*

Regina. *I know but it still seemed unfair.*

Kathy. *Yeah. I kept thinking to myself, 'Why did this happen to a person who was active in church and with family and friends?'*

Me. *How did you feel?*

Kathy. *At first I was in shock.*

Larry (Kathy's husband). *Yeah, for me all I could think was 'un-believable.'*

Kathy. *When the doctors gave us the complete diagnosis—the spinal cord injury and paralysis—I wondered what type of quality of life you would have? Right then, I knew that the family was now forced to pull together, stay strong and help you through. If we didn't have faith, we needed to have it now.*

Larry has been in the family so long until we embrace him as a blood brother. He and Kathy were high school sweethearts and have been married over 40 years. Together they established and minister as marriage mentors of their church.

Kathy is the oldest of all my siblings. Growing up, older sisters are often thrust into situations which naturally bring out their nurturing instincts. She is also the organizer of the bunch and without hesitation she assumed her role from back-in-the-day as big sister taking charge and taking care of me, the younger sister.

I especially recall the months I was in rehab at Mid-America Rehabilitation Hospital. Kathy worked within close proximity at the Sprint headquarters in Overland Park, Ks., in human resources.

In the mornings before going to work, Kathy stopped by Mid-America to dress me until I was able to dress myself. Even then, she still stopped by to help. She also kept my clothes laundered. With her experience and expertise in human resources and insurance benefits, she was extremely helpful in understanding and interpreting my insurance coverage and filing claims.

No matter the crisis or better yet, because of the crisis, I still had to (as Tressa often says) "handle your (my) business."

For Tressa, recalling that night was most difficult. She sighs, and then takes a deep breath.

Me to Tressa. *You can do it.*

Tressa. *This is so hard. I get too emotional.*

She composes herself to start sharing.

Tressa. *Friday, May 9, 1997. I got a call from you to say you had just gotten off work at Southwestern Bell. This was your part-time gig. It was about 11 p.m. You told me that you had left your billfold at your full-time job, KCATA and needed gas money to get to work the next morning. You were headed to KCATA to get your billfold.*

Me. *I remember the call.*

Tressa. *Since I lived off 63rd & Paseo, I told you it was too late to* *drive that far and to come by my apartment so that I could give you $5 to put gas in your car.*

Me. *It was late and I didn't let on, but it had been a long day. And I was tired.*

Tressa. *So, you could get your billfold the next day.*

Me. *It made perfect sense.*

Tressa. *In the midst of my waiting, (she pauses) I fell asleep and was awakened to the phone ringing about 12:39 a.m. When I answered it was Idella, Daddy's wife on the other end. She started with, 'You don't know?' 'Know what,' I asked? She said, 'Anita was in a bad car accident on Troost. The police called your Dad and he's on the way over there (to the hospital). They're life-flighting her to Truman, I think.'*

Me. *And when you hung up from Idella's call?*

Tressa. *I remember feeling like I had just been hit with two tons of bricks. After I called Regina. I sat tearfully asking God to help you. Then it hit me (she pauses again). Had I not told you to come get the money, this would not have happened. Then I got angry at myself for falling asleep (another pause). If only I had I just stayed awake, I would have known that something happened.*

Tressa's sharing reminded me of a conversation we had several months after the accident. In this conversation, I sensed that Tressa had guilt bottled up inside. My family's concern about my well-being was obvious, and after this conversation with Tressa; it was confirmation. I knew there was justifiable concern about how my family handled the tragedy. But it took me totally off guard that Tressa could even remotely think she was to blame.

As we spoke, Tressa's voice cracked; she choked up and started to cry. I intentionally cut her off before allowing her to finish what she tried to say. "It's not your fault," I reiterated. "What happened to me was not your fault." And I sternly meant every word.

I didn't want to hear her say that. Instead it was my job to put the thought out of her mind and I was up to the task.

As far as I was concerned, it was the Enemy's tactic to consume Tressa with a false sense of guilt and feeling responsible. To think that she had internalized blame, suppressed and carried fault for weeks. I wondered if she had shouldered responsibility, prompting her to do whatever she could to make it up to me. I wasn't having that; and I was adamant.

So I had no problem cutting off her comment before she could get it out. I needed to console and reassure my sister, while I nipped that nonsense in the bud and responded with conviction, "This (the accident) could have happened anywhere at any time."

Clearly, this situation justified my need to be concerned about my family. From the outset, it was important they follow my lead—my spirit to believe God, my discipline to comply with medical instructions and therapies, and my determination not to be defeated.

How I handled this experience was key and directly related to my family's spiritual, mental and emotional reactions and well-being. Simply put, as long as I was upbeat and remained optimistic they could draw from my energy; they could follow my lead. Likewise, they were unhappy campers whenever I was disturbed or upset. Their disposition was a direct result of mine.

Obviously, while gathered in the hospital waiting room my family didn't know what to expect from me. No doubt, there were underlying tense and anxious moments but they chose to save face with camaraderie and humor.

Tressa. *We were watching episodes of the program 'Cops' on TV. Daddy kept us laughing with his wise cracks as the drunken man tried to get out of being arrested.*

Daddy had a way of keeping others at ease when the circumstance dictated otherwise. This trait was a testament to his strength when considering the fact that he got the initial call from the police officer. He was the first one on scene in the emergency room. According to my stepmother, Idella, days later Daddy shed tears as he reflected and described to her my injuries that he saw even before I was cleaned and put in a hospital gown. When he left their home, he expected to find me being treated for injuries from a "fender bender." After his call to her from the hospital, he told Idella "They weren't sure I was going to make it."

My teenaged youngest brother, Carlton, was not present at the hospital. Idella broke the news to him the next day.

Carlton. *I was scared I was going lose you. I wasn't ready to deal with that kind of devastation. All I could do was pray for you, Sis.*

Me. *You know you did the most important thing?*

Carlton. *Yeah. Then...oh God...when I saw you getting better...*

Me. *What?!*

Carlton. *I look at you and it gave me (emphasis on 'me') hope. I mean I read my Bible and I know Pop's preaching. But I now see that all things are possible with God. I know God can change situations that look impossible. Miracles are possible with God.*

Me. *I want you to remember that. Daddy and Idella would want you to remember that.*

Carlton. *Sis. I think you are a strong person. In all that you go through, you always keep going. You don't give up.*

I constantly do for Carlton what he did for me when Idella told him about the accident; I pray for him and for good reasons. I cannot imagine what it is like to lose both parents before turning 30 years old.

Daddy passed away in 2004 and Idella passed six

years later. Now who will he turn to for guidance, to feel as though he is connected? Carlton is without both parents and I feel a strong sense of responsibility to him. Carlton is the youngest. Although he is shy, he is a gifted musician. He composes chords and plays the keyboard by ear. Just as Carlton spoke of God working a miracle in me, I am praying that he knows the same God will work in his life.

My older brother, Cleotis, Jr., and his wife, Pam have been married over 20 years. Together they are the founders and pastoral leaders of a church in Raytown. During the week, Jr. follows his passion, devoted to assisting and teaching men who were previously incarcerated the skills needed to re-enter society as responsible citizens, fathers and employees.

Jr. didn't rush to the emergency room, which may seem strange. (Oddly, I can't help but recall Jesus' four-day delay to return to Bethany after learning Lazarus was sick; Jesus had His reasons.) Likewise, Jr. had his reasons.

Jr. *On the night of the accident, I remember receiving the call that you were involved in a car wreck on 85th & Troost and taken to St. Luke's Hospital on The Plaza. Being that I lived in close proximity, I drove by the scene of the accident to assess the severity.*

Me. *What did you see?*

Jr. *For the most part, the accident had been cleaned up and it was* difficult to determine how serious you were injured; until I arrived at St Luke's.

Me. And what did you see then?

Jr. Nita, when I walked into the emergency ICU and saw you lying in the bed, I was deeply saddened. You appeared to be badly injured with all the medical equipment and the steady stream of doctors and nurses in and out of your room.

Me. Seeing a roomful of white coats and scrubs can be unnerving.

Jr. The preliminary reports were a very badly broken ankle and a bruised spine with the possibility of paralysis.

Earnestine. But Aunt 'Nita, your development has trumped the reports of doctors on numerous occasions.

Me. Quite honestly when I asked Dr. Kelly, my doctor of physical medicine, if I would walk again. He always smiled and answered, "We'll see."

Earnestine is my niece, Regina's oldest child who was pursuing a Bachelor's Degree in Fine Arts at Howard University. I make a concerted effort to keep planting seeds when we talk. She is creatively gifted, packaged as a songbird, dancer and actress. I refuse to let up encouraging Earnestine because God has graced her for fulfilling service, using those gifts.

Earnestine. My recollection of the day I learned of the accident is quite vivid, almost as if it happened yesterday. It was the spring of

1997 on a Saturday afternoon. I received a phone call from my mother, whose tone of voice gave me the impression that something was wrong.

Me. *How did you feel when she broke the news to you?*

Earnestine. *Aunt 'Nita, as Momma recounted the story of your accident, feelings of disbelief and anger came over me. Before the accident, Aunt 'Nita, you were always the most active out of all your siblings; always on the go.*

Shonte. *I'm going to be honest. My initial reaction was I did not understand and I struggled with 'why?' Why did something so tragic happen to such a good person? That was the question that immediately came to my mind. Then when I saw that you took the brunt of the injuries for an accident that wasn't your fault... ummm...'why?'*

Janel. *When I came to the hospital I was upset. You were in an accident because a young boy was driving drunk on his prom night? I was so upset, very angry.*

Jr. *Nita, just the sight of you was hurtful because no one expects to one day see a loved one in such a horrible condition.*

To learn of Jr.'s reaction lets me know how much he was affected. He doesn't react as quickly and openly emotional as the sister siblings or my nieces, but he is no less sensitive to hurt. As I have watched him on many occasions, Jr. just wants to get to wherever a person is hurting, so that he can do what he can to ease the pain.

Jr. *Oftentimes when a loved one is hurting, you do whatever it takes to bring them through. The obvious thing to do at this particular time (the night and days following your accident) was to pray and provide the support needed for such a time as this.*

Shonte and Janel are sisters, Kathy's and Larry's daughters. Janel is the younger of the two who is always willing to help whenever she can. Recalling that moment of her first hospital visit brought out Janel's sensitive side; she was moved to tears.

Janel. *There you were in the hospital consoling Shon and me, telling us it was Ok. We were in your room crying and you took it so calmly. And that turned my anger. I began thinking, Wow. She is really strong because you kept saying to us 'just be thankful' you were alive.*

Shonte, on the other hand, has always asked the probing questions. She has always been "my little conversationalist." She is assertive and never shy about initiating dialogue. I love to watch her in action. She listens attentively, taking it all in and processing her thoughts before she responds. But forget about trying to pull the wool over her eyes because she will instinctively yet intelligently blow your cover.

However, I don't think she expected to get a rational answer to her "whys." I just think she genuinely had difficulty accepting what happened to me. Someway, somehow, something about what happened made no sense and yet had to be resolved.

Eventually, inquisitive Shonte finally came to terms with her own questions.

Shonte. *Later the revelation came to me that God uses people and circumstances as tools to share a word with others who are going through unfortunate circumstances. Aunt Anita, I'm glad that I now understand that these are some of the ways God uses to expose His goodness to others.*

Jr. also has a knack for showing that he can be keenly observant. Don't mistake his calm, quiet demeanor as detachment. When you least expect it, he will open up. Like the old E.F. Hutton slogan, "When E.F. Hutton (Jr.) speaks; people listen."

From simple actions to huge sacrifices, early on throughout my ordeal, Jr. observed how the family rallied as though he had a ringside seat watching one round after another.

Jr. *I remember watching our Dad comb Nita's hair. I remember our Mom making sure Nita received the best medical care. I remember my sisters staying by Nita's side around-the-clock. I remember the determination in Nita's spirit to get through this tragedy. As she recovered, I remember the joy that she projected to all who visited. While we were trying to be a blessing to you, Nita; I remember thinking (after all she was going through) she was being a blessing to us.*

This "blessing" Jr. refers to was none other than the overflow of what my family gave to me. The blessing of their support, prayers, and seeing me as someone they valued, despite the dramatic changes, motivated me to reciprocate with that same spirit.

Earnestine. *Aunt 'Nita that is what amazes me so. You encouraged us more than you realize. So I couldn't help but to give back to you what you gave to us. As a means of encouragement to you, I remember sending you a recording of my rendition of an old gospel song titled, 'Be Grateful.'*

Earnestine knows about my love of gospel music. She knew I owned a collection of music from as far back as the 80s. Gospel music especially is timeless and gets at the heart of the Christian experience. To this day, I still have the cassette. I don't intend to part with it. (I guess I should convert it to digital format, though).

Earnestine. *More than you may realize Aunt 'Nita, we are all grateful for the progress you have made over the years. And yet...we are still trusting God for complete restoration.*

Janel. *You have touched my life and been an inspiration. Here you are—someone whose whole world has turned around. It was awesome watching the way you handled the situation. You gave us so much to think about, so much to be grateful for.*

Shonte. *I'm glad, Aunt Anita, that you even took the time to consider how we felt and reached out to us. I'm sure this book is* *going to be all that God wants it to be to reach people and draw all of us closer to Him.*

The family's stories gave me insight on their individual struggles, questions and resolutions. As you can see, each had to process what they saw and/or heard related to my injuries and prognosis. They had to get past the initial shock. Their need to turn all that they were feeling over to God and trust Him more took front and center. This kind of reaction should never be taken for granted under any circumstances. Whenever anyone is faced with challenges and uncertainties out of a near-tragic situation, trusting God can be a fearful walk across a tight rope instead of a casual walk in the park.

As the days progressed, my health improved. My health was my primary focus. However, there were so many other areas in my life that had changed. The domino effect from the accident meant adapting and preparing me for what seemed to be an avalanche of unknown new normals. I could not set aside doing whatever it took to regain muscle function and strength.

Here is where family comes in. My family was instrumental in helping me take care of areas in my personal life that needed attention. As I look back, I cannot recall ever feeling overwhelmed or anxious. It was as if they were my angels taking the load off, easing my mind and keeping me from needless worries.

This way, I could stay focused. I don't think they will ever realize how much they mean to me. They took care of my business as they took care of me.

I recall the first time my family had to rally yet again because of a subsequent health scare. It was in July 2001, when I underwent surgery to replace a pump device that was initially implanted in 1998. The pump was needed to transport muscle relaxer medication into my spinal canal because I suffered from severe spasticity. High dosages of oral medication were insufficient to keep my muscles from jerking my body around so intensely, until sometimes the muscles spasms would thrust me out of my wheelchair and onto the floor.

Needless to say, I was especially thankful when my health insurer determined that I was a candidate for the pump implant (See *Daddy's Devotion* chapter).

The summer of 2001 was my first pump replacement, three years following the initial implant. The procedure was supposed to be relatively easy and only required an overnight stay. The surgery went as planned. However, the post-surgery turn of events were unexpected and happened fast.

At 11 a.m., I was being prepped for a one o'clock procedure that would take no more than 90 minutes. Then I would be in recovery for about two hours before moving to a patient room.

All of that went off without a hitch. I knew that I was in my room around 4 o'clock because I was gearing up to watch my favorite afternoon TV show, *Judge Judy*.

That was the last I remember. My next memory was not until the next morning. In between those times I ended up in ICU. What on earth happened?

The story came from two sources – the attending nurse and my sister-in-law, Pam. According to the nurse, a routine post-surgery visit to my room to take my vitals turned into a physical struggle with her. My blood pressure had shot up sky high. I became so agitated until I ripped the IV needle out of my arm. She called for assistance to restrain me to the bed. Medically and in layman's terms, my actions were the result of being overmedicated by the combination of a high dosage of muscle relaxer injected into my pump and the anesthesia that was still in my system.

Eventually, I lost consciousness. I lapsed into a coma.

The muscle relaxer dosage was injected at the same strength as the normal level prior to surgery. In hindsight, the surgeon realized after the surgery he should have started at the lowest possible dose then gradually increase its strength over the course of a couple of days.

According to Pam, "I was one of the first to arrive at the hospital" after the calls to the family. Pam told me the family nervously waited for about two hours.

Tressa's patience got the best of her, sensed something "wasn't right" (as Tressa put it) and began questioning the medical staff. Shortly afterwards, the doctors came to the waiting area. It was then the family realized the seriousness of the situation.

The family was allowed in my room. Pam said, "You were totally out of it, in a coma state and you appeared lifeless." At that time the doctors could not assure them the condition would reverse itself but encouraged my family to talk to me. "She can hear. So keep talking to her," they were told.

No doubt the news was disturbing. Just a few short hours prior, a simple procedure and recovery as planned took a turn for the worse. Still, the family followed the doctors' suggestions.

After about a couple of hours, I started to respond. "But you were not making sense," Pam recalled. They each took turns talking to me. However, I was told I repeatedly answered Tressa yet would not answer Regina, at all.

It appeared that I was coming out of the coma. The signs were so encouraging, until it was time. Let the camaraderie begin.

As I gradually regained consciousness my gibberish and nonsense talk set the stage for some of my family members to make jokes and poke fun at the things I said. Leave it to Tressa to teasingly console Regina by telling her something like, "It's ok. She (referring to me) never makes sense anyway."

As the talking and camaraderie continued, my family was put at ease. My vitals showed signs of improvement. Around midnight or so, family left the hospital. They were relieved that I was at least out of the woods.

"Even still, we decided the next day we would start early and take shifts to come and be with you," Pam said. "I decided to take the early shift, to get to the hospital at breakfast time."

Here is where I remember this experience. The next morning, Pam walked in my hospital room and suddenly was surprised to see that I was awake, alert and had already finished my breakfast. Puzzled, I wondered, *Why so surprised?* Pam detailed what happened the day before.

When she told me that I was hooked up to monitors and tubes, it gave me chills. The scene she described seemed worse than the hospital ICU scene the night of the accident. What Pam witnessed the morning of her visit was a sharp contrast to what she saw the day before. While writing this chapter Pam recalled, "You had just finished your breakfast, and the only thing you were concerned about was getting your hair combed," she laughs. "That's when I knew you were alright." When Pam left the hospital that morning, she called family with this report, "You know she's alright when *all* she wants is her hair combed!"

Throughout our conversation, parts of what Pam described was hard to believe. Then again, with God it's not hard to believe; when I consider the numerous times God intervened on my behalf to reverse the outcome of other situations.

Add this to, other chapters filled with my testimonies of God's intervention to turn around and take control of close-call circumstances. God again demonstrated to my family and me that I was in His hands. Thankfully, God has blessed me to live to tell it.

Moments like these continue to convince me of God's faithfulness. Whenever I encounter situations that seem to want to end with a period, God punctuates them with His proverbial comma. His intervention makes the statement that His work in my life is "to be continued."

Testimony after testimony, God has an indescribable way of magnifying the areas in life that really matter. For me, family is one of those areas. With the Lord Jesus as my anchor and lifeline, my family knows how to pull together to help pull me through. With precision, they managed taking control and following through.

I recall listening intently to a message by Bishop T.D. Jakes titled, *I Got This*. The message is based on the account of the paralytic man who was unconventionally carried to Jesus while he lay on a mat. Four faith friends climbed the roof of an overcrowded house to connect him with Jesus.

Bishop Jakes addressed issues from several angles, relating paralysis and dysfunction with the challenges of the church, the tendency to be comfortable just lying on the mat and my favorite point, "hooking up with people who can take you somewhere." This illustration was an eye-opening "ah-hah" moment for me. In my physical dysfunction, being hooked up with a faith family that surrounded me, carried me and willingly shared their abilities to make up for my limitations, magnifies why my family matters so much to me.

Collectively my parents, sisters and brothers, in-laws, nieces and nephews taught me that family matters as I faced my uncertain future; I didn't have to face it alone.

Family matters when even my best attempts to claim God's promise to "keep you perfect peace, whose mind is stayed on me" (Isaiah 26:3), needed their assurance that whatever is "...intended to harm me...God intended it for good to accomplish what is now being done..." (Genesis 50:20). I believe instinctively they knew there was a greater purpose for my life. And I definitely needed their support to keep me on that path.

I had to go down that road – the road leading me to face unforeseen obstacles and unpleasant situations. Yet and still, I also had to follow my purpose, despite the pain in order to make the progress God destined for me.

In doing so, I learned that family matters when I found myself struggling to release my vulnerability. At times it was so hard to surrender my independence to dependence upon them and doing things their way. They proved to me over and over again that it was okay. During times when I had to forfeit my independence and relinquish my personal space, if you will, I craved reassurance. No matter what I needed – help around my apartment, cooking meals, physical assistance – there was no need to feel inferior.

Family matters in times of setbacks (and believe me, there were many). I had to decide if setbacks would overshadow any progress I previously made or would they serve as a springboard to more progress. My family would not allow me to succumb to the former. For progress overshadowed by setbacks could very easily become my justification for giving up, and quitting was not an option.

And finally, family matters when my I needed a spirit lift, a boost to shield me from negativity. I needed their camaraderie and humor to remind me my situation could have been worse; my situation would get better.

Over time, my physical healing became evident. I will never forget the day when I walked publicly for the first time. My sisters, brothers and in-laws were in on a plan to pull a fast one on our Dad. Nevertheless, the surprise was worth the effort it took to put our plan in motion. To get the details, you will have to turn the pages to the *Daddy's Devotion* chapter.

Keep Turning: Family Matters

Going back to Jr.'s observations, he was definitely on point, especially when he referenced Mother's diligence to make sure I received the best medical care. As previously stated, I heard Mother say numerous times to doctors, nurses, family – whoever she felt the need to remind, "Do whatever is best for Anita."

It had to be a struggle for Mother knowing that there were some things she wanted to do for me, but could not. She had to yield and rely upon the medical staff's expertise. Yet she never backed down from charging them with the responsibility to do what was best for me.

Her insistence was justified. In the hospital room was someone who was more than a patient requiring medical attention and more than just an injured daughter out of the woods from a severe automobile accident.

Mother was at the bedside of a daughter whom she almost lost but, by God's grace, was given back to her.

Keep turning the pages for more on Mother's story.

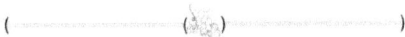

After four months in the hospital and rehab, the time to be released and return to my apartment finally arrived. Tressa and Kathy brought me home and helped me to settle in. They inspected the apartment to ensure whatever I needed was within reach and the apartment furnishings provided clearance for maneuvering my wheelchair.

After a final check, it was time for them to leave. As they walked out of the door, I overheard Tressa comment, "I feel like a parent leaving her child behind on the first day of kindergarten." That feeling comes with mixed emotions. On the one hand, the parent is nervous about leaving the child behind. On the other hand, the occasion marks an important milestone in the child's life.

I had reached that milestone. This was a definitive turning point. From that day forward, I had to learn to live more independently as a paraplegic.

My family had been exceptionally supportive. They carried me through a period of my life that called for my accepting my condition as one who is physically disabled, not an easy thing to accept. However, their support constantly reminds me of those faith friends who in Luke 5:15-26 carried the paralyzed man up to the roof and down into the crowded house to get him to Jesus.

God continues to prove that He is true to His promise of restoring my health. So with each milestone comes the opportunity to move on and advance to the next phase.

I am forever grateful to God for my family, their love, care and support. You will see why as you turn the page, read the tribute to my family and relevant *Globe* articles that reveal how much they mean to me.

My Family Tribute
Originally published May 6 – 12, 1999
Reprinted with permission from the
Kansas City Globe

The month of May is the first time families get together in large numbers since the Christmas/New Year's season. May has its own set of celebrations. In May, families gather for Mother's Day. Graduations from pre-schoolers to college grads are reasons for family celebrations. Families also get together for Memorial Day holiday. Whatever the occasion, at family gatherings people can talk and laugh, reminisce and predict, reunite and bond. I, for one, am big on family gatherings.

Two years ago in the month of May, my family came together at a time unplanned and unexpected, yet hardly festive. This particular gathering was in response to the news of the serious head-on collision in which I was involved. They nervously rushed to St. Luke Hospital's intensive care unit in the early morning hours of May 10.

My father received the initial phone call from a police officer who apparently recognized my last name, knew some family members and took it upon himself to make the call. My father had no clue of the accident's seriousness, thinking it was probably a fender-bender. When he arrived at the hospital, what he saw and heard from emergency room staff was troubling. He then had the disturbing task of making sure the rest of the family was contacted and summoned to the hospital.

They gathered to hear the prognosis of my condition and to be updated on the outcome of surgeries I underwent within a 30-hour period. In ICU's waiting room, they were together praying and visiting with other relatives, church members, friends, co-workers and colleagues. (By Mother's Day afternoon, word of the accident had spread). Periodically, they gathered in my room for a private quiet time with me, to keep watch at my bedside, collect their thoughts and wonder what the next moment would bring. And although I fondly cherish family gatherings, I would have given anything to spare my family the pain and anguish of coming together Mother's Day weekend in 1997.

In fact, I remember a conversation I had with my mother. I expressed regret that I was unable to honor her that particular Mother's Day. She answered, "God gave me back my daughter. That's gift enough for me."

I know it is impossible to turn back time. So, I decided the two-year anniversary of my accident would be an opportunity to bring my family together in this column. I want you, the *KC Globe* reader to know how much I appreciate my family's steadfast love, attentive care and untiring support. I realize they, too, have been affected by this experience. Yet, they continue to motivate and inspire me to persevere.

From time to time, others would ask if I needed anything. I appreciated their offer to help. I would pause and try as hard as I could to think of something. Usually,

I came up empty and often responded, "I can't think of anything." That was mainly because my family had so rallied around me and attended to my needs and wants, I literally wanted for nothing.

Two years after the accident, that same spirit exists. From the toddlers to the parents, my family continues to outshine and outlast this crisis by praying and pulling together. They are united with one agenda in mind – whatever is best for Nita.

Many times I am moved to tears at what they do and the spirit they demonstrate. They are my partners in prayer. They extend a shoulder to cry on and a listening ear when I need to express my hopes, share my victories large and small, confess my fears and vent my concerns. When the need arises, they are my advocates of personal business and health issues. They are my cheerleaders applauding my efforts. But they also scold me when I hint at passing up a challenge. When I'm away from home, they keep tabs. They call to check on me at work. Even when I'm out with friends if my cell phone rings, I know one of my sisters is "just checkin'."

I spent three weeks in St. Luke's Hospital and several months in Mid-America Rehabilitation. Some days, they came and went in shifts. Other times, they converged on my hospital room at the same time. In the mornings, family was there to help me dress and get my day started. They were there at bedtime until I was ready to go to sleep. They were present during therapies. When my family gathered at the hospital, quiet visits were rare. Most of the time camaraderie was the order of the day. The most innocent comment or action yielded outbursts of laughter. This would set the stage for one session after another of poking fun at each other. And if someone other than family just happened to be present, join the fun. Or else without warning, risk being the butt of the joke.

I especially looked forward to Sundays. The family would leave church services, and then meet together at a restaurant for dinner before coming to visit me. I waited for their arrival like a kid on Christmas Eve night wide-eyed and anticipating Santa Claus. Selfishly I knew I was in for a laughing-good time. Whoever coined the phrase "never a dull moment" must have taken a sneak peak at such moments with my family.

To this very day, my family has been consistent in pulling together as I learn to walk again and use my lower body. Thus, I close with this poetic tribute I pulled together to celebrate and honor my parents, sisters, brothers, in-laws, nieces and nephews:

> I am grateful to God for you, my family.
> You walk by my side
> Hand in hand, in spirited support,
> Patiently proving I'll "never walk alone."
> God knows I appreciate you, family.
> You walk before me to
> Shoulder my burdens,
> Protect me from needless cares
> And clear my pathway of obstacles ahead.

challenging myself at greater levels of activity. (But I also have to be careful not to overdo it).

In other words, although I have reached another milestone in my recovery, I must continue to move forward. I cannot stop. Dare that I give up.

I remember the day when I told a family member that my days of physical therapy were ending. She expressed sadness because she thought the therapy would continue until I was able to walk with canes. She wondered what I would do.

But I knew that this milestone was in no way the end. In fact, this milestone, like graduation, was another beginning. It required more of me, my independence and motivation from a human perspective.

Spiritually, it further revealed the reality of living with an enduring faith at a totally new level. The faith that I had three years ago is definitely not the same level of faith I now possess. I'm experiencing a level of faith in God that prior to May 1997 was unimaginable. I'll elaborate in next month's column.

Until then, keep the faith.

God has given me you, family.
Ever walking behind me
With the compassion, courage and
strength of character
Needed to encourage my every move.
And when I get weary or tired along the way
Surrounded by your footsteps and
Inspired by your rhythm,
Family, I resolve
I can continue taking steps towards
healing and wholeness.
— Much love, Nita

Until next month, keep the faith.

Moving On With Milestones

Originally published June 1-7, 2000
Reprinted with permission from the
Kansas City Globe

I recently attended my nephew's commencement ceremony – the Raytown High School Class of 2000. I was bubbling over with pride, not just for my nephew, but also his sister who, in early May, earned an undergraduate degree in musical theater from Howard University in Washington, DC.

That night, however, I was so happy for all of the Raytown grads, but there was one grad in particular. This young lady, at senior high school age, was about as tall as my five-year-old niece. I, like so many in the church auditorium, watched with intrigue as she marched down the aisle with fellow graduates to the traditional *Pomp and Circumstance*. Her short stubby legs climbed the stairs. She took her seat to await the anticipated march across the stage.

When that moment came, she stood near the mike. It was as if all eyes were on her even before the announcer called her name. There was a rumble in the atmosphere as practically everyone geared up for a resounding congratulatory applause. Her name was called and as she walked across the stage to receive her diploma, it was as if the audience could not stop clapping, whistling and cheering for her. Everyone present that night recognized that this physically challenged high school senior turned gradua[te] reached a milestone, despite her abnormality.

Personally, I took my feelings a step further[. In a] brief moment with this complete stranger, I [felt a] certain kinship. For persons such as me, who li[ve] against the odds, to accomplish anything n[ew] deserves commendation.

I was a bit misty-eyed but I managed to ho[ld back] tears. It was not a time to be self-absor[bed or] introspective. For it was this grad's proud mom[ent,] a time to be preoccupied with me. Still etche[d in my] mind and stored in my memory is that celebrat[ion] for this young grad, who enthusiastically and [proudly] walked across the stage to receive her diploma.

I know all too well the experience of [reaching] milestones, especially since the past three yea[rs. Most] recently on May 11, I completed weekly [physical] therapy sessions at Mid-America Rehabilitation [Center] in Overland Park. Although it was extremely d[ifficult to] part with the caring and competent team o[f] therapists and administrative staff, I knew tha[t day] eventually would come; simply because I had [reached] the level of physical progress that minimized [the need] for therapy.

Now it is up to me to continue app[lying the] exercises and movements I learned. More th[an ever, I] have to demonstrate my commitment to my[self] without the promptings of therapists. I must [keep a] weekly schedule of strength training and [...]

Faith Friends
Originally published August 31 – September 6, 2000
Reprinted with permission from the
Kansas City Globe

As I concluded in my July column, this is the first in a series of upcoming writings on the faith experiences of some Biblical personalities.

Three of the four New Testament Gospels are about Jesus healing a paralyzed man. For your reference they are Matthew 9:2-8, Mark 2:2-12 and Luke 5:15-26.

Any miraculous occurrence sparks intrigue and tends to capture the imagination. Here are my thoughts on what makes this healing miracle story so unique.

Four friends carried a paralyzed man on a mat to Jesus. They had to fight their way through a crowd that surrounded the house outside. They got close enough and realized the house so jam-packed with people inside, until there was absolutely no room for them to enter.

Facing these obstacles, how would they get to Jesus? With man on mat, they climbed onto the rooftop, uncovered the roof by digging through a thick layer of clay, wooden beams and branches, then made an opening wide enough to lower their paralyzed friend before Jesus.

There is more to this story, but I'll stop here; because I want to devote this month's column to the faith of these friends.

The admirable actions of four friends amazingly prompted Jesus to respond, "When he saw their faith." Their persistence to get the paralytic within physical proximity to Jesus undoubtedly was worth the effort.

"Excuse us. Excuse us, please. Coming through," could have been their plea while making their way through the outside crowd. Or, they could have waited until the outside and inside crowds cleared. In other words, they had logical options. Instead, they were poised to take extreme measures. Out of a sense of desperation, they struggled their way to the top of the house. They had to synchronize and balance their movements and strength, while carrying their friend on a mat. Once on top of the house, they ripped apart and forced their way inside from the rooftop.

Everyone in the house was awestruck and no one objected to their actions. There was no denying the evidence of their faith, so how could Jesus deny them a favorable, gracious response? Their actions eventually turned into a double blessing for their friend. They believed that if their helpless friend's condition were to change, Jesus would be the only one to make it happen. In addition, they were willing to do whatever it took to help ease their friend's suffering.

The conclusions I have drawn illustrate the character of selfless "faith" friends. Their actions were solely on behalf of their friend who had an obvious need. That's selflessness. Jesus was the only one who possessed the power (ability and authority) to meet that need.

Whether or not He would was not an issue for the friends. They knew that He could. They believed Jesus would and that was all that mattered.

That's faith. They were willing to do what they could to help their friend. They compassionately, creatively and courageously pulled together.

Whereas their friend was helpless and weak, they were his strength. In an attempt to get to Jesus, the four friends did for the paralytic what he could not do for himself. They were genuine friends.

Their actions remind me of the countless number of people who prayed and continue to pray for me as I live to overcome my own paralysis. I think about the first few hours I was hospitalized, semi-conscious and literally unable to pray for myself. The prayers of so many pulled me through. If you want to experience an awesome demonstration of the power of God in someone else's life, tap into the power of prayer.

What about it *Globe* reader? It is doubtful that anyone asked you or me to climb and rip open rooftops to bring them into the presence of God, in order to receive a blessing. However, we are asked regularly to usher family, friends, acquaintances, co-workers, etc. into God's presence through prayer – simple, yet often-neglected act.

Think about the last time someone personally asked you to pray for them. Did you honor that request? Did you pray in faith, meaning that you knew God could and believed He would? Did you exercise compassion, creativity and courage that could alleviate someone else's suffering? In short, are you a "faith" friend? Only you can answer that.

Next month, we'll look at another person of faith.

Until then, keep the faith.

True to His Promises, God Is Restoring My Health

Originally published May 11 – 16, 2006
Reprinted with permission from the
Kansas City Globe

I had another topic in mind, but a recent experience is worth sharing with you.

Nine years ago, Mother's Day weekend on May 9, is a time I will never forget. My whole life changed in a split second. A head-on collision resulted in a spinal cord injury, that has left me partially paralyzed from about the mid-section of my body on down.

Last week in a conversation with my physical therapist and two other therapists, they reminded me that with the level of injuries I sustained and the weakness of my muscles, I am not supposed to be walking – not even using a walker.

Thus, I am keenly aware that I function with abilities within disabilities because of the power and grace of God. I'm living by God's healing grace rooted in His promises given personally to me. He promised me nine years ago in Jeremiah 30:17, "'But I will restore health to you and heal your wounds,' declares the Lord."

I've read this promise practically every day. And over time, God has added more. Another one in Jeremiah 31:3 says, "I have loved you with an everlasting love...I will build you up again and you will be rebuilt." And most recently, I began to mediate on Luke 5:17, "For the power of the Lord was present for him to heal the sick."

God led me to this Scripture the week of Resurrection Sunday during my 5 a.m. devotion. This familiar story is about the paralyzed man and four other men who, as a last resort, were determined to get this man inside a crowded house to Jesus. So they climbed the roof with man on mat in tow, and cut open the roof to lower him in front of the healer.

I read the story trembling and tearing up. I asked the Lord, Are you speaking to me? Then I prayed until my devotion time ended. Days passed. While at work, I began noticing a difference as I stood up and walked. I thought to myself something is happening. It was sort of scary yet exciting,

I felt more muscle weight on my left side – from my upper body down. Since my left side was the most severely damaged, I have had to "recruit" other muscles for mobility.

I'm writing this column on May 9, 2006. Nine years later, the Tuesday before this year's Mother's Day, the left-side muscle weight and strength I lost has returned.

Just think. For nine years, I favored and fatigued my right side obviously because it was stronger. For nine years, some of my left-side muscle strength was zero. But today, zero no more.

I am excited about the days ahead to build up that

strength through weekly therapies and weight training. And I'm still in this for the long haul.

Nevertheless. this experience is not just about me. Above all, it's about God and His showing me what He will do even with the impossible, as long as I allow Him. Ephesians 3:20, most of you know it, "Now unto Him who is able to do exceedingly, abundantly above all we ask or think according to the power that works in us." That power manifested itself as healing at work in me, and God is restoring my health.

That power is possible only through the blood of Jesus Christ. Sunday, I listened to Bishop T.D. Jakes' message, *The Blood Speaks*. He included in his message, *When I see the blood, I will pass over you*. We sang that song during Sunday worship. Another verse of the same song says, *There's power in the blood*. And yet another verse says, *There's healing in the blood*.

And many of us know, *The blood that Jesus shed for me, way back on Calvary. The blood that gives me strength from day to day, it will never lose its power.*

The power that flowed over 2,000 years ago from Jesus' blood is present for Him to heal today.

It works daily and it's all-encompassing. For power is not limited to targeting my health challenges. His power consistently takes care of me in every trying situation.

Because of His power I am more sensitive to His Spirit. He literally continues to meet me every morning for my devotions. He speaks to me through His word.

God intimately hears my open heart in prayer, and then positions my conscience so that I am aware of and open to His promptings throughout the day.

His power has brought meaningful relationships into my life. He has surrounded me with supportive family members, close and dearest friends, my church family, co-workers, colleagues, neighbors and health care workers. I couldn't ask for a better support system.

I shared the healing news with my mother Essie Prince and siblings last week. Mother, my father, the late Rev. Cle Otis Cobbins, Sr., my siblings and others were delivered near-fatal news nine years ago Mother's Day weekend.

Sunday, she thanked God for this Mother's Day gift - just like nine years ago when she thanked God for "giving her daughter back to her." The next day, she surprised me at work and had a beautiful arrangement of roses delivered to me.

Today, we can share in the awesome news as God takes me to another level of restored health. "God is not a man that he should lie, nor a son of man that he should change his mind. Does he speak and then not act? Does he promise and not fulfill?" (Numbers 23:19).

Have a blessed Mother's Day to all mothers.

Until next month, keep the faith.

How Sweet It Is To Be Loved By You

Originally published November 2013
Reprinted with permission from the
Kansas City Globe

This one is personal. In this column, I am going to let you in on my love life. It's an experience I don't mind sharing and you might want to pay attention, especially if you are not involved with anyone.

Now don't panic or get bent out of shape. This is not a column about me coming clean to expose a deep, dark personal secret. However, I am going to share openly and without reservation, "How Sweet It Is To Be Loved By You."

I'm sure you are wondering the you is who? To answer that, I will borrow from some of the lyrics to a Motown tune by the late Marvin Gaye: Verse 1: *I needed the shelter of someone's arms and there you were. I needed someone to understand my ups and downs and there you were.* Refrain: *With sweet love and devotion deeply touching my emotions...How sweet it is to be loved by you.*

Recently, I asked myself, "Anita, how do you know that you are loved by God? Better yet, what can you point to as evidence that you are experiencing God's love daily?"

These are fair questions to contemplate; the operative word is "daily." Like most Christians, I could make a mental mad dash to John 3:16, "For God so loved the world that He gave His only begotten Son..." And while this Scripture is true, in reality what does that love look and feel like daily?

While pondering these questions, I also resolved to be conscientious about living in God's love. You see, I know my family loves me. We often express and experience love towards each other, reinforcing how deep our love runs. Actually, the strength of our love inspired me one day to stop and seriously consider what God does daily in my life as an expression of love.

Since I have a running tab of how love is shown among my family, then why settle for God's love that is based solely on doctrinal and academic principles? It's time to refuse praising and acknowledging God's love merely as a church girl satisfying the rules of the game for "Sunday morning Christianity."

God freely loves as a powerful, intimate expression profoundly and personally experienced through Jesus Christ. When people show love, I know it. The same should be true for God.

I love this quote by Augustine, "God loves each of us as if there were only one of us."

Sadly, so many people would rather take a pass on God's love if it means opening up to a life in Christ. It is mainly because this Christ-centered love means taking a lifelong journey that is going to require challenging one's comfort levels and confronting sinful behaviors.

God never intended love to be so loosely defined

and expressed the way it is today. Every time, the Bible records God's loving actions, God is giving His all and offering His best despite the surrounding and adverse circumstances.

In Ephesians 3:16-19, the Apostle Paul captures the all-encompassing essence of God's love, which is through Jesus Christ. The apostle writes, "I pray that...Your roots will grow down into God's love and keep you strong. May you have the power to understand as all God's people should, how wide, how long, how high, and how deep his love is. May you experience the love of Christ, though it is too great to understand fully. Then you will be made complete with all the fullness of life and power that comes from God," (New Living Translation).

I wish there were enough testimony in me to fully understand the love of Christ. But since the complete revelation of His love is beyond my ability to do so, let me just share this much.

I know the width of God's love in Christ through my restlessness and sensitivity to reach out in various ways, so that others can also discover the joyous relationship God desires for them. Furthermore, God's love is so wide until at every turn, every angle His unfailing compassion faithfully goes to work helping me through inner struggles, brokenness, doubts and shortcomings.

I experience the length of God's love in Christ especially in my trials. This love continues to impress upon me, "You can make it. Endure and endure some more. It's always too soon to quit." I love hearing on the radio a song by The Williams Brothers who sing, *I've seen too many victories to let defeat have the last word.*

The height of God's love through Jesus strengthens me to keep looking up, when I have been knocked down or brought low. I can reflect on Jesus sacrificing His life on the cross and know that I am no longer sin's slave. I don't have to devil-down and live below my God-given potential.

I experience the depth of God's love in Christ when I refuse to settle for life on the surface. My conscious spirit tends to ask for and then seek more. I often tell myself, *There has to be more to life than this, more to church than this, more to God's word than this.* (You get my drift.) When this happens the quest is on to search for more and God continues to prove He will not disappoint. I am blessed with deeper insight, more revelation, strength and motivation.

Without God's love, my daily affairs risk being shallow, mundane and uneventful circumstances forcing me to just go through the motions. Thankfully, I don't have to spend one day, hour or minute wondering if God loves me. I know He does. And how sweet it is.

Until next month, keep the faith.

Chapter 9
A Mother's Day Gift from God

God gave me back my daughter. That's gift enough for me,
— my mother, Essie Prince.

I needed to apologize. The day finally came when I got that chance. I felt that I messed it up, royally. My siblings and I had made plans for a special Mother's Day. For the first time after years of Mother's Day gatherings, we planned a cookout instead of reservations at a restaurant. That restaurant scene is usually too hectic, crowded with long waits. The larger the dinner party the longer it takes to finally get seated, served and chow down. And if your family is like mine, the hungrier they are the less patient they are.

So we decided to go a different route and we were excited. We had assigned dishes to bring to the potluck cookout. We planned to gather at Kathy's and Larry's after going to our homes and pulling off our church clothes for comfort garb. We would relax then get ready to have the kind of unrestrained family fun we're used to having. No restaurants. No need to be on our P's and Q's.

But I messed that up. Oh yeah, the family still gathered – but at the hospital and not at Kathy's and Larry's home.

They gathered for medical updates on my condition, not for a celebration.

Why didn't I just go straight home? Was I really that low on gasoline? After all, I lived only six blocks from where I worked part-time. I contemplated these questions and other what-ifs time and time again. Each time, I drew the same conclusion. I wanted Mother to know how sorry I was she didn't get the Mother's Day she deserved and we had planned.

So one day in my hospital room it was just the two of us. I turned off the TV because I wanted to have a heart-to-heart. And I got that chance. I told her, "Momma, I am so sorry I messed up Mother's Day. I didn't even get a chance to get you a gift."

I expected her response to be something like, "No need to apologize" or "Don't worry. I just want you to get well." I didn't get anything close to what I expected.

Instead, Mother without hesitation responded, "God gave me back my daughter. That's gift enough for me."

Wow. I never saw that coming. Me? A gift? No one can begin to imagine what her response did for my self-esteem.

On the one hand, I always felt that this tragedy could have resulted in loss of my life. I am also aware my injuries, although serious, could have been worse.

On the other hand, I have been told by others that I am a number of things to them as they observe and experience my post-accident life. To some, I am "an inspiration." To others, I am "an encouragement." Some have said to me,

Keep Turning: A Mother's Day Gift

"You are a strong woman" or "a woman of faith and determination." My cousin, Rev. O.L. (Lee) Cobbins, Jr., often tells me that to his mother, (my Aunt Minnie) I am "her hero."

However when Mother acknowledged, "God gave..." and as I contemplated her words the realization that I was "a gift" put my thoughts about myself on a whole new and totally different dimension. It is moments like this when I come face-to-face with the power of words. Proverbs 18:21 says, "Death and life are in the power of the tongue."

I felt esteemed, affirmed and valued more than ever, although Mother was not putting me on a pedestal over my siblings. Mother recognized that this daughter came so close to being taken away from her. By the grace of God, I was given back. And there is no way to put a price on one's life. So for God to give life back is, in a word...priceless.

Furthermore, the fact that Mother expressed, "God gave *me* back *my* daughter. That's gift enough for *me*," lets me know that she considered this as something God did for her personally. She had a right to view this experience in a more personal way. Any mother would.

Mother remembered when she received the phone call from my brother whom she calls Otis. She was told the accident was just four blocks from where she lived. They tried to get to the accident scene but could not.

> *At that time I did not know it was my daughter, Anita. Otis and I finally found out she had been*

> *taken to St. Luke Hospital on The Plaza. Arriving there, Anita was unconscious. That was when it hit me. As her Mother, it was a hurtful nightmare. After being there four hours, trying to find out what happened, seeing that she could barely move any part of her body and hearing bits and pieces, hurt me to my heart.*
>
> *All I could do was go into a silent prayer and wait. But one thing I knew is that Anita was in God's care.*

Of all the human associations we have, the one thing mothers have over everyone else is the natural connection that began at birth while she carried that child in her womb. Mothers are the first to make that connection. In childbirth, mothers are the first to experience pain with the child. So I can understand why my situation affected Mother so deeply, so intimately–the thought of being separated from her child, especially when that separation resulted from a painful situation.

Nevertheless, she championed this experience wearing multiple hats. Mother kept close tabs with the doctors and nurses. She wanted to remain abreast of my medical progress and related health challenges. I had a caseworker assigned to help with insurance issues and facilitate my transition from the medical to the rehabilitation hospitals. Mother made sure the caseworker stayed on top of her responsibilities. Mother wanted me to stay focused and worry-free so that I could give my undivided attention to my recovery. Words are insufficient to adequately express

Keep Turning: A Mother's Day Gift

my appreciation, because the daily personal matters could have bogged me down and kept me distracted from what really mattered.

I could count on Mother to go to bat for me with such courageous and assertive determination until sometimes I shuddered to tell her about problems I encountered. If necessary, Mother would voice my concerns all the way to the top decision-maker, when I was at a loss of words to speak up for myself.

One Sunday while in rehab, I was scheduled for my first showering. Two nurses were assigned because I was still too weak to shower. Actually, they had to do all the work – transfer me to and from the shower bed and wash and rinse me. No problem, right? Wrong.

The nurses tossed me around on the shower bed as if I were a Raggedy Ann doll. Although they would support my body so that I would not slide off, once in position they carelessly plopped me onto the shower bed. This happened repeatedly. Finally it occurred to me; they mistakenly assumed that my paralysis included loss of feeling. Between the twisting, turning and plopping, they were hurting me. Oddly I was so stunned until I was speechless.

The ordeal – showering and dressing me lasted about 20 minutes. I was quiet yet upset the entire time. When they finished and left the room I could no longer contain my emotions and broke out sobbing. *Is this how paralyzed patients are treated?* The very thought was disturbing.

Keep Turning: A Mother's Day Gift

About an hour or so later, Tressa paid me a visit. She walked in the room and immediately noticed my facial expression as she stood at the door. From a blank stare into space in my room to making eye contact with her, she asked, "What is wrong with you?" She instantly knew I had been crying. I immediately opened up and told her what happened. "I guess they thought I couldn't feel," I said.

Tressa bee-lined out of my room, returned with the nurse and sternly pointed out, "Since she has been injured, I have never seen her *this* upset." To add insult to injury, the nurse responded defensively and unapologetically but vowed to exercise better care.

The incident was still unsettling for Tressa. She told Kathy and when Kathy arrived to visit, she took up the matter with the nursing supervisor. Oh but eventually Mother found out. And the next day, Mother went straight to the top. She called and asked to speak with the hospital administrator and no one else. I was not privy to what she said but that morning the nursing supervisor visited my room and apologized.

To do battle with Mother was to do battle with someone who refused to take no for an answer when "whatever is best for Anita" was at stake. That was Mother's position. And I could imagine Mother making her position perfectly clear, "I shall not be moved," (lyrics from

"Do whatever is best for Anita." I often heard Mother reiterate with the medical staff and caseworker. It often made its way in her casual conversations with those who visited me in the hospital and rehab, "Do whatever is best for Anita." Circumstance after circumstance, Mother would not settle for anything less.

I don't think she realized how much her support propped me up when I felt like I could not stand on my own. I remember so much about Mother, her actions large and small.

To know her is to know that Mother loves to cook *and* loves it when others enjoy her cooking. Her home-cooked meals were a welcome break from the hospital food. It never failed. Mother's cooking was the rave with the nursing staff and other patients just from the aroma alone, as their scents followed the smell of food past the nurse's station and down the corridor to my room. And Mother didn't help the situation. She proudly strutted through the corridor like the master chef who knew what she was doing. She was delivering food that was needed for an appetite "starvin' like Marvin" for a delicious home-cooked meal, while enticing others scents' along the way.

Mother just knew she had whipped up another mealtime masterpiece that I was eager to sink my teeth into. She loved to surprise me with any one of my fav dishes – chicken and rice casserole, barbecue anything and mouth-watering beefy brisket with her chunky potato salad. Her barbecue sauce was to die for. I recall other occasions whenever the mood hit, Mother would fire up the grill outside her apartment complex, in the dead of winter, early in the morning and barbecue. As far as I was concerned, Mother could remain in the BBQ-mood year round.

Mother's meals were not only tasty; they were plenty. She would cook enough food to last a couple of days. She took it upon herself to see to it the food was packaged to last and labeled with my name so that she could instruct hospital staff on how to store it in the fridge, and then leave instructions on how to heat the food in the microwave. *Naw she didn't; oh yes she did!*

To this day, Mother still cooks as if she is feeding an army. And when she calls and says, "Come and get it!", you had better be in your car and on your way before you hang up the phone.

Mother was also big on attaching cards or little notes sometimes to the food she delivered. She often expressed (and still does) how proud she was as she witnessed how I handled a situation that could have left me broken and bitter, angry at the world and feeling sorry for myself.

Although the cards were printed with their own inspirational messages, wherever there was unused space on the insides of the cards, Mother used it for her personal messages to me. She wrote all over those cards. It was as though Mother felt that the cards' pre-printed words were nice but didn't say enough. The words were insufficient to express the deeper messages she wanted to express to me.

Mother's efforts to further personalize the cards she purchased worked for me. I am a communicator by profession and words carry sentimental meaning and messages. I often thought, *Wow, she sees me this way? Mother feels this way about me?* Knowing this, I kept her cards close. In my alone times, I often read them over and over again. While hospitalized, I was like a wet sponge that could never dry up reading Mother's and the other stacks of cards I received daily. I preferred to soak up every word of encouragement, challenge, Scripture and inspiration that came with every card.

These are some of the priceless, lasting memories that are still near and dear to me. While I was hospitalized and in rehab I knew that I could rely on the genuine support, nurturing care and courageous advocacy of my Mother. Once I was released, Mother's care and work did not stop. She kept up those responsibilities and then some.

I remember when Mother planned and put together my first public birthday celebration. She invited family to lunch at a Western Sizzler restaurant and she took unapologetic pride in what she had planned.

I was still very much wheelchair bound. However, I counted every first-time experience as either a milestone I achieved or a benchmark that identified areas of fears and insecurities I needed to overcome. This gathering was a milestone. As the "gift" God had given back to Mother, I was also well aware that God had given me the gift of another year. Although my physical body had dramatically changed, I was alive. I reached another birthday.

There were family members present on both sides–the Cobbins and the Princes, plus my siblings. However in all of my exuberance, I still had to be cautious not to overexert myself socializing with all who were present, (although it was tempting to be at the height of my enthusiasm). I remember taking pictures galore with aunts, uncles and cousins. Photographs became a sort of visual storytelling journal capturing various stages of my progress, starting with my first birthday and public appearance several months after my release from in-patient rehab.

The birthday card Mother gave me dated 1/12/99 read on its cover:

> *For a dear Daughter to remind you how much you are loved.*

The inside inscription read:
> *It's easy to take things for granted in a family, to assume that you just know the things that somehow never get said. But maybe you don't know how special you are, how easy it is to be proud of you.*
>
> *Maybe you don't know how much it has always meant to have you as a daughter, to see you grow up so beautifully without ever growing away from those who love you.*
>
> *Well, in case you don't know, this is coming to tell you what a wonderful daughter you are – and how much you are loved. Happy Birthday.*

Keep Turning: A Mother's Day Gift

One of the rare times Mother did not write all over the card, she signed it with:

These are my words with much love and you will always be
in my thoughts and prayers,
Much love, Mother Essie.

The words in that card are true. How could I ever grow away from those who love me? That day, I was surrounded by family. I love my family. Just being in their presence assures me that I belong; I am connected. I can't explain why. I just know that every time I am with my family the occasions reinforce a deep sense of fulfillment.

I love being around family. And Mother knew that. So what better way to enjoy and celebrate this particular birthday than to be with those whom I love and who I know love me.

Mother also knew that I was committed to my faith in God more than ever. I could have angrily lashed out, feeling as though I got a raw deal. With a vengeance, I could have spent time and energy pursuing the legal resources at my disposal against the young man responsible for putting me in this condition.

Instead, I chose to be more Christ-conscious and faith-driven which stirred and revved up my motivation to embrace learning how to live through what is often called "the trials and tribulations" of life. I felt that it was important for Mother to see my spiritual pursuits coming from a genuine heart. Yet I did not believe in faking my feelings. When I was low in spirit, I would let her know even if that meant simply hearing sadness in my voice. Nevertheless, Mother knew I was determined and if I were to go down, it would not occur without a fight.

There were times when I shared challenges, frustrations or problems I encountered and Mother would give the "If I were you, this is what I'd do" advice. I listened. Sometimes I responded out of my faith choosing to wait on the Lord, remain prayerful and trust God for the outcome. Then she would say something like, "But I know you, Anita. You're going to let the Lord handle it."

One day I asked Mother to share what she has learned from me while observing me living by faith as a paraplegic. She chose to put her thoughts on paper:

> *I am truly grateful that Anita has always sought God for guidance. Her faith and trust in God have carried her through. As a young Christian woman, Anita knows she can't go at it alone. God has provided Anita the companionship, teaching and support she needs through other believers.*
>
> *The accident has not kept her from working a job, working in the church, preaching the word and living for God. And I am often asked, "How does she do it?" Anita has had many challenges in her life, been in the hospital many times, still takes therapy and drives herself wherever she has to go. But that's the way it is when you are truly God's child. Anita can do this because she stays on track with God.*

Affirmations such as the above mean more than I can put in words. I sincerely want those close to me see that I am serious about living by faith in Jesus Christ.

I know there are some believers who can relate to this. Think about the time when you made that conscious decision to change for the better. The greatest challenge and acid test of that newfound faith came from those closest to you. Why? Because those closest to you have reference points that involve your past and your present. They have some "I remember whens" deposited in their memory banks and are always ready to make a withdrawal to remind you about yourself from "back in the day." They will reference firsthand experiences and a timeframe to compare the way you were then with the way you are now.

I don't mind. After all, isn't that what change is all about? Consider the claim the Apostle Paul makes in II Corinthians 5:17, "Therefore if any man (or woman) be in Christ, he (she) is a new creature: old things are passed away; behold, all things are become new." Where is the noticeable newness if we settle for always reacting and doing the same thing, all of the time and over time with every circumstance?

Actually as new creations in Christ, the only thing that should be predictable about our behavior is that we are likely to "let the Lord handle it" or let Him lead us, show us, help us.

That said, I sensed a responsibility to prove to others God is real and Jesus Christ makes the difference in my life.

After all, God had proven Himself to me again and again in many different circumstances.

The words to an old yet timeless hymn come to mind. Every time I think of this hymn, I hear in my spirit Mother's voice, a second soprano range with sharp intonation sounding each note while enunciating the words:

> *There are some things I may not know.*
> *There are some places I can't go.*
> *But I am sure of this one thing.*
> *That God is real for I can feel Him deep within.*
> *Yes, God is real, real in my soul.*
> *Yes God is real for He has washed and made me whole.*
> *His love for me is like pure gold.*
> *Yes, God is real for I can feel Him in my soul.*

The very thought of Christ in my life seems to always boil down to being convicted, convinced and confident. I am convicted that God is real. I am convinced that the witness of God's existence begins within my inner self. I am confident that God loves me no matter what.

I glean all of these encouraging, life-changing and life-strengthening promptings from this song alone—this hymn I have heard Mother sing.

Mother and Daddy were blessed with singing voices and their singing talents were passed on to us. Society tends to zero in on the generational curses that are passed on to family members. I prefer to focus on being part of a family where generational blessings are within my immediate family and across family lines. Along with being part of a ministry family, I am a product of a singing family and fortunately it came from both parents. Still there is another trait in Mother's DNA that was passed on to me – the ability to speak. Mother is the first person in my family that I heard speak publicly.

I remember as if it were today, watching Mother "on the stage" before the church congregation while serving as the Sunday announcer. Her voice was also on the radio because our church, the Emanuel Baptist Church broadcasted live on Sundays at noon.

I now know that "stage" was next to the church pulpit. I remember her voice was so clear and distinct until to hear her was captivating. At my young pre-teen age, I didn't understand the announcements I heard. But I listened just like the older people and paid attention to that voice. Sort of like a fan undercover, I anticipated this part of the church service because something about Mother's voice grabbed and held my attention. Even when church service boredom made me antsy to get into some mischievous antics, I stopped long enough to watch Mother in action, to listen to her voice coming across the loud speaker. So I credit my speaking ability to Mother's genes.

My first memorable public speaking opportunity before a huge crowd was high school graduation when I stood as the senior class president and addressed my graduating class, the "Mighty Manual Cardinals."

My journalism skills first surfaced years prior. In fact, it was during a time when unlike graduation there wasn't

Keep Turning: A Mother's Day Gift

much to celebrate – the assassination of Rev. Dr. Martin Luther King, Jr. which resulted in several days of riots in cities throughout the country, Kansas City included.

There was widespread unrest. Almost each evening my eyes were glued to the TV news. I remember watching as news report after news report showed the destruction to buildings, the flames spreading across city blocks, the disorder and violence as people were being handcuffed and thrown into police vehicles. All of this was disturbing.

So one day I sat down and wrote a poem, my very first poem. From my eight-year-old perspective, I wrote how I felt about Dr. King's death; yet I questioned why the riots?

I showed the poem to Mother. The next thing I knew she had taken it to the *Kansas City Call*, the city's Black-owned-and-operated newspaper, to be published.

Mother remembered that time, as well.

> Anita has always shown the presence of a spiritual side that would get my attention, cause me to take notice. At the age of eight, during the riots in Kansas City, we stood outside our homes. There were cries because we did not understand why. There had to be a better way. We hoped the violence would stop. We were crying. We were afraid. The sound of sirens caused the families in the neighborhood to cling to each other, scared to death and wanting the sounds of the riot to stop. This particular day we were in the front yard of our home.

Keep Turning: A Mother's Day Gift

Anita was crying and asking what were we going to do? She looked at her Dad and said, "Let's go into the house and you pray. We did that, holding onto each other with Anita in the middle. Her Dad prayed, saying, 'God, you are love and families and babies do not understand why the hatred.'

Anita stopped crying. We went back outside. The violence was still happening. But as we talked with other neighbors, we agreed that God was still in control, in spite of what was happening.

About a week later when things had quieted down, Anita shared a poem she had written. And I took it to 'The Call.' I remember Lucile Bluford, the publisher stating, 'An eight-year-old had the answer. We all needed to pray harder than ever. And that God is the answer. And families need to pray together.'

Anita's poem was printed in 'The Call.' And I received calls thanking Anita for letting us know that God is the answer.

That was Mother, always collecting articles, papers, and schoolwork written by me. I knew she was proud of our accomplishments and recognitions when we were growing up and as adults.

The first recognition I received since being paralyzed was in January 2000. The local chapter of the Southern Christian Leadership Conference hosts the annual citywide Martin Luther King celebrations with events that span a full week. One of the events recognizes African-Americans throughout greater Kansas City who are nominated by their employers for their leadership and accomplishments.

I was nominated by my employer's (KCATA) executive leadership for my "unflappable performance style" when under pressure, "demonstrating the skill to expertly translate the perspective of our customers into highly effective customer information," and "an ability to maintain a 'big picture' view on KCATA programs and services." These qualities and my leadership in other community activities resulted in my being inducted into the class of 2000 Black Achievers in Business and Industry.

The recognition ceremony and dinner were held as one of the Martin Luther King events and Mother was right there to witness my being honored and accepting the award. We were joined by my KCATA Marketing Dept. co-workers, my oldest sister Kathy and my therapists, Deanna and Linda, who were willing to come as moral support and to assist me with walking to the stage to receive the award.

But guess what Mother had a blast doing? If you guessed snapping pictures, you guessed right. When Mother wasn't the taking pictures, she passed the task on to the therapists or stopped and enlisted the help of a passerby who would. It was fine with me. It was her night to enjoy, as well. After all Mother had to process and go through with me the past three years, I was humbled and encouraged the focus was on something other than the challenges of being paralyzed.

I worked towards resuming as normal a life as possible. However, I struggled not to allow my faith in God and my

Keep Turning: A Mother's Day Gift

faith that He would heal my body to fade. I had finally adjusted to my life as a paraplegic. My health improved. I returned to full-time work and resumed activities that allowed me to help others. My life was looking up.

Eventually the time had come. For some time Mother had longed to relocate to Las Vegas. She withheld her plans during the earlier, fragile years of my recovery. Finally, she followed through with her relocation plans in 2001, despite my quiet and sometimes vocal objections. Internally, my wishes wrestled against her desires. I did not want Mother to leave but I understood and had to accept the inevitable.

I tried not to let her see how I was emotionally affected just thinking about her being thousands of miles away. Although the wheels were in motion, I prayed daily and for weeks that God would intervene, do something to cause Mother to stay in Kansas City. But Mother had purchased her one-way ticket. Some of my siblings and nieces had helped her pack.

Eventually, those wheels literally were in motion. The moving van arrived. Movers loaded furniture onto the van. All signs pointed to Mother becoming a Nevada resident.

When it finally happened, I had mixed emotions. In the end, I realized Mother needed to experience a life of her own. I also knew that thankfully with God's help and the family's support, I would be fine. God has blessed me with a tremendous support system of family, friends, church members and co-workers. Plus, I realized that sometimes God has to wean us from whatever we have innocently and unconsciously relied upon as our security, so that we discover our true dependency rests with Him.

I think Mother knew that, too. She knew I was ready to let God be my source and provider of all I needed and desired in every way. With that, her leaving was actually a compliment to how I had matured as a woman of faith. Of course, I couldn't see that at the time. I see it now.

While away, we kept in touch. I especially loved hearing from her on my birthdays because she always surprised me in creative ways. For instance, one year she had delivered to my job a half-dozen, fully bloomed bright yellow roses surrounded by a beautiful arrangement of green leaves and baby breaths. The roses' fragrance filled my office. The atmosphere was rather picturesque, as the bright yellow rose arrangement radiantly beamed against the lights in my office. Because of the roses, my office was the immediate topic of conversation with co-workers who stopped by.

Another year, I received a package at work. When I opened it, there was a picture frame labeled "Radio Shack." I thought it was strange until I opened the frame. Mother had included a picture of herself and my niece, Cherish. Then I noticed the frame displayed a "play" button, a "record" light and a speaker component next to "mic." Now, I'm really baffled. My curiosity got the best of me. So I pressed "play" and out sounds Mother's voice singing *Happy Birthday*. Even after my birthday, I often played it so that co-workers could hear her beautiful voice.

Keep Turning: A Mother's Day Gift

Remember in a previous paragraph where I mentioned Mother's love for giving cards? One year for about one-and-one-half weeks I received a card in the mail every day leading up to my birthday. At first, I didn't understand why the daily cards. *What is she up to this time?* Once I received the actual birthday card, Mother wanted me to know that this was planned and just another gesture to surprise me in a unique way.

Fast forward to 2014, Mother is back in Kansas City. Last year, our 82-year-old Mother suffered a stroke. For about two months, Mother lost her speaking ability and left-side physical strength. By God's grace, her speech and strength have returned. Thankfully, her condition was not as serious as it could have been, although there were a few tense moments.

After observing Mother's weeks of recovery, I am deeply grateful to God. I know that by His grace, God has given Mother back to us, health, strength and all. I can somewhat relate to her sentiments years ago when she responded to me, *"God gave me back my daughter. That's gift enough for me."*

()

Chapter 10
Daddy's Devotion
...And you'll never walk alone.

M y siblings and I can be schemers when we want to, but in a good way. We schemed to make a late entrance at the St. John Baptist Church in Kansas City, Ks.

Every year on the second Sunday afternoon in October, the church held a finale appreciation worship service for Daddy and Idella. This particular service marked 15 years of pastoral leadership for Pastor Cleotis, Sr., and First Lady Idella Cobbins.

Also each year, Daddy's twin brother, Rev. O.L. Cobbins, Sr., and the Macedonia Missionary Baptist were the guest pastor and church. So yes, the fellowship between the two churches also made the occasion an annual family affair.

The congregation honored Daddy and Idella with tributes for the work the church accomplished each year. Capping a week of events, the Sunday afternoon program was the highlight.

We planned to purposely arrive late to church. We would meet together in the parking lot about 15 minutes after the start of service then prepare to make our entrance.

Once we were inside the church vestibule, we would strut towards the front of the church – late and together as a group. That was the plan, at least, part of it.

I will always remember the second Sunday in October of 1999. Our late and bodacious arrival was deliberate because it marked a major and memorable milestone since my injury. We schemed, anticipated and chose to use this occasion as my first public walk using a walker. Everything happened as planned. My siblings, in-laws, niece, nephews and I "crashed the church service" as a tribute to Daddy.

It's Showtime. Larry stayed behind with me so that he could push the wheelchair as I walked down the aisle. Kathy was ahead of us to video record me walking. After being helped to the vestibule, a St. John usher saw us through the entrance door window. Her face lit up as she saw me sitting in the wheelchair ready to stand up using my walker. She opened the double doors. Some of the worshippers turned and looked our direction, perhaps wondering why Kathy was in the aisle, moving backwards and video recording.

As they looked, they began to burst out with shouts and applauses. I saw some people tap the shoulders of other worshippers in pews in front of them to get their attention and point my direction. My cousin, Eric, was Macedonia's minister of music. He began playing the opening chords to *More Than I Can Bear* by Kirk Franklin. The music's slow, steady rhythm was perfectly in sync with my walking pace – a step with the right leg and a pulling drag on the left. Plus because I wore an AFO stabilizer on my left leg to support a condition called drop foot, the weight of the brace slowed my walk.

Keep Turning: Daddy's Devotion

The music was unplanned yet right on time. Eventually Macedonia's choir began singing the lyrics:

I've gone through the fire and I've been through the flood
I've been broken into pieces seen lightnin' flashin' from above
But through it all I remember that He loves me
And He cares and He'll never put more on me than I can bear.

As I continued walking from the rear to the middle of the sanctuary, the people's praises, shouts and applauses grew louder. By now, everyone was on their feet. The choir continued to sing. Whether they cried, clapped, uplifted hands or raised their voices in praise, it appeared everyone euphorically showed and expressed thankfulness to God.

I broke emotionally. I tried to hold back the tears to maintain my balance, but my emotions overtook my efforts. I gave in to the ugly cry. I looked towards Daddy's direction but still could not see him. The worshippers were on their feet, blocking my view. Some were watching me as if they were watching a bride procession down the aisle. Others were caught up in their praise and excitement. I wondered if Daddy knew why the praises, applause, hallelujahs and shouts grew as I approached and passed each pew.

So I looked toward the pulpit and noticed my uncle, Pastor O. L. Cobbins, Sr., stand and approach the podium. Over the celebratory sounds, the choir singing and the musicians' instruments, I clearly heard his deep, bass voice from the microphone as he rejoiced repeatedly saying, "Amen. Amen. Praise the Lord. Praise the Lord."

I kept walking, looking towards the area of the church where Daddy was seated. The choir continued to sing,

> No He'll never, put more on me. I said never, put more on me.
> Uhh. uhh never, put more on me
> His word said he won't. I believe it. I received it. I claim it.
> It's mine (My deliverance)
> It's mine (My healing)
> It's mine (My joy)
> It's mine
> No he'll never put more on me
> Than I can bear. Can bear. Can bear. Can bear.

When I was about three pews from the front, Daddy finally walked to the center of the aisle and watched me walk towards him. At last, I saw my Daddy. But the ugly cry got even uglier. I could hardly see the details of his appearance through my tears. He was a tear-filled blur in my eyes. That was ok. With each step I knew I was getting closer to embracing my Daddy.

When I did, I held on to the walker with one hand and put the other hand around his broad shoulders. I placed my face streaming with tears against his and repeatedly choked out, "Thank you, Daddy. Thank you so much. I love you so much. Daddy, I love you. Thank you for everything."

Daddy answered me with, "You're welcome. You're welcome, baby girl. Praise the Lord. Daddy loves you, too." The back and forth exchange lasted until I sensed my legs fatiguing, getting weak from being so worked up as I walked. We broke our embrace, I looked at Daddy and

Keep Turning: Daddy's Devotion

noticed his tearful, red eyes. Then I carefully pivoted using my walker for balance and turned towards the direction where my Uncle Otis stood. I signaled for him to step down from the pulpit and come to me.

When he did and we were close, I put my arm around him, as well. I expressed my appreciation to him for his love, prayers, support and for leading Macedonia to hold special prayer sessions on my behalf. Uncle Otis was one of my number 1 cheerleaders, rooting with conviction and his strong and unshakable faith in God's healing power.

Afterwards, I needed to sit down. So I turned to Larry who had the wheelchair ready and assisted me.

I did it. I completed my first public walk. I wasn't sure how it would go. At first, I was excited. Then I got a case of bundled nerves with knots in my stomach as I stood up. I took a few deep breaths and once I started, there was no stopping. Hearing the worshippers reactions, the music's intro, the choir singing and the blend of singing and music, I knew this was my moment to give God all He deserved. I knew that Daddy would, at a minimum, be proud of me. Most of all, I wanted Daddy to bask in the joy of God's affirmation, "Well done, good and faithful servant."

My first public walk was an indescribably memorable milestone and a worthy celebration that set the tone for the remainder of the anniversary program.

At an impromptu moment, I was allowed to express my sincerest appreciations first to God, then my family and the two church congregations. At one point in my comments, I remember saying, "Daddy, you know all those times you came to get me, and I was transferring from my wheelchair to the car? I had already been walking. I tricked you." To which, the congregation burst out in laughter.

When it was time for Daddy to comment at the end of the program, his comeback to me was his claim that he "...knew all along. I watched that girl get in and out of the car and I said to myself, it's going to happen. So you (he said to me) didn't fool dear old Dad."

Daddy left behind fond memories. At the drop of a hat, I will tear up just thinking about him. However, my tears are joyful tears as I recall Daddy's tireless and caring devotion to me throughout this entire experience.

Daddy stepped up in ways that kept my jaws dropping because I didn't expect him to be so devoted and nurturing. In fact, all of my family amazed me – Mother's loving commitment, my siblings', in-laws', nieces', and nephews' assistance that was well-coordinated and organized. I was always careful not to take them and their time for granted.

However, Daddy's devotion exceeded my expectations. Let me explain. He was born and raised in the country. He hailed from Lexington, Ms. Like his brothers, he worked alongside Granddaddy on the farm. He worked with his hands. When he moved to Kansas City, his jobs included years of working at a chemical plant and then later on he worked construction until he retired to pastor full-time. Plus, I recall occasions when he worked on his automobiles. How I still have visions of Daddy rigging the family car and

Keep Turning: Daddy's Devotion

his beat up work truck with hangers and wires and knocking out dents with a hammer. So my impression of Daddy was a man who was too rough, tough and strong to have a sensitive bone in his body.

Along with that, Daddy was short in stature with a muscular, stocky build. Daddy's physique complemented the appearance of one who spent most of his life doing some heavy lifting.

When I think of all of this, I never expected him to be so gentle. Daddy effortlessly channeled his sensitive, nurturing side. I never doubted for a minute whether Daddy was concerned about me. However I didn't expect him to be so intimately, attentively involved in my care. After all, aren't men supposed to man up? Be strong? Remember, "real men don't cry." *Oh really?*

My stepmother told me about the time Daddy cried during their conversation about the accident. I didn't think he would ever show his emotions around me. That Sunday, he did. And I was glad to see it with my own eyes because he was always busy helping me. I often wondered how he held it together.

For me, Daddy redefined himself. After I was released from in-patient rehab, he sort of became my "caregiver from across the state line." He lived in Kansas. I live in Missouri. Mother was my in-state caregiver. She lived about 10 minutes from my apartment.

Daddy had to drive the distance to take me to my medical appointments, on personal errands or just to spend time with him and "away from it all." He made me feel as though I was somebody worth his time to crisscross states whenever I needed him and whenever he just wanted to spend time with me; he was so carefree with his time.

When we were together; we talked and the topics were endless – the Bible, of course; family; our churches; current news headlines; my progress and challenges. Some days, Daddy was full of wise cracks. At times I could not stop laughing. Other times I wondered if his jokes were meant to be funny, although he was the only one cracking up.

Without him knowing it, much of what Daddy did gave me the will to fight for my emotional stability. Believe it or not, there were many days when I needed that emotional reinforcement. The pain I experienced daily, the multiple trips to medical appointments and therapy sessions, the loads of medication I needed regularly, the hair loss, and changes in my weight and health of my skin were constant reminders of my changing physical condition and appearance. My body was broken, no longer functioning as it once did. My physical appearance had changed.

At times I struggled to feel good about myself. I could have easily caved under the weight of the many negatives that typically come with a life-altering illness. However, being with Daddy took my mind off having an inferiority complex and low self-esteem. This side of Daddy helped to love me back to wholeness along with the collective attentiveness, support and care given by Mother, my sisters, brothers and their spouses and children.

Keep Turning: Daddy's Devotion

It always helped being around Daddy because he said and did things that always made me feel as if I mattered. Endearingly he often referred to me as "baby girl" or "puddin'." I am not the youngest girl and perhaps too old to be either. But if that was who I was to Daddy; then I had no problem with going back a few years to be the "baby girl" he took pride in helping.

Remember I am not only writing about Daddy, the devoted one. I am also writing about a preacher and it goes without wondering, whenever he had a spiritual message; it was mine to pay attention. His central message to me was to "trust in the Lord." Despite my struggles, Daddy stressed trusting God to always provide the strength that is needed. The complications I encountered would lead me down the path to overcome if I continued to trust in the Lord.

Daddy often pointed out, "We cannot lean to our own understanding and call ourselves trusting God." He based this principle on Proverbs 3:5 and 6, "Trust in the Lord with all thine heart; and lean not unto thine own understanding. In all thy ways acknowledge him, and he shall direct thy paths," (KJV).

Trust, like obedience, is a challenge for most believers. We can easily relate to the desperate father in Mark 9:14-29, whose son was possessed with a spirit that robbed the son of his speech and often threw him to the ground in convulsions leaving him stiff as a board.

Since Jesus' disciples lacked what was needed to heal the man's son, the father brought the son to Jesus. Jesus tested the father's level of belief saying, "Everything is possible for one who believes." Immediately the boy's father exclaimed, "I do believe; help me overcome my unbelief!"

For many believers, here is where the rubber meets the road. On the surface, we say we believe or trust God. However at the core, we struggle to believe. We don't need help overcoming surface trust, because we tend to settle for trusting God only on the surface. Instead, we need help overcoming unbelief or our lack of trust in God at our core.

When the father confessed "I do believe" that was on the surface. When he went deeper and confessed "help me overcome my unbelief!", he exposed the heart of the problem. He looked deeper and was unwilling to neutralize his position. Otherwise, he would have remained stuck in a rut, risking an opportunity to see Jesus as the last hope and the only one to heal his son. The father needed help and was not ashamed in the presence of Jesus to admit it.

Learning to stand, balance and walk again was a 20-month process that above all required my trusting God. Whenever I lost my balance, I recovered and kept walking. Sometimes I fell; I got up and tried again. My muscles stiffened tight and I pushed through the pain. The physical complications were a formidable foe against my struggles to walk by faith. In this corner...physical pain! And in this corner...spiritual gain!

It took a deep-seeded resolve on my part to keep trusting God, because some days it looked as if God chose to renege on His promise. So when Daddy was led to "preach" to me about trusting God, I was all ears.

Whenever Daddy and I were together, I continued using the wheelchair which meant I had to wheelchair transfer to get in and out of the car. Each time, he patiently watched and waited. After awhile, I was able to stand, balance and walk using the walker while in therapy but I kept it secret from him. I wanted to surprise Daddy and the pastoral anniversary was the perfect occasion.

As I reflect on some of my most difficult experiences, Daddy was right there. I remember one night during my earlier days at Mid-America Rehab. I was in intense pain. A burning sensation ambushed my body and traveled from my upper waist down my legs. I felt as though I was on fire. I had never experienced this type of pain, the sensation felt trapped inside as it cycled through my nerves and muscles. I would not wish this pain on my worst enemy.

I tried to minimize the pain's intensity by tossing and turning in my hospital bed. I could not get comfortable no matter the position. My moans and groans turned into cries and appeals to the nurse on duty for pain medication. To my dismay, she could not administer medication without the doctor's orders. Worse off, she had difficulty reaching the doctor.

I didn't care. I pleaded for something, anything that would eliminate this agonizing pain.

Evidently my pleas seemed to bounce off the walls. The nurse would not budge and that angered me to tears. The more I tried to push her to do something about my pain, the more she resisted. She saw that I needed help. She saw me crying. I'm the patient in pain and she was more concerned about protocol?! Waiting to hear from my doctor was inexcusable. After all, "wasn't another doctor on duty?" I argumentatively insisted. Why not call and consult with him or her? The telephone was on my bed.

The next thing I knew my anger peaked. I picked up the telephone receiver and hurled it so that it landed at the foot of the bed. It was an impulsive reaction out of mounting frustration, anxiety and anger boiling over. In my mind, waiting on relief translated into no relief in sight, no doctor, just more excruciating pain and discomfort.

Daddy jumped up from his chair. From across the room he hurried to my bedside, locked me in a bear hug and started praying as I cried out, "It hurts. Daddy, it hurts!" I heard him pray, "Lord, take away the pain. Help Anita." This went on for several minutes. Whereas I cried out for pain pills; Daddy called on God in prayer.

As he prayed, I gradually calmed down. My loud cries turned to chokes then whimpers even though the pain never subsided. The nurse had left the room. I felt helpless having lost that battle. Like it or not, I had to wait until the doctor surfaced to order pain medication.

Once Daddy saw that I had settled down emotionally, he stepped out of the room. Awhile later, he returned. I was still in tears. He sat down in the chair. I noticed him squirming as if he, too, was getting impatient. He rose from

Keep Turning: Daddy's Devotion

his chair again and walked out of the room. I could hear his and the nurse's voices. They both returned to my bedside.

Eventually the doctor returned the nurse's call and ordered medication. I was still angry although there was nothing I could do except take the pills. Shortly afterwards, I fell asleep.

The next morning the nurse's assistant woke me to take my vitals. It also was time to prepare for breakfast and take my morning meds. The nurse from the night before came in to check on me. I felt much better. I told her that I had never experienced that type of pain. The burning sensation no longer plagued my body yet was still fresh in my mind.

She told me, "Your father didn't go home until after midnight. He stayed until he was sure you were alright."

Early on in my recovery, Daddy often stayed with me past visiting hours and late into the night. Sometimes he came after he had visited earlier the same day. Some mornings, he picked up where Kathy left off helping me finish getting dressed by putting on my shoes, socks and leg brace.

Daddy tried his hand at combing my hair. The hairstyle did not matter to me. Some hair strands ended up in odd places on my head. Some hair swooped to the side. Other strands poofed on the top. Since Daddy gave it the good old college try, I decided to proudly wear his fashionable hairstyles—swooped, poofed and all.

And how can I forget the lunchtime and dinnertime

feedings? Thank goodness, Daddy was feeding an adult and not an infant. He would shove a fork filled with food in my mouth while I still had a mouthful from the previous serving. I couldn't chew and swallow fast enough, while he also talked on his cell phone. His attempt at multitasking took on a whole new art form and sent chills through me. Daddy was rather heavy-handed. Each time he put the fork to my mouth I felt pressured to open wide but try not to choke or cough up food.

This happened enough times until I finally wised up and simply asked Daddy to wait until I swallowed before the next bite. *Why didn't I think of this before,* I asked myself?

Nevertheless, these were some of the simple pleasures representing some of my best moments that even today are fondly worth remembering.

Daddy and I were together one day to witness the miraculous outcome of another difficult situation. The problem surfaced in late 1997 even though God's solution was manifested months away. As I regained physical strength, my activity level increased. Ironically, with increased activity I began to experience severe spasticity.

The best way to describe this condition is when tight muscles snap into position after a period of inactivity. It is commonly known as muscle spasms. The onslaught of spasms was so acute and painful until, my whole body would suddenly and forcefully jerk from one position to another. Sometimes the spasms would hit hard enough to throw me out of my wheelchair onto the floor.

The only way to minimize the spasms' intensity was to lie flat on my back on the floor. The prescribed muscle relaxer medication was at the highest oral dosage. Still it was not enough.

While at home, obviously most of my time was spent on the floor watching TV, reading, writing or napping. *What a life?* This was my life, for about eight long months. Some moments I was down in the dumps. At one point, I lapsed into depression (See *I Lost My Joy* chapter). Other times I tried to encourage myself, clinging to the hope of my eventual healing. I looked forward to outpatient physical therapy and the exercises but dreaded going home only to end up on the floor, on my back. My attempts to size up the situation swung back and forth like a pendulum between hope and despair.

After several consultations with my doctor of physical medicine, he recommended my case to pain management as a candidate for a pain pump implant. The doctor warned the procedure was expensive and insurance carefully scrutinized patients' cases before determining if a patient receives a pump.

My initial appointment with the neurologist was mid-July of 1998. Daddy and I met this doctor for the first time. While in the exam room, the spasms continuously kicked in. Oddly I was glad the doctor saw firsthand what I had experienced for months. The doctor discussed the success patients experienced after receiving the pump. However, he, too, reiterated the possible delay in insurance approval.

I guess he did not want to get my hopes up. But what choice did I have? Insurance delay was a much better option than insurance denial. The whole time we're talking, I am having rounds of muscle spasm episodes.

After about a 30-minute visit, the doctor stepped out of the room. He left the door partially open and we overheard his conversation with a representative from my health insurance provider. He gave information on my profile, summarized the automobile accident and the resulting injuries. He concluded with his diagnosis of my condition that qualifies me for the pump. Afterwards, I noticed him saying less. I could tell he was listening and answering questions in the affirmative. I felt anxiety kick in as I wondered what the doctor would report back to us.

When he returned, he appeared puzzled and yet relieved. His perplexity gave way to the good news that insurance approved me for the pump implant. It was on the spot with no delays. No additional paperwork. Just a flat - out approval.

The doctor himself was surprised as he broke the news to us. I was extremely thankful, amazed and excited. As I breathed a sigh silently I kept saying, "Thank you, Jesus." At last, I could see light at the end of this painful tunnel.

The next step was scheduling the surgery. The doctor had gotten over his momentary shock and began looking at his availability the following week. His schedule was open and he was ready to suggest a date. Daddy mentioned that he was scheduled to be out of town that same week for the

Keep Turning: Daddy's Devotion

State Convention's Congress of Christian Workers, but he would cancel his trip.

Wait one minute. Rewind. No way! I wanted Daddy to keep his plans. With that, I surprisingly threw Daddy and the doctor a curve. What happened to the urgency to undergo this pain relieving procedure? Well...it took a back seat to my stronger desire that Daddy take a well-deserved, long overdue break. The doctor suggested the following week and I insisted *that* would be the week. I put up with painful spasms for months. I could endure two additional weeks. I had a chance to give something back to Daddy. This small sacrifice paled in comparison to his selfless devotion to me.

So right there in the doctor's office, we set a date. The surgery that was supposed to take months waiting for approval was instead scheduled. I consider this another testimony of God working on my behalf, despite the odds and past experiences of other patients living with a similar condition. God had already planned the approval and timing for a procedure He knew I desperately needed. The wait was expected to last months because of insurance. The wait only lasted two weeks because of my insistence.

Daddy enjoyed his involvement in the national and state conventions, as well as the local association of churches. He held offices at the state and local levels. Years prior to the accident, I worked alongside him on the local level serving as president of the Sunshine District Association Junior Mission. After five years leading young adult women ages

18 to 35 in mission work, I stepped down but continued to keep close tabs on his work and leadership.

The following week Daddy and Idella traveled to the State Congress. Judging from his voice during phone calls, I could tell Daddy was relaxed, enjoying his time away and free from worrying about me.

July 1998, after about eight months, I finally underwent the procedure. Daddy seemed more excited for me than I was for myself. Throughout this situation, though, Daddy's devotion was the prescription for getting me through those tough times. He and Idella worked together. She kept him on schedule with his commitments to me. I realize I was not Daddy's only responsibility. Yet I never felt as if I was in competition with Daddy's other obligations.

Daddy's devotion was a large part of his personality. I noticed his devotion caring for Granddaddy after he was moved from Mississippi to a Kansas City, Ks., nursing home. Daddy literally visited Granddaddy every day, as my uncles, aunts and in-laws tended to him in every way. Granddaddy passed in 1995.

When Uncle Otis' health began to fail, Daddy spent an inordinate amount of time at his hospital bedside. Our beloved Uncle Otis went home to be with the Lord in April 2002. Daddy was often quiet. He appeared introspective and deep in thought. Sometimes Daddy was hard to read. *Was he on the verge of shutting down or opening up,* I asked myself? Either way, I did not push. Daddy needed to be free to contemplate life without his twin brother without my inquisitive interference.

During Uncle Otis' homegoing celebration, it was time for the final family reviewal. Daddy was the last brother to approach the casket. I had an urge to get up and go stand with him. I decided it would be best Daddy have this moment alone. As he returned to his seat, our eyes met. I saw grief in Daddy's eyes. I believe I can speak for all of my siblings wishing we could do something to console Daddy and help him get through this season of sorrow. The best we could do was be there for him.

After the family reviewal, something extraordinary happened. The funeral attendants were draping uncle's body and closing the casket. All of a sudden, the pastors in the pulpit rose to their feet, then the choir members, deacons seated at the front of the church, the family and the entire congregation. The Macedonia Missionary Baptist Church was filled to capacity and when the casket closed, everyone was standing and applauding.

I was moved by the spontaneous expression. I concluded that this moment symbolized honor given to my uncle, a man whose influence took root in my early years as a Christian. His teachings, counsel and loving support grounded me in the Christian faith. His life spoke volumes and reminds me of something I have heard my parents say, "Don't forget the bridge that brought you over." I will always be grateful to God for Uncle Otis because he laid a faith foundation that anchored me in some of my most difficult circumstances as a young, single woman in Christ. He was that bridge that often compelled me to cross.

Now back to Daddy's devotion to me. He taught me something which led me to contemplate and size up this trait called devotion. In general when devotion is given in a genuine, unassuming fashion, it can be powerful. When the devoted person fails to realize the positive affect he or she has on others that is when you know the devotion is real.

Our time together deepened our relationship. Daddy's devotion proved to me I would never walk alone. However, one day all of his devoted actions would slowly but surely change. A few months after Uncle Otis' passing, Daddy was diagnosed with cancer. Initially, the cancer was treatable through surgery and he was eager to get it over with.

My world began to shatter when his illness surfaced. My life with Daddy, as I comfortably and contently knew it, was about to drastically change. His initial cancer diagnosis was supposed to be easily treated surgically, then a brief recovery period and Daddy would be on his way to a clean bill of health.

Unfortunately, Daddy's health took a turn. In short, the doctor led the family to believe other vital organs unexpectedly and adversely responded to the treatments. It was difficult visiting him week after week, lying in the hospital, hooked up to medical equipment and tubes throughout that were supposed to maintain reasonable function of his organs, while he laid in the bed lethargic, unresponsive and unable to communicate with us.

Keep Turning: Daddy's Devotion

For about eight weeks, this was our Dad's life. It seemed as though our prayers were not heard. At times, the only change in his condition was another procedure or surgery in response to another new health issue.

Eventually, the family began to question the doctor's competence and approaches to Daddy's medical care. It was unconscionable that Daddy was in such poor health prior to having a simple procedure and brief recovery.

The entire ordeal weighed heavily on the family. We were discouraged and worn out with the frequent hospital visits and numerous last-minute summons to the hospital when medical issues surfaced.

I vividly remember the latter half of a stormy workweek in October 2002. An unexpected, frantic phone call from one of my sisters delivered a troubling update on Daddy's condition. He was being taken to surgery...again; his fourth procedure since being admitted mid-October. Apparently, something unforeseen had gone wrong.

I left work in a nervous panic, under emotional pressure, struggling to pray and searching for divine comfort.

By the time I finally arrived at the hospital and was helped to the surgical waiting area, my family had just finished with the doctor. Based on his report, the looks on their faces were disturbing. In short, Daddy's condition had reached a critical point, he was heavily sedated and he would eventually be moved to ICU. The doctor's report to the family concluded with a strong suggestion not to keep watch at the hospital. Instead, we should go home and get some rest. Eventually, we left the hospital.

On the way home, I had mixed reactions. One moment I was numb. Other times, I tearfully wept. At the same time either way, I tried driving cautiously on the interstates because it was a dark, stormy evening. The windshield wipers and defroster could not work fast enough against the torrential downpour which made driving difficult. "This sickness is not unto death" entered my thoughts again and again. I knew it was a Scripture. I was familiar with the words but I was so distraught until I heard it and I didn't hear it.

After a 30-minute drive I finally arrived home around 8 p.m., entered my apartment and as soon as I sat down, I broke down emotionally. The words, "This sickness is not unto death," came to me again. So it dawned on me to pray about what I kept hearing. I managed to choke out this prayer, "Lord, you teach us in your word to 'try the spirit by the spirit.' If this is you speaking and not my flesh, then I need you to reveal the Scripture."

The response was, "John 11." I did not believe what I heard and argued with my thoughts that John 11 is about Jesus raising Lazarus from the dead.

Next, I decided to search the phrase in my New International Version Bible concordance. I ran across a similar phrase referenced in Philippians 2:27. It read, "Indeed he was ill, and almost died. But God had mercy on him, and not on him only but also on me, to spare me sorrow upon sorrow." I thought, *What a comfort!* I felt as though God was speaking directly to me. Still, I reasoned that the Scripture I was seeking is printed in red letters (representing Jesus' actual words), and Philippians does not include red-letter text.

I continued the search this time consulting my King James Version Bible concordance. To my amazement and relief, I found the Scripture in John 11:4, "...'This sickness will not end in death. No, it is for God's glory so that God's Son may be glorified through it'."

God responded to my desperate cry for solace, answers and insight – anything that would help me deal with what was happening to Daddy. In moments like these, God's word is revealed with perfect timing. Psalm 34:15, "The eyes of the Lord are on the righteous, and his ears are attentive to their cry..." God was speaking all the while during the emotional drive home. Indeed, He was compassionately attentive to my cry. God lovingly responded to my request to prove that He was the one speaking. Still I had to take the initiative. I paced back and forth through passages of Scriptures for confirmation that Daddy's sickness was "not unto death."

I had to ask. I was desperate to hear from God. Only seven short months prior in April, Daddy's twin, Uncle Otis, went home to be with the Lord. I thought surely the family would not have to lay another loved one to rest in less than a year. Would this be by divine order to reunite the brothers so soon? If so, I was not ready to accept Daddy leaving us; I was not prepared to let Daddy go.

As the days passed, it was confirmation that this recent turn of health events was not Daddy's time to go. However, his condition lingered. The days dragged on for weeks.

Finally, Idella's patience and willingness to allow the doctor to keep trying different approaches reached their limits. Ironically, one day at physical therapy I confided in Deanna, my therapist, about Daddy's condition. Sometimes a listening ear and shoulder to cry on were just what I needed before I could begin physical therapy. As always, Deanna comforted me but took it a step further. Based on my description of Daddy's health, she suggested a well-respected, highly recommended chief physician at St. Luke. She wrote his name on a sheet of paper and gave it to me before I left rehab.

Two days later at work, I received a magazine that profiles top local professionals monthly. My department subscribes to the magazine and in this particular issue medical professionals were featured. I just happened to thumb through the pages when I ran across the name of the same physician Deanna recommended. I read his profile.

Immediately that morning, I called Idella. I shared some of Deanna's glowing comments and the doctor's profile as one of Kansas City's top physicians. Idella wanted the phone number. I could tell she was adamant about Daddy moving to another hospital under another physician's care. We ended our conversation.

Around noon, Idella called back with the news that her

efforts to reach the St. Luke doctor paid off. She first spoke with his nurse. She described to the nurse Daddy's initial diagnosis, the multiple surgeries and her lack of confidence in Daddy's treatments. She was excited when the nurse committed to getting her message to the doctor, who at the time, was performing heart surgery.

I heard a demanding insistence in Idella's voice, "I want Cleo out of that hospital TO-DAY." And she stressed, "TO-DAY." Her patience had run out. To Idella, no matter what the doctor tried there were always more questions than answers. We talked a few minutes more, then ended our second conversation.

Around 4 o'clock that afternoon, I called Idella again to get an update. She answered, but this time she sounded hurried. And she was. Daddy was being transferred to St. Luke and the physician was expecting his arrival by 4:30.

I felt a sense of peace. Daddy was on his way to another hospital and under another physician's care – a notable chief surgeon, at that. He was not in St. Luke long before undergoing another surgery. But that was ok with the family. We were apprised of different treatments Daddy would receive. The surgery was successful. Within a week, Daddy was conscious, alert and talking. The following week, his dialysis was discontinued. He no longer needed treatment for his kidneys. Daddy was back and we were thankful to God.

At the other hospital, it seemed as though he was dying, just lying in a hospital bed, like a zombie and hooked up to medical equipment. He was unable to communicate. Although alive, Daddy was not improving. It was then when I begin to feel the weight of missing Daddy.

We spent so many intimate, quality moments together until the very thought of his inability to help me left a huge and painful void. A penetrating sense of loneliness deepened just thinking about it. I am not referring to him actually leaving this life and no longer present to help. This pain was because I could not bear the thought of him no longer interacting with me with his devoted care and assistance. Sadly, that time came.

January 27, 2003, he was released from St. Luke. His focus was now on managing his own illness. About two months following Daddy's hospital release, he was back to his old self – spending time with family and his friends, ministering to the St. John family in every way, community meetings and resuming his responsibilities as moderator, to name a few.

He sealed his position among family, friends and the faith community as a living testimony determined to have a life, as if he knew he could die any day. Aside from seizing opportunities to share his testimony, the only indicators that Daddy had health challenges were the wound pack he wore for a few weeks, his walking with a cane and change in his weight. Although his physical health changed, Daddy was driven and more motivated than ever.

And my thoughts were fixed on Daddy living a long time with no end to his life in sight. Nevertheless, I gradually began adjusting to demonstrate to him and prove to myself that I could take care of Anita.

I remember when he addressed the association as its newly-elected moderator. The August 2003 annual session convened at my church, Metropolitan Missionary Baptist Church. I was beaming with pride not just because Daddy was now leading the association but also because Daddy laid out and articulated a vision and recommendations for the association's consideration and vote that night.

I was preoccupied with his address followed his sermon based on Matthew 22:37-39, "And Jesus said unto him, 'Thou shalt love the Lord, thy God with all thy heart and with all thy soul and with all thy mind. This is the first and great commandment, and the second is like it. Thou shalt love thy neighbor as thyself'."

I was amazed and captivated witnessing his strength, endurance and the way Daddy communicated plans and programs for the upcoming year in his first year. This new moderator standing before us that night previously spent six months in the hospital and rehabilitation after undergoing eight surgeries. I was caught up comparing the man I watched that night with the man whose bedside we often rushed to and stayed beside.

Daddy was passionately and powerfully delivering his sermon simply titled, "Love." The congregation responded with applause, shouts of, "Amens! Praise the Lord!" Daddy's address and sermon were well-received.

Keep Turning: Daddy's Devotion

He began to move away from the podium. His delivery grew intense and fervent. He stepped towards the edge of the pulpit. I along with others around me gasped. I didn't think Daddy was going to do it. *Oh no. He's not.* Well, he did. In one swift, sweeping motion he leaped from the pulpit, which sits about 3 ft. high, onto the sanctuary floor. As he preached and paced, my heart raced. I did not know about anyone else but Daddy literally scared me. I was afraid he may have injured himself in some way. Daddy, however, just kept preaching and pacing. Finally he returned to the pulpit climbing the three steps this time. As he ended his sermon, the crowd was on its feet joyfully celebrating what we all had witnessed. But...this moderator's address would be Daddy's first and last.

The following week Daddy called me at work. He came to the job for an unexpected visit. The first time he came to the job unannounced was over 10 years ago to deliver the news that my cousin, Ronnie Cobbins, was murdered.

While we talked, I cautiously yet curiously asked him, "Daddy, is there something wrong?" He just smiled and answered, "No...I just came to tell you I love you." "Ahh. I love you, too, Daddy." It was a touching and sentimentally special moment. I wasn't sure what came over him. Days later, another turn in Daddy's health led me to conclude his visit was no accident. Friday of that week while enjoying a fellowship in St. John's basement, Daddy became ill. He was rushed to the hospital by ambulance. We later learned that Daddy had suffered a seizure and tumors were found on his brain. Daddy underwent radiation, yet his condition was graver than he let on. Let me explain.

After Daddy passed, Idella told me that it was at this time when the doctors informed him he had six months to live. His condition was terminal. Still Daddy never told us. Instead with every setback, Daddy's spirited faith in God took front and center. We could count on Daddy to work with the strength and stamina he had even though radiation darkened his skin. He lost weight and began using a walker. After this extended hospital stay, Daddy was placed in a nursing home for further rehabilitation.

There were times Daddy summoned the family to visit him. We crowded around his bed to hear him open his heart on several subjects. The subjects were spiritual in nature with one overriding message – love each other and take care of one another. The love message was our take away each visit. It never dawned on me Daddy was sharing his final discourse, just as Jesus did with His disciples in John chapters 13 to 16, before facing His ultimate suffering and death. The only difference, Jesus on several occasions informed His disciples He was leaving them. Daddy never told us.

I remember Thanksgiving 2003. Three churches, St. John Baptist, Macedonia Missionary Baptist (my late uncle's church) and Zion Traveler's Baptist gathered for the annual holiday worship service. Daddy was scheduled to preach. His health was noticeably failing. I didn't think he could endure a 30-minute sermon. But he did. Then I thought,

Keep Turning: Daddy's Devotion

Surely Daddy was not going to sing, too. But he did. The whole time I thought Daddy would at least stand and support himself on the walker. Instead, Daddy set aside the walker as though he had not experienced a sick day in his life.

I have so many fond memories of Daddy. Today those memories serve as treasures that I often draw from to lift my spirit and encourage myself to keep going. In his message from I Samuel 30:6b, *Ziglag - Or David: Encouraging Himself in God*, C.H. Spurgeon noted that David did not, at first, attempt to encourage anybody but himself. Spurgeon wrote, "Some of the best talks in the world are those which a man has with himself. He who speaks to everybody except himself is a great fool!"

My life as an active paraplegic calls for many days and nights of long talks, encouraging myself and reflecting on memories of Daddy that also serve as lessons he instilled and taught me.

First, Daddy taught me to accept myself and be grateful to God for the health and strength I have, despite being paraplegic and the physical changes that are the result of my condition. I witnessed how Daddy embraced the change in his physical appearance. He took it in stride. After his first round of radiation, he lost his hair. He decided he liked being bald. After all, to him baldness was the new look of the young fellas.

Over time, his sporadic and eventual loss of appetite became evident as Daddy went from a stocky, muscular physique to a thinning, frail frame. Yet many times Daddy would call me and cheerfully greet me with, "This is your handsome Daddy!"

Secondly, I am more sensitive to spending time with, calling and praying with people who are hospitalized or shut-in. Daddy made time in his schedule to visit and comfort family, friends and strangers alike in hospitals and nursing homes. I think of the words Jesus shared with His disciples in Matthew 25:40, "...'Truly I tell you, whatever you did for one of the least of these brothers and sisters of mine, you did for me'."

And finally, I learned from Daddy that when you least expect it, what you do for others can have a profound impact upon their lives. I have already discussed the actions Daddy performed taking care of me. He channeled an inner-"maternal" side, that instinctively rose to the occasion. This man from the country worked on the farm and with his hands. In his adult life, Daddy performed heavy labor while working in a factory, at a chemical plant and construction. Yet with those same rugged and rough hands, he tenderly did whatever he could to nurture me through my post-accident experience.

I appreciate Daddy all the more for all that he did, as I lived to regain and maintain as much muscle function as the Lord allows.

I honestly did not realize until Daddy's health began to deteriorate how much I depended upon him. This turning point was the most difficult to accept. I was losing the one who deeply affected my life. It was if I unconsciously put my spiritual and emotional well-being solely into his hands. Hands there were being weaned from me, little by little.

I believe he was aware that although physically he was weakening, God was enlarging his spirit. Based on this, Daddy believed he had the strength he needed to endure. Many people knew about some of his health challenges. In spite of his illness, we either saw with our own eyes or heard the news from others that he kept going. When people saw him at Peachtree restaurant, it was a testimony that God had given him the ability to drive himself across the state line to his favorite eating place where he could sit, dine and fellowship with friends. Perhaps his fellow ministers were encouraged and inspired when he attended Baptist Ministers Union meetings, supported the district and state brotherhood events and other church services.

St. John Baptist Church members were with him weekly and could attest to his preaching on Sundays, teaching on Wednesdays and whatever he could do to minister to their needs throughout the week.

When he attended family gatherings, we could not help except to thank God that Daddy was still with us.

Daddy was motivated. He was active seemingly with boundless energy while on the move. He refused to allow his ailing and frail physical frame to deny him the privilege and opportunities to serve God, be with family and even formulate plans while serving as moderator of the Sunshine District Association of Missouri-Kansas-Nebraska.

In all of this, Daddy's mind remained sharp and strong.

He also maintained his sense of humor.

As divine strength was being perfected in Daddy's physical weakness, I believe Daddy had accepted being taken on a journey that ultimately resulted in him being absent from the body and soon present with the Lord.

Daddy's physically weakening condition emerged as God's opportunity to display strength that defies human, rational understanding. We saw Daddy active, going places and doing things himself. No one drove him. Few people did things for him. I don't recall Daddy sending other deacons, church members or ministers on visits to pray for and minister to others. Daddy lived to help others. He did all of this and more himself.

One of his greatest joys in his final days was when he proudly gave Tressa away in marriage to James on New Year's Day in 2004; 28 days later Daddy passed away. Before leaving, Daddy preached his last sermon on Sunday, January 18. After that Sunday worship service, the church was near empty when Daddy came out of his office and entered the sanctuary. He approached the chairman of deacons. And as a final pastoral act, soft-spoken Daddy transferred leadership to him saying, "Deacon Hollinshed, you're in charge. Deacon Hollinshed, you're in charge." With that, Daddy struggling slowly to balance while using his walker, took his final and quiet walk up the sanctuary aisle and out of the church. I believe Daddy knew he would not be returning to the pulpit, not returning to St. John.

The next day, Daddy and I shared our last intimate

conversation in his home Martin Luther King holiday. I was off work and decided to spend time with Daddy. The visit lasted a heartfelt three hours. He was now bedridden. The cancer had spread to his bones. His condition was deteriorating and he lived with extreme pain. Still, he never complained or let on, but I could see it in his countenance.

During my visit, we talked and skipped around topics. He kept bringing the focus of our conversation back on me. He asked more than once, "You doing alright?" My response was always the same, "Yes, Daddy. I'm fine." It was hard looking Daddy's direction. He tried his best to deal with his physical pain without me knowing it. He wanted to give his undivided attention to me and I was not going to spoil his intentions by inquiring about his health.

However his attention was on my health. We would make eye-to-eye contact and Daddy advised me repeatedly, "Take care of yourself." After awhile, I wanted Daddy to rest; it was time to leave. I pulled myself up from the sofa using my walker. I walked towards Daddy, leaned over balancing myself so that I could kiss Daddy goodbye. He tried to raise up and could only elevate his head. Still we were too far to get close enough. Most of all, I saw pain in his eyes. I said, "Don't strain yourself, Daddy. Just relax." I held on with one hand, kissed my fingers with the other hand and placed those fingers against his lips. Daddy kissed them and we exchanged "I love yous." That was our last heart-to-heart conversation.

Two days later on January 21, Daddy informed Idella he needed to go to the hospital. He told her, "You should probably call an ambulance." Daddy could not walk. The Sunday evening of his last sermon, it took Tressa and his new son-in-law, James, about two hours struggling to move Daddy out of his car, carry him down about 15 concrete steps, through the outdoor patio and into his house. After he passed, Idella told me medical records showed Daddy had suffered a broken hip. She concluded the fracture was probably from a rear-end collision they were involved in about a week prior.

Daddy was taken by ambulance to Providence Medical Center. It would be his final hospital trip. The cancer had reached an aggressive stage, but I was still clueless that Daddy was dying. As we visited and kept watch at Daddy's bedside, his demeanor was quiet. Because Daddy was pain-sensitive, he was morphine-dependent. And still, in all of his suffering he never complained. Instead, he would thank the nurses for keeping him comfortable.

I honestly thought Daddy would hang on and eventually return to the nursing home. Or could it be I was in denial? I think girlfriends Delores, Brenette and Diann believed I was, although they never said so. The following week on a Wednesday, they graciously offered to come and get me so that I could visit Daddy. They helped me to his room then turned around and left to go to the waiting room so that I could be alone with him.

By now, Daddy cannot communicate although according to the nurse, he could hear. My emotions swelled. My heart was crushed. I was at my lowest as I looked upon the face of the love of my life, who was on the verge of transitioning from this life. Since he could hear, I had some things I needed to say and wanted Daddy to know:

> *Daddy...It's me...Anita. I had to come be with you...Daddy, I really don't want you to go...but I know you're on your way to finally be with Jesus, and Granddaddy, Grandmother, Uncle Otis, Uncle Otha Bell, all those other brothers and your sister...I want you to know how much I love you...I will always love you even after you're gone. Know this...I am SO...proud...I...am SO...proud...to be YOUR daughter...*

A few minutes later, Regina entered the room. She caught me with my head resting against the bedpost, wiping tears from my face. Now I am overwhelmed with grief, deep in sorrow. I think reality, although struggling its way, was starting to set in.

The room was respectfully quiet. Then my pastor Rev. Wallace Hartsfield, Sr., entered the room. He put his arm around Regina and as he looked at Daddy, he began sharing his thoughts. Regina listened more attentively to him than me. I was grievously consumed with thinking, *What am I going to do without Daddy?*

Pastor Hartsfield's visit was relatively brief. Before leaving, he prayed for us but he did not leave immediately after the prayer. Instead, he stepped aside. I wasn't exactly

Keep Turning: Daddy's Devotion

sure what he was doing until he finished. He handed me a notecard and asked me to read it when I got the chance. He had stepped aside to pen these words to me:

> *A note of encouragement from your pastor. My dear Daughter Anita. In recent times in my own life facing the hurt and pain in others' lives, I have referred them to your faith and tremendous strength. I want <u>you</u> to say over and over to <u>Anita</u> that the God who has brought you is the same God who will bring you and carry you consistently. Baby, I love you and am here for you. Pastor Wallace S. Hartsfield.*

I didn't intend for my grief to indicate a diminishing of my faith. However God knew the difficulty I faced as the inevitable began overtaking the answered prayer I was seeking. I had held on and held out hope that God would allow Daddy to remain with us a little while longer.

I stayed in the room a few minutes more then I wheeled myself out of Daddy's room to look for my girlfriends. They had food for me to eat since it was my meal and meds time. We began sharing lighthearted conversation. At one point, Brenette zeroed in on my need for this visit with Daddy. "You seem relaxed," she noticed. "You needed to release your father." Brenette was right. My last words to him, going through the period of tearful sorrow and processing questions in my mind turned out to be my pathway to peace and acceptance; I was no longer in denial. This visit was my moment of release.

Keep Turning: Daddy's Devotion

When Daddy passed at 10 o'clock that next morning, I remember Idella sharing with me his transition. She said she previously asked him to promise her he would not leave unless she was with him.

Idella got up that morning and hurried to get dressed to get to the hospital. She said she entered his room at about 9:57 a.m. And his eyes were open as if he was looking for her. (His eyes had been closed for about a week). After telling Daddy she loved him, she mustered up the courage to say, "I know you're ready. You can go now."

With that, Daddy took his last breath and closed his eyes. He had kept his promise to Idella. Daddy died.

Off all the chapters in *Keep Turning the Pages*, this chapter was the most difficult to get through without my having to stop periodically and get past the tears. At times, I had to put the writing aside because I bawled like a baby.

Daddy's passing was the first in our immediate family. As you can see from my story, I clung to hope until almost 24 hours before he passed. Perhaps I was the sole hold-out whom God had to gently free from the fear of being without Daddy. And so, He orchestrated that final visit the day before. I had to let him go but I still carry Daddy in my spirit. I remember his counsel whenever I am hit with situations to forgive hurts I did not deserve. When others reach out to me for help through difficulties, I often ask myself, *Lord, how can I help and what would Daddy do?* I draw strength from the well of memories Daddy left behind, especially when I recall him reminding me to "take care of myself" in those physically and emotionally tough times.

Ironically, I recall it was Daddy who nudged me into the arena of independence when he suggested I work to buy myself a pair of shoes. Then I guess I got too independent for my own good.

So after a few divine teachable moments, I learned to be careful not to impose my will upon God. Is Daddy doing it again – impressing upon me to take care of myself? I didn't take it that way.

Instead I would rather focus on how Daddy's devotion became a life-changing, ok-now-I-get-it object lesson. His devotion enabled me to equate God's love, devotion and care for me. In Daddy, I saw a new dimension of my worth through God's eyes. I knew that God would be with me always and forever, even in the midst of being separated from my loving Dad.

Whenever I fall short of my own expectations to care for myself, I hear in my spirit one of the most meaningful and favorite of Daddy's songs. No matter the number of people in the congregation when he sang this song, as far as I was concerned, Daddy sang *Someone To Care* to me:

> *When the world seems cold,*
> *And your friends seem few,*
> *There is someone who cares for you.*
> *When you've tears in your eyes,*
> *Your heart bleeds inside,*
> *There is someone who cares for you.*

When your disappointments come,
And you feel so blue,
There is someone who cares for you.
When you need a friend,
A friend till the end.
There is someone who's a friend to you.

Chorus:
Someone to care someone to share,
All your troubles like no other can do.
He'll come down from the skies,
And brush the tears from your eyes.
You're His child and He cares for you.

I lost my job, my joy and yes even my health as I knew it. God blessed me to return to employment. He restored the joy of my salvation and my health continues to be the result of His healing grace. Nothing compares to no longer having Daddy around.

Like an innocent child forced to come to terms with why things happen, I often contemplated, *Daddy's not coming back. Now what? What do I do?*

Well...life goes on. I need to go on. Daddy would want me to hold on to what he proved to me before his health failed, (Anita) *You'll never walk alone.*

And so now, my life is characterized as one in which I am encouraged to walk on by faith each day.

Chapter 11

Walk On. By Faith

God is always poised to position our lives towards purposeful living, Anita.

( )

The *Kansas City Globe* headline read, "Over 2,500 Attend Homegoing Celebration for Rev. Cleotis Cobbins, Sr."

As the family processioned into the Metropolitan Missionary Baptist Church sanctuary, it was a humbling sight. Eventually, the church filled beyond its capacity. The lineup of program participants represented the many circles in which Daddy traveled – the State Convention, the Sunshine District Association, the ministers' organizations, St. John Baptist Church, friends and former co-workers, and of course, the family.

As I walked down the aisle, I looked towards the front of the church. The pulpit and the combined choirs representing Association churches and the St. John Baptist church lined from one end of the choir stand to the other. The overall sense of honor and recognition given to Daddy was a tribute to his legacy. Daddy was remembered as "A Loving Family Man, Faithful Servant and a Dear Friend."

When I arrived at the hospital the day he passed. I was wheeled into his room and strikingly his appearance was a sharp contrast to the man I said goodbye to the day before (See *Daddy's Devotion* chapter).

His countenance radiated peace. It was as if Daddy had returned to a youthful appearance. The radiation had darkened his skin color but I noticed his color had returned. The texture of his skin was smooth as a baby's bottom. In his face I saw his father's features – nose, chin, cheekbones and all.

During his homegoing celebration, my brother, Pastor Cleotis Cobbins, Jr., referred to Daddy's appearance. He recalled, "I anticipated a sad and somber atmosphere. Much to my surprise, I could not believe how peaceful and healthy he looked." Jr. continued by sharing, "The night before, I saw the battle raging inside his body. And I said, 'God, this doesn't look like a man who has just gone through a battle.' 'The Lord said, Yes it does. When you are connected to me, this is what you look like when the battle is over'."

Truly Daddy was a living testimony who proved the power of divine strength that is available to anyone who dares to trust God wholeheartedly.

In his sermon during the homegoing, Pastor Hartsfield, Sr. highlighted Daddy's determination to keep going in spite of his illness. "Undoubtedly, C.L. (Daddy's name affectionately among pastors and ministers) had gotten so far along in his faith until death did not bother him at all. He started living dangerously because he was so sure. And that is a good feeling to have," Hartsfield concluded.

Keep Turning: Walk On By Faith

For me, the occasion also was a sort of prelude and preparation to my acknowledging God's call upon my life. Something strange that I could not shake lingered with me. The days leading up to the homegoing were fast-paced and at times chaotic. Anyone who has experienced the required responsibilities when preparing for a funeral can relate. The undertaking can overwhelm your attention, energy, schedule and emotions. While I was going through all of this, there was God also vying for my attention. With the tension between grieving and this strange restlessness in my spirit, I fought to stay focused.

Even during the celebration as I shared, "A Living Testimony"–memories of Daddy, the Spirit of God weighed heavily upon my spirit. I wasn't sure what was happening then. But I know it now.

Isaiah 6:1 says, "In the year that King Uzziah died I saw also the Lord sitting upon a throne, high and lifted up, and his train filled the temple." This verse implies that it took the death of this king before the prophet's awareness of God came into focus. Or, Isaiah 6:1 could also mean that the prophet saw God's awesomeness in ways previously unknown to him triggered by King Uzziah's death.

I prefer to embrace the latter view. Daddy was no longer physically present. God moved upon my life when I was vulnerable and sensitive. I had to live on and be open to whatever God desired of me.

I know God is with me daily through every situation. I make it a point to not only acknowledge God's presence but also strive to yield to Him. I know that through the Holy Spirit, God works in, through, with and upon me. I can be under pressure or experiencing a season of peace, my intimate awareness of God's presence and active role is not an issue.

However with every turning point I referenced in this book, I saw and experienced God's awesomeness in ways previously unknown to me, Daddy's passing included. God consistently revealed His faithfulness, compassion, provision and unfailing love at new and exciting levels. With each new level, I discovered the new person within, which wet my appetite for more and stimulated an insatiable hunger that was never satisfied to stay at the same level. Perhaps this is the Scripture's underlying message in II Corinthians 5:17, "Therefore, if anyone is in Christ, the new creation has come: The old has gone, the new is here!" (NIV).

The call to the ministry was the first immediate opportunity and test after Daddy passed way. Once I realized the calling, I accepted it without hesitation. Still I could not tell anyone. My church had yet to allow women to preach. My family was grieving. Most of all, it was not the appropriate time.

I was joyfully ready for this transition. So I decided my "pulpit" would be in the monthly *Globe* columns. I was just fine and content with this approach. I have to admit the opportunities were invigorating and therapeutic. For almost four years, I had settled into a flow, putting my thoughts on paper, sharing inspired concepts, principles and personal stories. Cranking out columns gave me a rush...until the Spirit began speaking to me...again.

Father's Day, June 17, 2007. I worshipped with my cousin, Pastor O.L. (Lee) Cobbins, Jr., at Bread of Life East church. I made this my annual Father's Day ritual. Father's Day was still an emotional time and I preferred to be around family.

After every worship service, Lee and I would hang out and just talk. This particular Father's Day was no different. Seated next to me, Lee leaned back in his chair and towards me as he pointed to and envisioned my placement on the church pulpit. He said to me, "I am going to invite you to speak and share your testimony." I then heard another voice say, "Preach."

I recognized that voice and sort of laughed to myself as I responded in agreement with Lee. Three days later on a Wednesday, I received a phone call from Rev. Wallace Hartsfield, II, who was the Assistant to the Pastor and preparing to succeed his father upon the senior Hartsfield's retirement. In a nutshell, Hartsfield, II, cut to the chase. It was time to announce my calling, time to come out of the *(Globe)* columns and go public. His subtle urging was apparent. What could I say except to agree?

Within those three days I had already attempted to reach Pastor Hartsfield, Sr., to request a meeting. The following Wednesday on June 27 that meeting was my opportunity to finally reveal God's call upon my life. He did not question the call although he confessed his long-standing struggle with the issue. Nevertheless, we agreed to meet again for further instructions and assignments.

In 2007, Pastor Hartsfield and the church were in transition because of pastor's retirement. I fulfilled the ministerial requirements but the year was coming to a close. And time was running out to schedule a date for my initial sermon.

Fast forward to December 31, 2007. The annual Watch Night service was also the setting for Pastor Hartsfield, Sr.'s final recommendations to Metropolitan. A few days prior, Pastor Hartsfield, Sr., called and asked me to be present for the service. To my surprise, he included in his final recommendations to the church the announcement and acceptance of women in the preaching ministry. I was one of the first two women. Together, we made history at Metropolitan. Along with that I am the first, and so far the only, woman preacher in my family.

The day I preached my initial sermon, April 27, 2008, I was focused on the message, *More Power to You*, (Ephesians 3:16-21) and my need to remain sensitive to God's direction. Still my thoughts were also on Daddy. He would be so proud and I took the gift given me by my siblings and in-laws as confirmation. It was a white minister's jacket with gold trim, and I wore it as a symbol of consecration by my family and their affirming me to this new ministry. It was also another demonstration of their support as Daddy's spirit echoed reminding us to "love one another."

Keep Turning: Walk On By Faith

So, here is my timeline of some major turning points:

May 1997	January 2004	December 2007	August 2014
Anita in near-fatal, head-on collision	Anita's father's passing & her ministry call	Anita's ministry call made public	First book, *Keep Turning the Pages*

One way to interpret the timeline is to span 10 years: 1997 to 2007; from the car accident to the history-making public announcement of God's call upon my life to preach His word, and 10 years: 2004 to 2014; from Daddy's passing/my preaching ministry calling to publishing my first book.

Or one could equate the timeline in seven-year intervals, using the number seven to represent the Biblical number for completion – every seven years a major occurrence towards a new turning point. Based on this, I see my life summed up this way: God framed and orchestrated my circumstances, so that out of tragedy I am living proof God makes good on His promise of Romans 8:28, "And we know that in all things God works for the good of those who love him, who have been called according to his purpose."

God did not thrust me into the difficult situations. Instead God led me through and brought me out, each time ushering in a new beginning and preparing me to advance to new levels and greater responsibilities. Despite hurts, disappointments, distresses, failures, suicidal thoughts and pain, the Spirit of God never gave up on me. Each time, my faltering spirit longed and was ripe for an infusion of power and influence that was beyond my ability to produce. So there I was with my broken self yet perfectly positioned for revelation, renewal and restoration that only God can give.

This was my mirror and how I viewed myself. Many people who describe and esteem me as strong would be head-scratching shocked to hear me confess that only I saw Anita as struggling and weak yet willing to be kept in God's will. I struggled and I know it. I was determined to understand an authentic, practical faith that is based on Scriptures but unique and applicable to whatever I was going through.

My pastor, Rev. Hartsfield, Sr., was one who viewed my life differently. The year after Daddy passed away he approached me after a Sunday service and observed, "If ever I've seen an overcomer, I've seen it in you." I had led the song, *For God So Loved the World* during worship. It is one of my favorite, heartfelt songs because my world depends on God's amazing, unconditional love that no one can match or rationally explain. As a personal testimony, the messages I sing are an overflow of my gratitude to God. Whether singing or serving, I always desire to offer and pour out the most grateful, sincerest and highest expression of myself.

Having lost my health, with Daddy's passing, the year I struggled financially because of unemployment along with other trying circumstances, Pastor Hartsfield witnessed my repeated resilience and efforts to re-establish my life with a committed faith in God and determination.

I am adamant that my faith in God will not be based on a façade that is often associated with typical church-goers.

There is a time and place for religious activity that should never ever define, dictate or dominate the incredible relationship God graciously offers through Jesus Christ. This relationship targets the sum total of a person's life. Why limit interaction with Jesus to a mere 90 minutes to two hours on the day of worship? When the church music stops, the sermons end, the prayers close with "amens," there remains a transformative life to be lived.

So I cannot knowingly allow myself to get caught up in the movement to disprove Jesus' claims on His identity and His teachings, no matter how much pressure, popularity and acceptance the movement gains. I would rather pursue the full benefit of growing "in the grace and knowledge of our Lord and Savior Jesus Christ," II Peter 3:18. My faith in Him, my struggles, hunger for God's word, Spirit-driven ministry aspirations and abiding relationships continue to confirm that knowing Jesus is worth the pursuit.

Furthermore, I am unwilling to accept the kind of faith that is often the topic of misinterpreted, God-inspired Scriptural messages. Since becoming a Christian I have longed for a faith that accepts Biblical truth, teaches me to apply relevant principles and leaves the outcome to God. To clarify, I have not mastered faith. I absolutely have no basis for being high-minded and self-righteous, although I am living this life and loving it. Yet any attempt to drum up my own visions of spiritual and personal grandeur will only result in wasted energy and time. I simply know that I have the capacity to exercise childlike faith in God. And if I choose not to use it; it would be my loss.

Therefore, I choose to walk on by faith–maximize my opportunities and time according to the Apostle Paul's assertion in II Corinthians 5:7, "For we walk by faith not by sight." In some Biblical references the word "walk" gets at the heart of Christian conduct. The Christian walk should strive to align with and be supported by an honest verbal testimony. My testimony begins with me trusting God and then conducting myself according to that trust.

Thus, I choose to believe in God's infinite abilities. God cannot be confined to human senses, abilities or reasoning and faith is fully aware of that. As a matter of fact, faith will insult everything human about us. Faith co-exists with senses, abilities and reason, then audaciously reserves the right to defy whatever we see, feel, possess, do and think.

Perhaps this is why I am intrigued and committed to walk on by faith–to keep conducting myself according to the beliefs I express. I read instances of faith's defiance over human limitations in the Scriptures and I am moved to draw from those experiences whenever I face challenges. Every time I beat defeat, my spirit leaps with exuberant anticipation, "God. What more will you do?!"

Human limitations says over 5,000 people cannot be fed with just two fish and five barley loaves – impossible.

Human reasoning questions the integrity and reject the message of a man who followed Jesus; but under intense pressure switched, and publicly denied Him three times to avoid mounting opposition. After all, once a denier always a denier. Right?

Human wisdom sees God's blessings only for those who do everything right – that is, performance-based blessings.

But I thank and praise God. For when I read how Jesus fed multitudes just by using a young boy's lunch, I see faith proving Jesus' ability to provide using the endless supply that is at His disposal (John 6:1-14).

When I read into the denying disciple-turned-anointed Apostle Peter's bio, faith in God confirms that anyone can conquer their flaws and failures, be used to finish strong and still make a difference in others' lives (Luke 22:31-34, Acts 2:14-41).

From reading Jesus' reaction in Luke 18:11-14, Biblical faith cautions against a righteousness that can be sincere but self-driven, based on human effort without genuine confession and repentance.

Therefore, I vow to walk on by faith first of all because God's provisions have never failed me. True there were times when I lacked and was in desperate need. At the end of the day, though, my needs never went unmet. At some point, eventually God provided. He met my needs His way and in His time. Yes, there were situations that caused me to ask, "Lord, why?" However, I have never felt the need to expand on that question and ask, "Lord, why did you let me down?" Truth told, God has never let me down.

Secondly, I have purposed in my heart to walk on by faith because whenever I am confronted with situations that are not in my best interest, God uses what is meant for evil and turns it for His glory and my good, (Genesis.

39:50). What I love about God is He doesn't just defeat the Enemy. God prepares tables before me smack dab in the Enemy's presence (Psalm 23:5). To make matters worse, God often transforms some of those experiences into opportunities for ministry, because I am supposed to live according to God's purpose and not circumstances. Now I see that.

If I lived entrenched in my circumstances then I enslave my life to endless frustrations. Why? Because I would miss God's plans and purposes that are at the core of my being. I would allow the wrong reactions to the difficult and tough times overshadow urges to live on the level of my potential.

Thirdly, I am keenly aware that the only reason areas of my life are scripted by circumstances is because God's plans and purposes require my need to go through a process. Process stirred me to learn more, being a teachable student of a purposeful life avoids a stale existence. I am motivated and so devoted to God until digging deeper to grow taller comes naturally.

As I walk on by faith through the process, fulfilling whatever God desires gradually comes to focus. Moreover, I discover who I am from His perspective. And once I settle the issue of my identity within the context of situations, get ready because I am ready to flow, fly and fight.

To this day, I have assumed the challenge and obligation to use the adversities of living with a spinal cord injury as stepping stones to purposeful living. As a personal creed, I believe, "my healing will not come full circle unless and until I can help someone else." Serving God and others, only then will I be satisfied.

God did not spare my life to pursue positions, be dogged by circumstances or to devil down and go my way doing my own thing. It is the Lord who lifts me up where I belong, not Anita. However, He is the one positioning me so that I can passionately and purposefully allow Him to get the most and best out of my potential.

Just as He did for Peter after his faith failure. It took a process for him to recover. Before a small group of people, Peter falsely claimed, "I don't know Jesus." When he was converted, the Spirit of God lifted Peter to boldly stand before a multitude with a stirring message of truth that convicted them to believe in the same Jesus they previously rejected and condemned to death.

Finally, I choose to walk on by faith because no matter how many times I have had to repent–that is, change course from going or doing things my way–He was faithful and just to forgive and give me another chance.

God proved His investment in our lives when He gave His all and best in Jesus as the perfect sacrifice. To chase after substitutes is to squander God's investment. Even if I live righteously and religiously on my best days, what a slap in God's face to even think these are acceptable substitutes worth more than Jesus' sacrifice. Jesus died so that I could live as a transformed testimony of the good work God has begun in me, "...being confident of this, that he who began a good work in you will carry it on to completion until the day of Christ Jesus," (Philippians 1:6). This verse is proof positive God is committed to His work in our lives, but we have to be willing. So, I cannot conform to others' demands and circumstances' plans, while also letting God do His work. I don't have the capacity to cater to both sides. I lack the smarts to successfully play both ends against the middle then arrogantly expect God's investment to payoff.

I suppose in every page of *Keep Turning the Pages* I have attempted to expose you to life-changing, personal and intimate experiences that have been worth knowing God, believing in Jesus and living within Holy Spirit power, along this faith journey. Whatever you have read – loss of my job, loss of my joy, my youngest sister's illness, the challenges to regain my health or my beloved Dad's passing – be encouraged because my living has not been in vain.

I vow to walk on by faith because this journey elevates my optimism about the days ahead. The fulfilled measure of my faith has yet to reach its end, since faith is dynamic. The full measure of God's blessings and work in me has yet to culminate. I refuse to live in order to make do. Yes, I desire to keep telling God's stories written in the pages of my life.

In more recent years, there have been more challenges, new relationships, more opportunities and a newer vision for ministry. In all, God has been right there motivating me. And since I will never walk alone, I walk on by faith.

So, until *Keep Turning the Pages, Part II*, keep the faith.

About the Author
Anita L. Cobbins

In the summer of 2003, Anita's then-pastor, Rev. Wallace S. Hartsfield, Sr., shared this observation, "If ever I've seen an overcomer, I've seen it in you."

These words were expressed as Hartsfield witnessed Anita's determination to re-establish her life after a 1997 near-tragic, head-on collision left her partially paralyzed and with other related-health issues.

Since then, Anita's faith and determination have been a personal challenge to use the adversities of living with a spinal cord injury, as stepping stones to a life of purpose. Although paralyzed, life for Anita is now about "taking steps towards healing and wholeness."

Thus by God's grace, Anita has launched *Faith In God*, a ministry that integrates media and personal appearances as a way to reach and share with others the reality and power of the faith walk, based on her daily experiences and major situations she has encountered.

Years ago, Anita was inspired to write *Keep Turning the Pages* following the automobile accident. Today, Anita lives to overcome paralysis, regain use of her lower body, endure the daily challenges and discover the reality of a genuine, uncompromising faith in God.

She is determined to know firsthand what it's like to face her adversities, go through trials and learn all that she can from every aspect of her life. With the turn of each page, the reader will follow along and see how God faithfully does just that – turn Anita's tragedies into testimonies of triumph.

To family, friends, co-workers, colleagues and church family, Anita inspires many as a principled, spiritual motivator and leader who values the importance of staying focused in order to pursue and accomplish what matters most.

She is considered an active, independent paraplegic who despite her condition, still uses her spiritual gifts, skills and talents to serve and minister to others. As Anita lives and waits to experience the full manifestation of God's healing grace in her life, she will also tell you, "my healing does not come full circle unless and until I can help someone else."

Helping others has been her driving motivation behind ministries such as the A.B.L.E. (Abilities. Barriers. Limitations. Empowered.) Support Group Ministry. Anita established and coordinates this ministry at her church that reaches out, encourages and celebrates the abilities of persons with disabilities and those living with chronic and life-altering health challenges.

Since 1999, she has been a featured columnist for the *Kansas City Globe*'s religious column titled, "Expect a Miracle." In some of the monthly columns, Anita's inspirational writings take the reader on her journey of faith with Jesus as the faithful companion and Lord.

Anita is a member of Metropolitan Missionary Baptist Church located in Kansas City, Mo. Dr. Wallace S. Hartsfield, II, is her pastor. Along with the A.B.L.E. Ministry, she devotes herself to making "full proof" of her ministries (II Timothy 4:5) through preaching, teaching, evangelism and singing. Anita serves as an associate minister, Sunday Church School teacher and also in Metropolitan's evangelism and music ministries.

Anita also shares her knowledge, strategic planning and execution expertise as a communications and marketing consultant, primarily assisting community organizations and area ministries.

In addition, Anita accepted God's call to preach the same year her father, the late Rev. Cle Otis Cobbins, Sr., passed away in 2004. Four years later, Anita preached her initial sermon and was officially licensed on April 27, 2008, making history as one of Metropolitan's first women preachers.

Anita's family line is marked by a legacy of preachers, pastors, teachers, singers, musicians and creative arts. All are instrumental in preparing and encouraging her to fulfill more than two decades of ministry.

Her father and his twin brother, the late Rev. Otis Lee Cobbins, Sr., left behind a powerfully influential legacy for the future generation to follow. In addition, Anita's older brother and 11 cousins are currently serving as pastors and ministers in Kansas and Missouri.

Anita deeply loves her family. She highly praises her family for being her lifeline and solid support system throughout years of living as an active paraplegic and despite subsequent health-related setbacks.

Anita is a communications and marketing professional and has been employed in the marketing department at the Kansas City Area Transportation Authority, Kansas City, Mo., since 1990.

In 2009, Anita was recognized among the *Kansas City Globe's* 100 Most Influential African-Americans. She was chosen for this honor representing the local media and marketing/communications category, along with *Kansas City Star* and KMBC TV 9 media professionals.

In 2000, Anita was inducted into the Black Achievers Society in Business and Industry, an honor sponsored by the Southern Christian Leadership Conference (SCLC) of Greater Kansas City.

Anita is also a member of the Public Relations Society of America, Inc., the American Management Association, National Association of Black Journalists and Delta Sigma Theta Sorority, Inc.

Anita earned an undergraduate degree in Journalism and Mass Communications (Radio-Television Broadcasting & Production emphasis) from Kansas State University, Manhattan, Ks. She completed her graduate education at Webster University, Kansas City, Mo., with a dual Masters of Arts degree in Media Communications and a Masters of Arts in Marketing.